Identifying Child Molesters
Preventing Child Sexual Abuse
by Recognizing the Patterns
of the Offenders

Carla van Dam, PhD

Identifying Child Molesters
Preventing Child Sexual Abuse by Recognizing the Patterns of the Offenders

Pre-publication
REVIEW . . .

"**G**rooming is a difficult concept for most people to grasp, as styles can vary. Dr. van Dam's work goes a long way in clarifying this concept for a lay audience. I consider this now to be the definitive work on the subject. I believe it will be extremely helpful to parents in their effort to protect their children from sexual exploiters. Previous efforts in this area focused on teaching children to try to control adults (by saying no, by telling, etc.). Such efforts almost by definition will have limited (if any) success. Dr. van Dam's book now provides parents and others with the tools to recognize when and how to intervene."

Roger W. Wolfe, MA
Co-Director,
N. W. Treatment Associates,
Seattle, Washington

Identifying Child Molesters
Preventing Child Sexual Abuse by Recognizing the Patterns of the Offenders

Carla van Dam, PhD

HMTP

The Haworth Maltreatment and Trauma Press®
An Imprint of The Haworth Press, Inc.
New York • London • Oxford

Published by

The Haworth Maltreatment and Trauma Press®, an imprint of The Haworth Press, Inc., 10 Alice Street, Binghamton, NY 13904-1580

Cover design by Monica L. Seifert.

Library of Congress Cataloging-in-Publication Data

van Dam, Carla.
    Identifying child molesters : preventing child sexual abuse by recognizing the patterns of the offenders / Carla van Dam.
        p.   cm.
    Includes bibliographical references and index.
    ISBN 0-7890-0742-8 (hard : alk. paper)—ISBN 0-7890-0743-6 (soft : alk. paper)
    1. Child molesters—United States—Identification. 2. Child molesters—United States—Psychology. 3. Child sexual abuse—United States—Prevention. I. Title.

HV6570.2 .V36 2000
364.15′36—dc21   00-033546

CONTENTS

Foreword   vii
        Gavin de Becker

Acknowledgments   xi

Introduction   1

Chapter 1. The Problem   11
  Case Studies   12

Chapter 2. Knowing It Is a Problem: The Need for Clarity   41
  Clear Definitions   41
  Guiding Treatment   43
  Guiding Research   44
  Guiding Relationships   45
  Guiding Interventions   46

Chapter 3. Why It Is a Problem: What Is the Harm?   57
  Psychological Issues   60
  Moral Issues   69
  Cultural Issues   71

Chapter 4. Prevalence: How Often Does It Happen?   75

Chapter 5. Characteristics of the Child Molester:
** Who Does It?**   81
  Demographics   81

Chapter 6. The Grooming Process: How Do They Do It?   89
  Sexual Attraction to Children   90
  Justifying the Interest   92
  Grooming the Adult Community   96
  Grooming the Child   103

Chapter 7. The Social Climate That Helps Foster It:
Turning a Blind Eye   **115**

Attitudes Toward Children   115
Attitudes Toward Women   117
Societal Denial   122
Molester Denial   127

Chapter 8. Visible Grooming   **137**

Current Prevention Strategies   138
Visible Grooming of Adults   142

Chapter 9. Setting Boundaries to Help Prevent
Child Sexual Abuse   **161**

Intervening with a Potential Child Molester   161

Chapter 10. Summary   **195**

Appendix: Legal Definitions   **201**

References   **205**

Additional Resources   **219**

Index   **221**

Foreword

A mother named Olivia told me of taking her six-year-old daughter, Juliette, to the small fenced playground at their local park. Most of the children there were brought to the park by a parent, a few by babysitters or nannies, one by a grandparent. After a short while, Olivia had intuitively connected each child to his or her guardian. In one case, it was because child and adult resembled each other. In another, she saw a man encourage a boy who was hesitant to let go at the top of a slide; she heard another parent warn her daughter to stop hitting a smaller child. Soon enough, Olivia had accounted for every adult in the playground but one man, one man she didn't like.

He was about forty, clean-shaven, with short hair. He was sitting on a bench watching the children play, but not focused on any particular child. He had nothing with him, while most of the other adults had something they were keeping an eye on: a doll, a toy, or else a whole bag of the things parents seem always to be carrying around when they go out with their kids. When Olivia saw the man leave the playground alone she was relieved he had gone. Sure, he might have stopped by just to get the joy most of us feel in the presence of children playing, but she didn't think so. *I don't trust him. What was he doing here anyway? Glad he's gone. I'll watch for him in the future. He seemed like a child molester.*

Seemed like a child molester? On the basis of what? This is an outrageous and unearned condemnation, a secret discrimination so intolerant that it would be illegal in any other context. The man came back to the playground a few minutes later and Olivia saw his son run up and hug him. She'd misconnected the boy to another adult, but Olivia quickly forgave her prejudice. After all, she told me later, "I was just protecting my child."

I asked if she felt bad for having falsely accused the man in her mind. *Nope.* Did the experience make her reluctant to judge people so quickly in the future? *Nope.* Even though he turned out to be just another parent, did she regret her suspiciousness? *Nope.*

I praised her for her self-confidence and pointed out, "To effectively protect Juliette, you'd need to be just as willing to entertain suspicions about people you know."

"That's not quite as easy," Olivia responded, "because then I'd feel terribly guilty."

Carla van Dam's work shows us that such guilt is misplaced. Juliette, like any child, is far more vulnerable to someone the family knows than to a stranger. And Olivia, like any parent, is far more resistant to suspecting someone she knows. Those people we are willing to suspect are inherently less dangerous than those we refuse to suspect. We may suppress an objectionable thought about a neighbor or a family friend, but the only way to really banish a thought is to consider it. In fact, we show greater integrity and greater love for our children when we are willing to consider any thought.

The goal is not that you distrust a man or teenage boy merely because he has access to your children, but rather, that you be willing to listen to yourself when you do feel distrust. It makes sense to pursue suspicion rather than immediately abandon it since it's a fact of our species that some of the adult males molest children. Expecting those particular males to look glaringly different from all others has proved to be an ineffective strategy for preventing sexual abuse. Popular, but ineffective.

Most people consider the behavior of sexual predators to be a mystery, but Dr. van Dam refuses to call it a mystery. Rather, predatory behavior is a puzzle. Based on years of direct experience helping families affected by sexual abuse, and years of studying predators, Dr. van Dam knows the pieces of the sexual abuse puzzle, and she shows us their shapes and their colors. You'll see that most of them are already familiar to you. Above all, *Identifying Child Molesters* will leave you knowing that you never have to wait for all the pieces to be in place before you act.

Of all the serious harms that could come to a child, sexual abuse is the most common. Unfortunately, the odds are getting worse, not better. More mothers are working, so more children are spending their days in child care facilities. Divorce is on the rise, and the increasing number of remarriages means more sexual abuse by stepfathers in the home. Sexual crimes against children are also increasing of their own accord as the abused grow up and become abusers themselves. Because the predators so often molest more than one child, the number of victims is increasing exponentially.

One in three girls and one in six boys will have sexual contact with an adult. According to a study by the National Institute of Mental Health, the average molester of girls will have about fifty victims before being caught and convicted; the average molester of boys will have an astonishing 150 victims before being caught and convicted. Most will have plenty after being caught as well, some even victimizing as many as 300 children throughout their "careers."

All these predators have a process by which they gain access to and control of victims. Thanks to Carl van Dam's exceptional work, there are children who might have become victims—and will not because their parents read *Identifying Child Molesters*. Like me, after you've read this book, you'll want to share it with as many parents as you can.

Gavin de Becker
Los Angeles, California

ABOUT THE AUTHOR

Dr. Carla van Dam is a clinical and forensic psychologist working in the state of Washington. She consults with various organizations, provides psychological reports and evaluations, trains professional groups on issues regarding child safety, and teaches university courses. She has a PhD in Clinical Psychology, and is licensed in both the state of Washington and the province of British Columbia.

In 1986 she received the Canadian Medal of Bravery.

Dr. van Dam is a member of the following organizations: American Psychological Association, B. C. College of Psychologists, Association for the Treatment of Sexual Abusers (ATSA), its Western Affiliate (WATSA), and the Pacific Northwest Neuropsychological Society. She has published articles, books, and pamphlets on the topic of child sexual abuse.

Acknowledgments

This book would not have been possible without the help and assistance of many people. Linda Halliday (now Linda Halliday-Sumner) has been a tireless informant, educator, and advocate who was actively aware of the relevance of this topic before 1980 and who has continued to be a leader in this field. Throughout the years she has provided insight and an ever-deepening understanding of the personal and professional complexities involved in protecting children from child sexual abuse. Her contributions are visible throughout this book. Special thanks also go to Iris Rucker and Jan Lewis, who provided endless mentoring through crucial phases of professional development and who continue to share their expertise, support, and friendship. There have been many others along the way. Chuck Bates has tolerated years of long walks and discussions to hone and develop the ideas in this book. The work could not have been done without his help, loyalty, encouragement, and support.

Special thanks also go to the many families who so generously talked about their experiences to help others avoid the heartache they have had to endure. They are not named, but their courage and pain should help everyone remember the importance of this topic.

This work was also greatly facilitated by a number of sex offender treatment providers whose support and assistance was instrumental in making this book possible: A sincere thank-you goes to Roger and Florence Wolfe, Marcia Macey, Susan Moores, and Michael Barsanti. In addition, Charles Regets, Charlene Phelps, Lisa Johnson, Ruth Harms, Christina Maleney, Cindy Spano, and Jan Coleman have also helped along the way. Also, a special thanks goes to Bob Geffner, the Senior Editor of The Haworth Maltreatment and Trauma Press, who made this publication possible, and to Amy Rentner, for her thorough attention to editorial details.

Introduction

This book was written to help readers know how to better protect children from potential child sexual molesters long before any abuse might otherwise occur. This will be accomplished in the following two ways:

1. *It will identify those who might molest.* By reading this book, the seemingly invisible steps that typically precede child sexual abuse will become visible. No longer will the charm that molesters typically use to endear unsuspecting adults work. Instead, those very moves will be correctly identified and understood. Through reading the stories of countless molesters, their families, and their victims, readers will be able to more accurately recognize when they have become the targets of a molester's charm. Correctly identifying this attempt to charm as opportunistic behavior will give readers the necessary perspective to stop it.

2. *It will describe what to do when encountering a potential molester.* Understanding the behavior molesters typically exhibit when trying to charm adults to obtain access to children will dictate what must be done. By becoming familiar with this terrain, readers will have both the required understanding and skills to know what to do and the courage and strength to follow through with the necessary actions. Such responses will appropriately curtail an offender's access to children and subsequent opportunities to molest.

Only by unmasking this process and working together can the adult community directly stop the child molester from having continued, unimpeded access to society's children.

*　*　*

Fred appeared to have it all: everyone in the community adored him. He was smart, gregarious, good-looking, and twenty-one years old. After graduating from high school, he was accepted at an Ivy League university but decided to complete his studies locally to ease the financial burden on his family. Such responsible behavior made him seem mature beyond his years, and only added to his good reputation.

He continued to attend all the high school functions, where he was always greeted as the returning hero. Younger teens latched on to him, eager to catch his eye and be included in the inner circle, which he generously and graciously allowed. He knows all the kids by name and has looked after a number of them at one time or another. Many of these children have accompanied him to the movies, on all-day outings to the lake, or on overnight camping trips in the mountains, reveling in the status of having been chosen for such an event.

Fred's social skills amazed parents, as he graciously talked to them, and recognized their children's special qualities. In high school, he participated in programs to help elementary school children and volunteered as a camp counselor. But while the others who did this were also absorbed in sports, academic studies, and social activities, Fred continued to make time for his young charges. After graduation, his contemporaries dispersed to various colleges and universities or became busy in their new jobs. Their involvement with the younger children was an activity they did well and enjoyed, but it did not define them. Fred, on the other hand, remained in the local community and continued to be totally immersed in activities with adolescent children.

He paid for his college tuition by helping children: he drove a number of kids to soccer practices, tutored other kids in math, and baby-sat three children every night so their mother could work the graveyard shift. When time permitted, he also baby-sat for a number of other families.

Some ugly rumors were floating around. At the local school, some of the children heard that a twelve-year-old child named Mark told his parents, "Fred showed me his privates." The parents went to the police, who told them, "It's just your son's word against Fred's. Even if it happened, it was consensual." Fred's lawyer told Mark's parents that if they continued spreading rumors about Fred they would be sued for slander. They became anxious about having gone to the police, worried about how to help their son, and learned that the disclosure to police impacted Mark at school. The children at school asked Mark, "Why would you say such mean things about Fred?" How Mark had been identified and how the other children have learned of these events remained a mystery.

Most kids rallied behind Fred, isolating Mark and making him feel even more like an outcast. Then, a very popular boy at the school told his friends, "I know this is true. I know Fred did this to Mark. He tried to do the same thing to me, but I told him to buzz off." Two days later, this boy found his torn gym clothes in a dumpster, and he was told by a number of older kids to "quit spreading rumors about Fred." Another girl at the school said, "My best friend's sister knows Fred. She says he didn't rape that boy. They just traded blow jobs." This did nothing to diminish or tarnish Fred's reputation, but it did help to further ostracize Mark. Despite these rumors and allegations, Fred continued in all his activities with children. The parents and children rallied behind him, while Mark's parents feared legal repercussions against them for trying to help their son.

Stories similar to this one take place daily in every community. In each case, the molester in question is seen as above reproach, and the children and their supporters feel defensive and afraid. This is how most molesters operate, and they are so successful, it is a wonder that any molesters are ever charged or convicted. Understanding this process is essential for protecting children from sexual abuse.

Molesters typically sexually abuse children only after they have first charmed adults into believing they are above reproach. This is a premeditated approach hundreds of molesters describe using. Only after the adults have embraced them with wild enthusiasm do they begin to molest the children. This book identifies this predatory pattern and provides the tools to prevent its occurrence.

If it were easy to stop molesters, this book would not be needed. Their unbelievably winning ways handily turn the adult community into covert allies in the seduction of children. In case after case, adults become incredibly charmed by someone whose behavior should be worrisome. Instead of alarm, they respond to that charm like deer caught in the headlights of a car, not only failing to protect children, but, subsequently, also vociferously defending the molester when allegations do arise.

This book will help prevent this from continuing to happen by providing the right perspective to correctly identify risky behavior that might otherwise look wholesome and desirable. Recognizing such behavior will save adults from being taken in by those whose interest in children should be cause for concern. This will protect children from situations in which child sexual abuse would otherwise predictably have occurred.

Current child sexual abuse prevention strategies are primarily geared toward stopping abuse from continuing after it has already begun. This kind of prevention requires children to be in charge of their own protection. They are taught about "good touch/bad touch," told to say "no" to those who try to harm them, asked to relay this information to trusted adults, and instructed to keep telling until they are believed. Rather than relying on children to be the principal line of defense, it is time for adults to take over the job of protecting children by no longer giving molesters access to them.

Doing this means recognizing the seemingly charming behaviors child molesters initially use to lull adults into compliance. This typically precedes the grooming and assault directed at children. Correctly identifying these behaviors generates opportunities to intervene long before children are at risk. This means adults have to understand molesters and recognize their methods. Many find this too distasteful. Like ostriches burying their heads in the sand to avoid danger, these people prefer not to know anything about this topic.

Unfortunately, ignorance is not bliss, but an invitation for offenders to abuse children. Molesters play to the abhorrence this topic engenders, utilizing the discomfort to smooth over any discrepancies or clues that might arise, ensuring adults provide unwitting tacit support and collusion in their access to children. Adult inaction is tantamount to abdicating the task of looking after the health and welfare of children.

The information in this book will not shed new light on how to protect children from the infrequent assaults by unknown individuals called "stranger danger." Nor will applying the principles in this book automatically ensure protection from all child sexual abuse. Rather, this book is directed at intervention against those molesters who look "too good to be true." They are identifiable precisely because of the elaborate strategies they use to successfully endear themselves to adults. The very behavior that wins them carte blanche to ensure unimpeded access to children fits an identifiable pattern. Seeing this behavior in the correct context will help adults to better protect children from harm.

Much has been documented about child sexual abuse in the past three decades, but this extensive literature still does not explain why adults are often blind to the sexual abuse of children. Little has been written on how this sexual abuse remains invisible to precisely those adults most responsible for the care and safety of children. Instead, when a case is reported in the popular press, readers wonder how it could have happened. They question how other parents, teachers, and friends could have been ignorant about an offender in their midst. They erroneously assume such a person would automatically not be likable and feel smug that it could never happen in their community. They marvel at how any reasonable adult could have entrusted the care of children to a sexual predator.

This book will make visible the maneuvers these molesters use, seemingly effortlessly, to successfully ingratiate themselves into everyone's lives. It will also provide the necessary tools to nip this process in the bud, by preventing such people from having access to children. It is important to learn these strategies, as over 95 percent of child molesters typically are known, loved, and trusted individuals who are already firmly entrenched in their communities. It is this insider status that molesters go to such trouble to establish and maintain because that is what allows them to be regarded as trustworthy and "above reproach."

Extensive interviews with hundreds of such molesters help identify how they gain their insider status, which ensures any subsequent abuse is invisible to the adult community. By understanding these dynamics, professionals, parents, friends, school staff, and other community members are more likely to recognize the grooming that so smoothly undermines the usual defenses established to protect children from harm. Failure to recognize this process results in the inevitable incredulousness experienced when allegations against well-liked and respected people occur. These allegations, tentatively made by barely articulate and/or frequently troubled youngsters, and possibly supported by anxious parents, are then pitted against the eloquent denials of the established, successful, and exceedingly well-liked adults being charged. This book will elucidate this process. Without intervention, the continued tolerance will inadvertently encourage the molester to proceed with impunity, at the expense of the children whose disclosures are all too often discredited.

The information provided here comes from numerous sources: the scholarly literature and popular press, stories from families whose children have been molested, as well as husbands, wives, and children who have been preyed upon. In addition, detailed descriptions have been provided based on extensive interviews with hundreds of child molesters. Many of these offenders, in a study conducted by the author, have identified their carefully planned siege on families precisely for the purpose of helping to protect children (van Dam, 1996). Their material describing how they groomed adults to obtain access to children will sound repetitive. This is because their stories are so similar.

Although all identifying information has been altered,* the stories will sound stereotypical, so that the molesters cited may resemble individuals known by the reader. That is because, in all likelihood, such people are part of everyone's lives. Any resemblance should result in opportunities to practice the safety measures recommended in this book. Thus, the repetitive similarities between the cases described here and individuals known to the reader should serve as an opportunity to protect children from potential or continued sexual abuse.

It is not the intent of this book for the reader to begin reporting friends and loved ones to the police, nor is it necessary to prove that

---

*A few cases in this book describe molesters by name. The Bouchard family requested this. Their willingness to come forward has ensured that Margaret Carruthers no longer has free access to further molest children, as she has been convicted. The Bouchards believe remaining anonymous only further protects the molester. In the cases of Robert Noyes and Mary Kay Letourneau, the material provided in this book is a matter of public record, with both of them also currently serving prison sentences.

any person who fits the profile described in this book is a molester. What is intended is the prevention of potential abuse. That means, when someone fits the described profile, following these suggestions will provide the tools to engage in socially appropriate responses to stop the process, which will protect children from potential harm. Such proactive responsibility will ensure that adults reclaim the job of protecting children rather than hoping children will tell about abuse after it happens.

Many of the chapters in this book provide an overview of the field. The topic of child sexual abuse frequently engenders extreme views and emotional reactivity that only helps to distract everyone from the primary concern of creating safer environments for children. This book will help put the topic of child sexual abuse into perspective to give the reader a better understanding of the field. The following descriptions provide a brief overview of each chapter:

- Chapter 1 lays the foundation for understanding how the community can so often be naive to the very behaviors that should make it wary. Five case stories are introduced to exemplify many of the principles under study. These cases are crucial for correctly understanding the dynamics of child sexual abuse and are referred to throughout the rest of the book, as they illustrate various issues under discussion.
- Chapter 2 provides clear definitions of what constitutes child sexual abuse. Failure to address such abuse frequently occurs because people do not know what constitutes child sexual abuse. This confusion helps to protect molesters while further victimizing children and their families.
- Chapter 3 covers the many ways that child sexual abuse impacts society. The harm caused by the abuse is discussed to help the reader understand the importance of this topic to the health and welfare of children. This chapter delineates how child sexual abuse affects those who have been victimized.
- Chapter 4 addresses the prevalence of child sexual abuse, which occurs with such epidemic frequency that over one-fourth of the population is directly affected. The subsequent impact on friends and family only increases the relevance of this topic in everyone's lives.

- Chapter 5 summarizes the characteristics of child molesters, to remind the reader how ubiquitous they may be, and to dispel the reader of any mistaken notion that a child molester may be identified by looks, clothes, or social class. Molesters are found in all segments of the population, and they are often extremely successful and well-liked members of society. As a result, the molesters discussed in this book are especially unlikely to be identified.

- Chapter 6 describes how molesters groom children. The protocol child molesters use to access and groom victims seems to follow a set procedure. This chapter discusses how they go about talking themselves, others, and their child victims into enabling them to abuse.

- Chapter 7 describes how social attitudes impact child sexual abuse. Although child sexual abuse occurs in many cultures, certain societal attitudes toward women and children help it to flourish. The social/cultural mores that inadvertently foster and support further abuse are described.

- Chapter 8 provides the framework to help readers identify potential molesters. The recognizable behaviors molesters use to charm and manipulate adults are described. By understanding these behavioral patterns, adults will correctly identify worrisome mannerisms that might otherwise appear likable and acceptable. Recognizing the behaviors provides the framework for preventing child sexual abuse.

- Recognizing potential molesters is the first step. Chapter 9 provides the tools for intervening and stopping contact before opportunities for abuse ever occur. Adhering to the steps listed in this chapter will stop potential molesters from obtaining opportunities to abuse.

- The same dynamics that make child molesters difficult to curtail at the individual and community levels are described in Chapter 10, to summarize how they are played out on the national and international levels. Molesters increasingly use arguments of individual liberties and freedom to blur boundaries, whereby they obtain acceptance as a discriminated-against sexual minority.

This book provides the necessary overview to thoroughly understand the topic of child sexual abuse. The tools for initiating prevention strategies to stop sex offenders are primarily covered in Chapters 8 and 9. Many readers will find this topic emotionally stressful. Others are already very familiar with the predatory nature of the molester. Some may be personally experiencing the complexities of the dilemma, as they and/or their children are being targeted. For those who need to know immediately how to protect their children, Chapters 1, 8, and 9 provide the necessary framework and initial understanding needed to know how to proceed.

Chapter 1

The Problem

This book is about child sexual molesters whose charm, respectability, and agreeable demeanor ensures their easy access to children. A closer look at these molesters and the community's response to them will provide a useful framework to help end this victimization. Seeing precisely how molesters operate and how community members frequently become their adamant defenders will help readers be less naive and correctly recognize these behaviors as attempts to charm them for the primary purpose of victimizing their children with impunity.

Though the stories presented in this book will seem preposterous to some, similar events in other communities fail to meet with local outrage. In one town, for instance, the man voted Citizen of the Year was convicted on a number of child sexual abuse charges. Prior to his conviction, he had successfully run the annual community fair, utilizing young students to manage the booths. Despite his conviction on numerous instances of child sexual abuse, the very community whose children he had molested appealed to the courts for his temporary release from prison to run the fair.

Since such community reactions are common, understanding them may be useful for improving protection strategies. This can best be done by hearing those individuals who molest describe how they target and manipulate adults to gain access to children. A number of people sexually molest children. Their age, sex, and occupation follow no pattern, although molesters do tend to choose lifestyles that will give them access to children because this ensures easier opportunities to molest. This may be done through career choices, selected hobbies, or marriage into families with children (Salter, 1995; Halliday, 1985). Thus, the opportunities to molest are endless: Child molesters may become youth group leaders, social workers, ministers, coaches, bus drivers, and so forth. With educators, the most frequent arrests and convictions are among physical education teachers, with the second most being among music teachers (van Dam, 1996). This is primarily because these specialties traditionally provide increased access to children outside school hours, with ready opportunities for intimacy, which are then exploited (Salter, 1995).

It should be remembered, however, that most people who are attracted to these vocations or avocations are not molesters but, rather, that molesters are attracted to these professions because they provide ready access to children. Their extensive involvement with children and their families helps the molesters successfully create a positive community image. As a result, adults tend to suspend any doubts and tolerate behavior they might not otherwise accept in another context in which adult-child interaction is not expected to be so close. Again, remember, this does not mean that all adults working with children are molesters, but that all molesters obtain opportunities to gain access to children.

CASE STUDIES

The cases described in this book provide a framework to examine how communities embrace child sexual molesters in their midst. The names have been changed, but any resemblance to someone known to the reader should present an opportunity to apply the principles covered in this book. Throughout the book, these and other cases will be referred to as they exemplify the issues under discussion.

Case Study One

The first case involves a respected senior citizen.

Mr. Smith was a spry and boyishly young-looking older man. He retired after an illustrious and successful career and was known and respected in the community. He was fond of children and, in his retirement, dedicated his time and energy to them. His family described him as having the playfulness of a twelve-year-old, and the energy to match.

Children in the community knew and adored him. Those not acquainted with him usually became instant fans after playing his games, which involve getting money and candy. He arrived at birthday parties to play games that included guessing which hand has the money or which pocket has the candy.

Mr. Smith typically first engaged the children in his games, then talked to the parents. On an initial visit, he allayed parental concerns by naming friends and neighbors where he was a welcome guest. After reassuring parents, they looked on benignly as he played with the children, roughhousing, twirling them around, picking them up, and tickling them. These children, because of their size and weight, had not had any other adults twirl them around for many years. Yet none of this slowed down Mr. Smith. Adults marveled at how physically active he was with the children.

He was also seen at other functions where children congregate, equipped with shiny coins, candy, energy, enthusiasm, and physical games. Since retirement, he brought this enthusiasm to the schools, where he volunteered. Children seemed to love his attention, and many parents were enthusiastic about his involvement with their children. His dedication to children received ovations from parents at community and school functions. He helped families solve babysitting dilemmas, did not accept remuneration for his service, and brought the children treats.

Over the years, a few adults considered some of his activities and behavior inappropriate. Their concerns were largely ignored, but those who persisted in voicing their qualms were accused of being on a "witch-hunt" against a "wonderful man who contributed so much to the community." When doubts were expressed, many responded as if this were the first and only time any concerns had arisen. This helped silence those who would question his motives and ensured that each complaint was thereby treated as an isolated instance.

The complaints that occasionally cropped up were largely ignored. For instance, Mr. Smith was asked by one school principal not to help girls off the monkey bars. He responded by volunteering at a different school. Later he was advised by that school's administrator not to be quite as physical with the children. He ignored the advice. Parents were not informed, and the matter was dropped. Another time he was asked to not distribute money or candy on school grounds, but he ignored the request. Personnel in that school's administration changed, and the activity continued.

As a result of some of these behaviors, a few parents discussed Mr. Smith: Two parents mentioned initial discomfort with having him arrive at their child's birthday party unannounced and uninvited. Another couple described similar initial discomfort, but they experienced a change of heart after observing him with the children and learning of his community connections. They decided it must be okay primarily because he was such a respected member of the community and the children loved the contact. These parents overcame their initial concerns to become Mr. Smith's staunchest allies. The other two parents continued to have misgivings, kept their concerns to themselves, but watched their children more closely when Mr. Smith was around.

Two parents finally took their concerns directly to the school. Through the grapevine, they had learned about misgivings previously expressed by other parents. As a result they became adamant that a number of the activities, including the money- and candy-giving games, and the roughhousing and tickling, should no longer be tolerated on school grounds. Because this couple could not be placated and reassured, the school responded with a community meeting to air concerns.

At the community meeting, most parents were angry that anyone would be concerned about the "saintlike behavior of such a wonderful man whose actions were above reproach." A number of parents and teachers insisted that Mr. Smith not be held "accountable to the same standards." Other parents felt there was no cause for alarm, "as everyone knows sex offenders only abuse their own children. Therefore, none of these children were at risk."

A few adults dared to mention their concerns in this emotional climate: One teacher observed that many children shrank from Mr. Smith's touch, and one parent commented that her child did not like him. The school nurse expressed discomfort with the game of having children put their hands in his pocket to find candy. Another parent stated that the school's tolerance of this behavior on the school grounds created confusion for children. If it were acceptable to take candy from Mr. Smith on the playground, then it would be easier for these children to also assume that taking candy from others was okay. The couple who originally complained worried because he continued, with impunity, to engage in behaviors he had been asked to stop. Such failure to comply with school policies seemed problematic. However, over 250 other parents and teachers at the meeting were resoundingly supportive of this man whose love of children they felt was exceptional. The few dissenting voices were inaudible over the vociferous support.

The meeting ended with nothing changed, and Mr. Smith continued his activities. Those who complained about his behavior felt embarrassed about the unkind thoughts they harbored and kept quiet. The majority of parents were grateful to have such a wonderful resource: a man who tirelessly dedicated himself to the children of the community, providing them all with a grandfatherly figure who cherished their children.

When Mr. Smith is mentioned to those who do not know him, they are astounded that any community would tolerate such behavior. A man who spends his time giving coins or candy to children, or having them grope in his pockets for the candy, playing with them, tickling them, roughhousing with them, and ignoring local school rules seems odd. But they have their own respectable members of the community who are loved, and whose behavior is exonerated.

In reality, Mr. Smith's behavior was not "saintlike." He had children putting their hands in his pants pockets, ostensibly to get candy. He helped girls off the monkey bars by holding their bottoms. He ignored school policies and continued to hand out money and candy on the playground. And, despite being told not to, he continued to pick up kids, twirl and tickle them, as well as attending their birthday parties without parental invitations.

How did he gain and maintain such support that community members accepted behaviors that defied school rules? Why was he not held to the same standard as everyone else? This support might be a well-earned response for exceptional contributions. To be suspicious in the face of such generosity would be cruel. Yet covertly condoning inappropriate behavior and possible child sexual abuse is equally reprehensible. In the case of all those like Mr. Smith, a loss of innocence occurs when these behaviors are viewed unenthusiastically. However, popularity and approval may mask behaviors that should not be tolerated. Throughout this book, an examination of the literature and explanations given by molesters will provide a context for better understanding Mr. Smith's behavior, and the community's response to him.

Case Study Two

> *Mr. Smith does not provide an isolated instance of someone who enjoys incredible popularity, with inappropriate behavior tolerated, venerated, or overlooked. This second case involves a young family man just beginning a successful teaching career.*

Mr. Clay was a popular elementary school teacher. The community where he taught was delighted to have a male teacher at the primary level as a role model for the boys. He was actively involved in sports, taught physical education classes to all the young children, started a before-school gym club, and amazed parents with his attendance at all of their children's sports events. One mother reported:

> We were very pleased with him. My son thought he was just the greatest because he's really athletic and into sports, and so is my son. They seemed to have a really good relationship right from the beginning. . . . Mr. Clay's the kind of person who seemed to want to know each kid as a person, not just a student six hours a day. He wanted to go and see them in their different sports. He showed up at the baseball games just to watch my son play baseball. We were really impressed.

Another mother, who taught with Mr. Clay, had a son in his class. She was "thrilled" with this new teacher, and the friendly relationship her son had with him. She noted that he would pick up her son, throw him in the air, and tickle him whenever they met in the hallway at school. She assumed her son adored him, only to learn later that he did not really like Mr. Clay.

Shortly after school started, a number of the children in Mr. Clay's class began coming home from school late. For one father, this confirmed his son's enthusiasm for this new teacher: "My son stayed after school quite often. He was helping Mr. Clay do this or that." For one mother, however, it created difficulties, as her son was supposed to walk his younger sister home. She complained directly to the teacher because her son was coming home from school two hours late: "He told me they have to clean up the erasers and do their homework and said my daughter could just stay in the classroom and wait for him."

Just before winter break, three of the boys in the class who were all kept after school every day revealed to their parents that after school Mr. Clay would touch them under their pants. The parents conferred with one another, uncertain about what to do. After lengthy discussions, they finally went to the school to complain directly to the principal about what their sons had disclosed. The principal responded by telling them that "little boys that age can dream up some pretty wild stories."

The school principal, however, did subsequently conduct an investigation. After he completed the task, he spoke with these parents:

> I talked to this teacher, and I personally can vouch for his qualifications and have known him personally as well as professionally. What we boiled it down to is some wild imaginations and the three boys being really close.

The parents, despite being unsatisfied with this response, thought the matter was closed. One mother said:

> At this point, we hadn't come out and called it sexual abuse because it was hands down the back of the pants, and it was referred to as inappropriate touching, and nobody was really too willing to label it sexual abuse. We phoned different agencies to try to pin it down. Nobody wanted to call it anything, so we didn't know where we stood.

Even though the father of one of the boys involved worked for the police, one of the mothers reported:

We weren't really prepared to call the police and make it into a police investigation. From our children's point of view, and from Mr. Clay's point of view, we were really hesitant. It was an indiscretion, as far as we were concerned at this point. It was all vague: "Well, he put his hands down here." And, "Well, it was inside the pants, but fingers went to here." We were all still trying to protect Mr. Clay's reputation, and the possibility this was all blown up out of proportion and there was a mistake. At this point, my other son knew nothing about it. Nobody knew. Not even my best friend knew.

Through the grapevine, these three families learned another child had previously complained about similar touching by Mr. Clay. That child's parents had discussed their son's disclosure with the principal. Nothing had been done then, nor had the principal informed them of this prior complaint when they expressed their concerns. As a result, they became frustrated with the principal and therefore decided to complain directly to the school superintendent.

After lengthy discussion, the superintendent concluded:

If allegations do not clearly indicate sexual abuse, a gray area exists. . . . You already know my unease as it relates to initiating an inquiry through the process recommended by Child Protective Services. As previously discussed, I believe there should exist a court of discovery to screen frivolous or ill-founded complaints from those of substance. The very act of overt investigation carries with it a charge, a conviction, and a sentence, a situation which is repugnant to fair-minded people and, I believe, violates natural justice. Balanced against the need to protect the reputation, career, and livelihood of a teacher is the safety and well-being of the children. As you know, we initially, jointly, judged your children not to be at risk or in need of protection.

The school had ascertained the children's safety based on the fact that they no longer stayed after school with Mr. Clay. They did, however, remain enrolled in his class.

Once again the parents assumed the matter was over. Two months later, one of the families attended a local workshop conducted by two social workers experienced in working with child sexual abuse victims. Afterward they spoke with the social workers about their concerns regarding Mr. Clay. The social workers convinced them that the children had been sexually abused, and that "it was a classic case, and a classic case of a cover-up." The parents reported, "It was those two social workers who convinced us that the only place we should go, and the place we should have gone right from day one, was the police. So we did that."

As a result of their efforts, a police investigation was initiated. An officer was assigned to the case and interviewed the three little boys. One of the mothers summarized the policeman's interview with her son: "He was gentle, but to the point, and he wanted to be shown exactly where Mr. Clay had touched him." The policeman also interviewed a few other boys whose names were mentioned by the three boys he initially interviewed, but he got total denials from these other boys.

The mother who taught with Mr. Clay first learned about the allegations only when the police asked to interview her son, as his name had come up. She said:

> Immediately after the police interviewed my son, "I went directly to Jeffrey Clay, the teacher involved. I said to him, "The police contacted us last night about a problem that you seem to be involved in." Mr. Clay told me, "I didn't do anything to those little boys. I'm innocent," and "Would you and your husband stand beside me if it goes to court? Because I swear to God, I didn't do it."

The teacher and her husband agreed to support him.

Nothing came of the investigation, and the matter was again dropped. Two months later, on his lawyer's recommendation, Mr. Clay suddenly submitted his resignation. The original families involved later learned that yet another child had reported directly to the police about being sexually abused by Mr. Clay, this time providing details none of the other boys had admitted to the police: "He was very explicit, very definite, and extremely consistent. Jeffrey Clay had touched his penis and put a finger up his rectum." As a result of this latest complaint, an agreement was made between that family, the school, the prosecutor's office, and Mr. Clay's lawyer: Mr. Clay would resign from his teaching position and would agree to seek medical help. That family was told by the prosecutor's office, "You don't have enough evidence to lay charges. You're not going to get anywhere. Take this. At least he's resigning."

That family was never informed about the four other families who had lodged similar complaints that year, nor were the families originally involved in the complaints against Mr. Clay advised that another victim had surfaced: "We knew nothing. The police didn't tell us; the school board didn't tell us. The next thing we know, our kids come home from school and say, 'Oh, Mr. Clay isn't teaching anymore. He quit.'" The colleague he had asked to testify on his behalf said that she learned of his resignation the day it happened. That same afternoon she talked to her son about it, commiserating with him, since she knew how much he liked Mr. Clay. Her son's unexpected response was, "I didn't like Mr. Clay at all. He used to bug me." When she asked him what he meant, her son showed her exactly how Mr. Clay used to "bug" him, by demonstrating very sensual rubbing on the back, under the shirt, and down the back below the belt line. She said, "I went to the school the next morning. I immediately informed the principal of what my son had disclosed to me, and I said, 'Shall I phone the school district superintendent or are you going to look after it?' He said, 'I will look after it.' So I assumed from then on the district superintendent was involved and knew." Now six families had lodged similar complaints against Mr. Clay within that school year.

Mr. Clay's unexpected resignation, with the numerous rumors it created, resulted in the school holding a community meeting, ostensibly to educate the public about child sexual abuse. Mr. Clay's colleague learned for the first time at that meeting that other parents had previously complained to the principal about Mr. Clay, though they were yet unaware that her son had now also disclosed being abused. She joined the other three families, who had already been working together and felt frustrated because "there was nowhere to turn because we couldn't get out of the school with it. There was no support for us."

The teacher who had worked with Mr. Clay was cautioned by school personnel:

I was repeatedly called out of the staff room and told by the principal to keep my mouth shut, that anything I might say would be damaging to me. I said, "Well, I think it's the right of the rest of the staff to know what's going on here." The principal would not tell them. He forbade me to tell them at all because it was just alleged. So there's the ultimate protection for the man. I was running into my colleagues who were saying, "Did you know that some rotten parents trumped up these charges against this poor man?" Not just one person, many teachers said this. Nobody knew. It was all kept quiet. It was all part of a big conspiracy to keep it quiet. The superintendent did it. The principal did it. It seems that most people think that Mr. Clay resigned because of stress in his personal life, and he just didn't want to work with kids anymore.

A psychologist working at the school in the learning assistance program attributed the allegations to hysteria: "He was the last guy I would suspect for this sort of thing. He was heavily into athletics. He was a model teacher. He was progressive. He did neat things with his class as a whole." He believed Mr. Clay had been wrongly maligned and speculated that, "maybe, because he was young and energetic, might be the reason why these allegations are being made."

Another teacher in the school noted behaviors she had originally attributed to nervousness:

Mr. Clay used to come to school early, and when he talked to me in the hall, he would often grab a child who was walking by and put his arms over the child's shoulders. He was a tall person, so his arms would go down quite far. And he'd just talk to me and to the child while he'd be pushing his arms back and forth in front of the child. I just thought he was a little nervous because I was an experienced teacher and he was the new teacher.

She also remembered, with twenty-twenty hindsight, that when children were going to the morning gym club he sponsored, he would "pick up a kid, turn him upside down, pick him up by the legs. . . . I didn't think it was appropriate. My thought was, 'I'm sure glad I am who I am because some people wouldn't allow kids to have that done to them.' I feel now it was for looking down the baggy shorts. That particular thing was always done with boys." The kindergarten teacher noted that most of her students refused to go to the gym club on the days that he was there.

The four families who had formed an alliance were unhappy with how the situation was resolved, and they sent a letter to the school board to voice their concerns:

We, the undersigned parents, are deeply concerned about the circumstances regarding the resignation of Mr. Jeffrey Clay. Over the past few months, since our first complaints were brought forward, our frustrations with this issue have been growing. Have we really made every effort to ensure that this particular situation with Mr. Clay never reoccurs, and have we done everything possible to screen for other victims? Our main objectives are:

1. To assure ourselves Mr. Clay will not be able to resume teaching elsewhere as a result of no written record of these incidents on file.

2. That no child at the school will have possible later problems due to an experience that was never brought to light. The parents should be given every opportunity to question their children and follow it up with counseling.

3. Is the school district prepared to notify the parents of any schoolchildren who in any way had contact with Mr. Clay . . . concerning inappropriate behavior?

4. If necessary, is the school district prepared to assist those boys who have been, or might be identified as being, involved by providing a counselor, social worker, or therapist?

These families also strongly urged that a child sexual abuse prevention program be introduced into the school curriculum.

The following year the school did introduce a prevention program into the curriculum, but nothing further was done regarding the other concerns the parents had voiced. Other families were never informed about the allegations, and no counseling services were provided by the school district. The four families individually took their children to private counseling, with varying results. One parent went to the local psychiatrist, who told her, "Don't worry. Boys at that age are predominantly homosexual in their activity anyway, and there is nothing to worry about." One mother said:

> Maybe I'm making a big deal about it. I don't feel that we've been taken seriously. In some people's minds we've made a big deal about nothing. They tell us, "It was just little boys," and "It only happened for four months." You get the feeling, not from what is said, but from what is not said, that, one, your son did something wrong, and, two, you're making a big deal of it. You get this not only from the school system, but when you talk to other parents, or your doctor, and you begin to believe, "Maybe I should shut up. Maybe it's not a big deal. Then you think, "Damn it. My kid did not do anything to have this happen to him."

The other parents concurred, noting that people would trivialize what had happened by saying, "It was just touching." The mother who taught with Mr. Clay described her feelings:

> What makes me especially bitter was that the whole time he was abusing my son, he had the gall to have lunch with me every day in the staff room. And when the police were investigating, he even asked me if I would support him. He swore to me that he had done nothing wrong.

During the next year, the children started disclosing more detailed information, so the parents learned that the sexual contact with Mr. Clay had been much more extensive and invasive than they had previously understood. At the same time, the parents also discovered that the school district had hired Mr. Clay to work as a hospital homebound teacher, a program established to provide private tutorial services for children whose illnesses prevented them from attending classes. The director of that program had been told that Mr. Clay resigned from his teaching position for "personal reasons," but he now was interested in part-time work.

The parents were furious and decided to solicit help from the teacher's union representative because they wanted to be sure Mr. Clay could not continue teaching. Unbeknownst to the parents, however, the union representative turned out to be close friends with Mr. Clay's wife, and so when he attended the scheduled meeting with the parents, the agenda was different from what they had anticipated. The union representative arrived at their meeting to solicit support and sympathy for the "terrible plight of my good friend," Mr. Clay's wife, who would be put through some terribly humiliating and embarrassing ordeals should the parents proceed with a lawsuit:

> My concern is for Mr. Clay's wife. She's faced with a pretty horrendous problem. She has a series of steps to go through . . . the first bite is the threat of having a policeman arrive on her doorstep . . . the second threat is the publicity for her and her child.

He told them that Mrs. Clay had been unaware of any of the previous allegations, so they should have sympathy for her situation. He recommended a resolution that would prevent Mr. Clay from teaching, by presenting them with a letter from Mr. Clay's lawyer that stated Mr. Clay would give up his teaching certificate, with the reason identified as "cancellation for cause . . . cause being his reason or at his request." He presented the parents with a second letter from the therapist Mr. Clay had just begun seeing, which stated the following:

> Mr. Clay is seeking therapeutic assistance from me for his sexual proclivities . . . and will remain in treatment with me until his sexual problems have been resolved.

The union representative advised the parents to accept this arrangement and to agree not to press any further charges. He added:

> I gather it's very difficult to make a case stick . . . there is no point in not accepting this deal because my client, I mean Mr. Clay, will take it to court, and you'll lose it all. I want to make this perfectly clear. I'm not trying to make a deal for anybody. I'm just here to facilitate information.

He then gave them a contract from Mr. Clay's lawyer, whereby they agreed to drop the matter, with the explicit threat that if they did not do so, Mr. Clay would sue them for defamation of character.

The parents signed, and Mr. Clay succeeded in avoiding anything on his record to reflect the allegations that had been made. He subsequently reactivated his teaching certificate and has since taught the handicapped, as well as taken foster children into his home. Needless to say, his expertise, enthusiasm, and exceptional generosity to those who are needy has been very much appreciated by the community in which he now lives.

Case Study Three

> *The third case involves a very friendly blue-collar worker who successfully molested two generations of children, with impunity, for over twenty years, before any disclosures were credited.*

Mr. Martin was a hard worker, performing manual labor throughout his life. He was always ready to lend a helping hand to friends and neighbors and was handy at repairing "just about anything with a motor in it." A middle-aged gentleman, with an almost babylike innocence, he had an easy, ready laugh. He had been married three times. Although the marriages never worked out, he remained loyally supportive and involved with the children from each marriage, despite having fathered none of them. He married his first wife, who was suddenly single, penniless, and with three small children, after she had just left an abusive marriage. He took those youngsters under his wing to provide a good home for them. His wife turned out to be a drinker, so their relationship deteriorated over time, until he finally kicked her out and asked for a divorce, "when the kids were old enough to get by, and they could come and see me on their own. I never moved too far away."

He met his second wife through a friend. She had never been married, and "she was living on welfare trying to support these two little babies. I felt so sorry for them. Growing up without, you know, because she didn't have no money." He was making excellent money and was happy to share his new home with them. "I didn't love her at first. I just married her because it seemed like a good thing to do. I did it for the kids. I only started to love her after I got used to her." This marriage lasted approximately twelve years. Mr. Martin described how his second marriage ended:

But then she started treating me funny. She wanted money for all sorts of things I didn't want to pay for. She was starting to make up stories about things I was doing to the kids. She said if I didn't give her money, she'd go to the police. And she wasn't taking good care of those kids. So I kicked her out. She was mad. She tried to trump up charges about me touching neighborhood kids, but everyone knew it wasn't true. They all knew she was just out for revenge because she was afraid of losing her meal ticket.

He kept the kids, "which really impressed my friends, seeing as how they wasn't really my kids and all." He continued to provide for them but worried, since his work meant he was frequently away from home. "They needed a mother. So I found one." He married his friend's sister, who really needed the help. "She was living in a shack. She had a bit of a drug problem. Nothing too serious." He moved her into his house, and she not only took care of the children from his previous marriages, but the two of them began taking in foster children. "She cleaned up too. She quit doing drugs and did a good job raising those kids."

In addition to the wonderful home he provided for a number of stepchildren as well as some foster children, he was also called "Uncle" by his employer's entire extended family, in whose home he was frequently an honored guest, and for whom he often provided baby-sitting services. Over the years, the occasional suggestion of possible inappropriate touching cropped up but each time was attributed to ex-wives seeking revenge and money, or children "making up stories."

Mr. Martin was eventually convicted after he was caught molesting the child of one of the stepchildren he had previously abused. At that point, the other children he raised, their friends, and their children all confirmed these things had been done to them as well. None had ever told. Each assumed this had happened only to him or her, protecting the secret that allowed Mr. Martin to continue, without interruption, to molest all the other children in his sphere. His rambling explanations for each event only further confirmed his failure to understand the impact his behavior had on two generations of victims.

In defending himself against one of the allegations, he said, "I was only playing horsie with him. I never touched him or nothing." He explained some of the other allegations that had cropped up by adding, "I didn't know about sex or anything like that when I was growing up. I was never taught those things. I was only trying to understand what it was all about. I didn't ever mean no harm by it. I never hurt any of those kids. It wasn't like they said it was." One particular instance occurred because "there wasn't no lock on the bathroom door. I had kept telling them to get a lock put on it, but they never listened. I couldn't help it that the girl kept coming in the bathroom whenever I was in there."

In the case of the Citizen of the Year, there was no room for ambiguity. He was already a convicted child molester who also happened to have successfully organized the local fair. Out of convenience the community ignored the significance of his conviction and responded with overwhelming support in asking the courts to release him from jail to run the fair. In Mr. Smith's case, no suggestions of abuse were ever made. In Mr. Clay's case, numerous allegations kept surfacing and were handled as isolated instances, until finally a child who had been previously molested and whose family knew to go directly to the police resulted in Mr. Clay's resignation. In Mr. Martin's case, the occasional innuendoes that cropped up were easily ignored or blamed on the vindictiveness and anger of women scorned. He was convicted of child sexual abuse only after one of his former victims caught him molesting her daughter.

Case Study Four

> *This fourth case closely resembles the experiences described by those who dealt with Mr. Clay. In this case, however, events progressed far enough that this molester was eventually found guilty and given a life sentence.*

Robert Noyes, a schoolteacher in British Columbia, was finally arrested and subsequently tried as a dangerous offender in 1986, after molesting between fifty to seventy children (Halliday-Sumner, 1997c):

He stated [that] his first sexual involvement with younger boys was when he was 12 and he accidentally touched a 9-year-old, later developing into a molestation situation. Before he was twenty, he was caught playing with younger boys when he was employed in the capacity of a camp counselor. In the late 1960s he moved to BC [British Columbia] with his parents, enrolled at UBC [University of British Columbia], was an above-average student, and graduated in 1972. The accused worked in a group home before teaching. Shortly after getting his first teaching job at Balmoral Junior Secondary School in North Vancouver, he sought psychiatric treatment from the doctor who originally diagnosed his pedophilia. No alarms were raised where he taught. In January 1978, two boys he [had] molested for months disclosed [the abuse], and that night one of the victims called the accused to warn him. The accused then said he knew it was over, he went out of control, and he wanted to commit suicide. He contacted his family doctor and a friend, told them what he had done, and his doctor recommended he check into [the] hospital at UBC for treatment and group therapy. He did this the following day.

Although two mothers reported the incidents to the school officials, they were persuaded not to make a police report. They were given assurances from the principal that the accused was under treatment and would not be allowed to teach again. School and public health officials sought opinions from the accused's therapist on what to do about his teaching future. It was suggested [that] the accused could return to teaching if he were limited to [working with] high school students. A second opinion was not sought for fear of a lawsuit against the board by the accused. A medical health officer seconded the opinion and assumed his vague letter about the case, sent to the district school superintendent, would be forwarded to the education ministry.

The Supervisor told the health officer there was no legal process for handling the accused because there were no charges against him but offered assurances that no one consulting the school board for a recommendation would consider hiring him. In the fall of 1978, the Nechako Valley High

School in Vanderhoof, BC, did hire him, even though he admitted to the board he had a slight nervous breakdown and [an] ulcer, but he assured them he was cured. The hospital discharge papers stated he responded well to treatment and "was fortunate that his health officer did not recommend his leaving teaching." The accused further produced a letter from his doctor attesting "he was in good health and does not suffer from any condition that would prevent carrying out the duties of a full-time teacher." He also had a glowing report from Coquitlam Junior Secondary, where an official merely admitted he had been accused of molesting boys but had undergone treatment and should have a second chance at the high school level.

In July of 1980, he married and moved to Gibsons. He was a teacher in Gibsons, where there was another complaint. He was told to seek counseling and eventually transferred. The judge described the accused as an incurable pedophile. The accused had by then worked in Langdale, Vanderhoof, Coquitlam, Gibsons, and Ashcroft, BC. (pp. 198-200)

Throughout his teaching career he was treated by "at least ten psychiatrists" (Halliday-Sumner, 1997c, p. 200) with analysis, group therapy, and aversion therapy. A 1978 psychiatric report nevertheless described him as "arrogant and blind to the harm he caused" (Halliday-Sumner, 1997c, p. 200).

His sexual proclivities had been known by many throughout a number of school districts in the province. New allegations were viewed internally by the school system and handled as isolated instances. Each time he was encouraged to leave and given glowing letters of recommendation to facilitate a move to another district. In every community, therapists working with him knew about his sexual activities but kept quiet, despite legal obligations to report their knowledge. School district personnel also failed to report what they knew to the police, as each complaint they heard was handled separately. Every time people encountered indications of sexual improprieties, they assumed the information reflected only an isolated instance, encouraged everyone to keep quiet, and feared a libel suit from Robert Noyes should they discuss his proclivities. This case paralleled the Clay story, except that Robert Noyes was eventually convicted and incarcerated.

His conviction only finally occurred because of one little girl's response. The cloak of secrecy, individually maintained by numerous school districts and treatment providers who were all well aware of his sexual proclivities, began to unravel when this girl, who had previously been sexually abused by someone else and knew the system, called the police. She reported to the police that a number of the boys in her class were being molested by this teacher. Only through a thorough police investigation initiated by this elementary school child were each of those individual "indiscretions" revealed to be part of an ongoing pattern of abuse.

Case Study Five

> *Mr. Smith, Mr. Clay, Mr. Martin, and Robert Noyes thrive and flourish in every community. Yet they represent only part of the picture. Although many would prefer to assume only men sexually abuse children, this is not true. Unfortunately, women are also known to sexually molest children.*

Margaret Carruthers, a forty-four-year-old teacher in Canada, was convicted in February 1999, after twenty-nine-year-old Donna Bouchard took her to court for sexual assaults that had taken place fifteen years earlier. The teacher "began 'grooming' her student during the summer before she began grade seven, when Carruthers became her homeroom teacher and math teacher" (Wiebe, 1999b, p. A1). During that year the victim recounted her home life had become turbulent, and Carruthers was always very approachable. "By the end of grade nine, if someone asked me to identify my best friend, I would have said Ms. Carruthers" (Wiebe, 1999b, p. A1). In addition to teaching math and being her homeroom teacher, she also became her basketball coach and began inviting her to spend the night. The student valued the friendship and enjoyed the special attention from this admired and well-liked teacher. When the sexual abuse began, the student became confused and did not know what to do. While she did not want the abuse, she also did not want to lose this friendship. Donna Bouchard described what happened.

From the latter part of 1983 through to mid-1986, I was sexually abused by a woman, then my coach, teacher, teammate, and friend. What many people do not realize is that much of the grooming process begins long before the sexual advances do. Indeed, Margaret Carruthers, recently convicted of sexual assault [February 1999], though she has appealed the ruling, chose me long before she began "using me for her own sexual gratification," in the words of Queen's Bench Justice Robert Laing.

My name is Donna Bouchard, and more than a decade and a half later I am only now finding my voice. My story is not unlike that of other victims of sexual assault. Do not be fooled by the fact that I was offended against by a female, rather than a male. The dynamics are quite the same. They say hindsight is twenty-twenty, and I can certainly attest to that. However, if telling my story might help someone else to recognize the signs of sexual predators, to therefore avoid what happened to me, then tell it I will.

At a cursory glance, Margaret Carruthers held the image of a "perfect teacher," especially when I was in her grade-seven homeroom class in 1981. She coached several sports during my junior and senior high years, was a demanding math teacher, and appeared to love her work. She was the type of teacher who would be in her classroom, rather than the staff room, over breaks and noon hours. She was accessible to her students—made time for them, did little things to ease the difficult transition between elementary school and junior high. She wasn't "out the door" at 3:30 p.m. but usually stayed for an hour or two, marking papers in her classroom or talking with students and helping with sports practices. She'd say that she was single and therefore able to devote time that other teachers with their own families could not.

However, if one looked closer, one could see telltale signs that she was not merely a "master teacher." Miss Carruthers took special interest in some select female students and had several "pets" over the years. Indeed, she changed coaching assignments to follow these students through high school, altering her areas of "expertise" from sailing to canoeing; running to biking; basketball to volleyball to broomball, etc. I was one of these "chosen" students—the only one, to my knowledge, who has spoken out to date. The gift of her time was very powerful to a naive, impressionable, and confused thirteen- and fourteen-year-old girl such as I was at that time. Carruthers calculatingly began to single me out from my peers and family, isolating me, slowly and patiently. In everything she was very much the strategist. Several "markers" existed that should have been "red flags" to me, perhaps, but more important, to her colleagues, employers, school board members, or to my parents. While Marg could rationalize everything and explain things away logically, together as a whole, I believe they were indicators of her predatory and abusive nature. Allow me to elaborate.

Carruthers coached me in basketball from grades nine to eleven. In our school, grades seven to nine played junior basketball, grades ten to twelve played senior. I had played in grades seven and eight on the junior teams. Marg only helped out at practices but wasn't the designated coach or teacher supervisor. In addition to this sport, I also participated in drama and had the lead roles in plays throughout my school years. In grade eight, Marg began coming to rehearsals. She wasn't the director but volunteered her time doing set construction, etc. As the years wore on, Marg was increasingly vocal in her disapproval of the extent of my drama involvement—saying it took time away from training, and that it was an unnecessary stress, etc. When I was in grade nine, Marg began a senior team, which she encouraged me to play on. In that year [1983 to 1984], I was very busy with junior and senior basketball and drama. Prior to this, Marg had begun to assume the role of confidante or counselor, in addition to teacher and coach. I felt comfortable with her and would talk to her about issues pertaining to my own identity, my sense of "not belonging" in my family, my feeling unloved by my parents and misunderstood by friends, etc. I was spending increasing amounts of time with her, especially through that basketball season. It was during this time that I first began to stay at her home, a house trailer on the edge of town.

Marg was so successful in her efforts to isolate me from others for a variety of reasons: She treated me like a person, an equal, whereas others (especially teachers, parents) were treating me like a child. She wanted me to call her Marg, or "Mugs." She hated it if I called her Miss Carruthers. She'd say that I was different, I wasn't like other kids, or just "another student." She'd call me "D." She would often marvel at how mature I was for my age (like I was thirteen or fourteen going on thirty), that it was no wonder other kids didn't understand me because they were just that—kids. She knew how to get down to my level even though she was a teacher and I was her student. She made me feel special, as though I was worth spending time with. As I've said, that was very powerful. She was interested in what I had to say and really seemed to listen. She'd say she understood, she'd "been there," and she knew what I needed. She could see herself in me when she was my age, etc.

Any doubts I expressed to her regarding my parents or their love for me, she reinforced. She agreed that, since I was born less than nine months after their wedding date, I hadn't been wanted. She'd say she couldn't understand why they didn't love me, but it was okay because she loved me. She knew what kind of affection I needed. She encouraged me to lie to my parents and told me it was okay to be dishonest. I know that on more than one occasion, she led my parents to believe that trips to a nearby city were for the whole team, but it was just she and I who went. She'd buy me things: shoes, stuffed animals, meals, etc. She set up a bank account for my university education, paid for a creative writing course my parents hadn't been able to afford. She knew that my family's financial situation wasn't great and used that to her advantage. She said all of these were just "her way of helping out," and showing how much she loved me and how much I meant to her.

She attributed a lot more responsibility to me than to others my age. Therefore, despite the power differential, there was a significant role disturbance, especially after the sexual abuse began. She would make herself out to be the victim and began to confide in me about difficulties she was facing at work—with principals, etc. She would say that only I could support her or understand her. She didn't know what she'd do without me. She basically put me into a caregiver role. She began to give me alcoholic drinks—rum and Coke or liqueurs in coffee and hot chocolate when I'd stay overnight at her trailer. She told me to read books by Harold Robbins—a sexually explicit or graphic writer. (In fact, she had begun lending me books of her own as early as the summers following grades seven and eight.) At school she'd give me Tylenol or muscle relaxants even though staff weren't supposed to distribute these to students—but she'd say that didn't apply to "us." She'd often put little candies on my desk in her classroom—"Certs"—as a signal that she was thinking of me, or wanting to talk to me later. I learned to decipher these clues correctly.

As well, when I stayed at her place, there was a certain amount of invasion of privacy. She had cleared out the spare bedroom for me and said this could be "my room" (she knew I hated sharing with my younger sister at home). However, she'd come into my bedroom at any time or walk into the bathroom when I was showering (the doors didn't always close due to the shifting of the trailer in winter, she said). In coaching situations, she stayed in the locker rooms when we changed, saying that we should just strip in front of her because she wouldn't see anything she hadn't seen before, and that kind of thing. She was always so nonchalant and matter-of-fact about it, as though we shouldn't make a big deal out of it or question her decisions.

I knew I didn't like what she was doing, but I just thought that meant there was something wrong with me. I felt dirty, betrayed, ashamed, guilty, scared, and so very alone. Telling about the sexual touching became more a matter of telling on myself, rather than telling on her. By the time the sexual abuse was under way, Margaret Carruthers, a woman in her thirties—my teacher and coach—was my best and only friend. I was fourteen to fifteen years old and had no idea what was happening. I was spending more and more time at her trailer and less time with my parents. With my diminishing self-image and self-esteem, I rarely talked to my family when I was at home. I didn't think anyone at school would believe me, but more important, I had no idea how to even explain what was going on. In my own way, I tried to pull away from Marg—I would purposely avoid her at school or call her Miss Carruthers. She would give me "a look," and I knew she was angry. She'd throw chalk at me in the classroom, accuse me of playing games, of not knowing what I wanted, threaten to kill herself, be extremely cold and sarcastic with me in front of others. I wanted to die and began to think about killing myself.

I continued to spend some time with her, and she'd usually "pull me back in" within a short span of time. She was still my coach, and I couldn't imagine quitting the teams (I began to play broomball as well, which she played and coached). I didn't want to have to answer a whole lot of questions about why I wasn't playing on the teams or why I wasn't spending time with her anymore. Part of me didn't want to lose her either—in some way, I did love her, and I definitely trusted her. It was difficult because it wasn't just a "black and white" abuser and victim situation—at least that wasn't how it felt or certainly wasn't how she explained the sex. I struggled with my feelings toward her though. I still liked her, but I hated what she was doing to me. I learned to just dissociate and "shut down" when she began to touch me. I learned to touch her so that she wouldn't touch me. It somehow seemed to be the lesser of two evils, and I knew it hurt less. There was such an air of unreality to it all, too. I mean, I'd have to face her the next day—whether at the breakfast table or later in class and at practice. If she'd been "satisfied," then she was manic somehow, "on a high," acting as if nothing out of the ordinary had happened. I'd wonder if I had just dreamed it. I wondered what was wrong with me. While I wanted the sex to stop, I couldn't envision a life without her friendship. I was disgusted with myself.

What I know now is that nothing of the sexual abuse was really about sex as such. It was more an expression of her need for power and control taken out on me in a sexual manner. This is a fundamental point about sexual abuse that needs to be made clear to victims, but also to parents of children who have been victimized. Something that is especially difficult about same-sex abuse is that it often gets labeled as homosexual. When it's a male offending against a female, we don't label that "heterosexual" though! The dynamics of sexual abuse, whether male or female offenders with female or male victims, involve the exercise of power and control over someone weaker. Plain and simple. Abusing, or being victimized, has nothing to do with sexual orientation. People in my hometown of Debden, Saskatchewan (population 400), were often quick to label Margaret Carruthers as "the lesbian." Somehow they made that her crime. Nothing could be further from the truth. If Marg Carruthers were lesbian she would have had an adult female partner. She chose an adolescent—her student—that makes her a sexual predator, a sex offender, a pedophile. Educating people on that difference has been a daunting task.

Carruthers engaged in very common grooming behaviors. She was adept at manipulating my basic human needs for love, security, and affection; she accurately identified my areas of vulnerability and preyed upon them. She was skilled at isolating me from any resources (telling me that my parents didn't love me; saying derogatory things about my parents, brother, and sister), while simultaneously associating enjoyment and acceptance with such comments as "I need you" or "No one else loves/needs you like I do." She was adept at breaching my boundaries and justified everything she did in doing so. She told me, "You like this," "You want this," "You need this." I was further prevented from telling because of the relationship outside of the abuse: She remained my classroom teacher and coach; she attended some parties with my parents, etc. She made me feel like a partner in the activity ("I love you and you love me; no one understands what we have," "Let me show you how special you are to me; show me how special I am to you"), threatening to kill herself. In everything, she made herself out to be all I needed—and told me repeatedly that I was everything she needed. Pretty heady stuff for a kid to be hearing from a teacher over twice her age.

During the courtroom trial, Margaret Carruthers tearfully told the judge that the sexual encounters had been initiated by this seventh-grade student and that responding to them "was the biggest mistake of my life." Carruthers said Donna Bouchard seemed to need someone to talk to during her school years and Carruthers wanted to help. While Donna Bouchard said she felt Carruthers had used her, Carruthers countered that the relationship made her feel used too: "I was OK to talk to sometimes, but not OK to talk to other times. In the end, I felt like I was the one who got shit on" (Wiebe, 1999a, p. A2). Carruthers attempted to exonerate her behavior, indicating she primarily had been trying to help this student, even though "the relationship was difficult for me too. It doesn't mean that I never should have offered to help. Maybe it was just that you had a need, and I probably had a need too." She added, "perhaps I should have been more aware of the boundaries" (Wiebe, 1999a, p. A2).

As with the other molesters described in this book, earlier innuendoes existed. Once it became openly known that Carruthers molested students, one professional admitted to previous concerns regarding this teacher's involvement with three other girls. Another woman noted she had been "counseled to not have anything to do with that woman." Donna Bouchard had told a professional about the abuse while she was still a student, but "even though I told in no uncertain terms what Marg had done to me, this person did nothing with the information. My impression was that this person and her colleagues had something to hide—that their knowledge of Margaret Carruthers had long preceded Marg's coming to teach in Debden, and there must be some cover-up at play."

Donna felt a cover-up of sorts continued even after Ms. Carruthers' arrest in 1997:

> The school and school board responded by granting Carruthers paid stress leave and suspending her from teaching duties until a decision had been reached in the matter. Provisions of her release following arrest were that she not be unsupervised with anyone under the age of eighteen and that she avoid all contact (direct or indirect) with me. She held to the latter condition, but not to the former. She continued to coach and train a student who was still attending the school.

Carruthers is one of a growing number of female molesters who are currently being identified, charged, and convicted, joining their male counterparts as their behavior is correctly recognized as harmful to children. Typically, however, whether male or female, their community image and competent social skills ensure the abuse is overlooked, viewed as a onetime error in judgment, minimized, or blamed on the victim. Since they look so good, they continue to receive special accommodation and treatment, even when they are convicted. This is because they do not fit the stereotype image of a "dangerous sexual predator." They "present so well; they're punctual, usually employed, and in fact, they're so easy to deal with" they continue to "get away with it," as "probation officers let them slip out of sight" (Gannett News Service, 1995, p. A2). Summit (1989) summarizes this tendency:

We look only at the disparate, most superficial pieces as they present to our attention. We process those pieces serially, each as a novelty, never allowing them to coalesce into a meaningful whole, and never allowing a fresh and receptive analysis unprejudiced by previous dispersions. We may accept, one at a time, any number of surprising examples, each of which contradicts traditional knowledge, and still hold each as an exception with only peripheral significance. Unlike ordinary, unprejudiced discoveries, these clues are not allowed to add up to increasing understanding. Instead, like the plethora of medieval observations that contradicted geocentricism, such unwanted discoveries only increase the intellectual challenge to explain them away. (p. 419)

As the previous cases show, each community had enough reason to be wary, instead of suspending disbelief and allowing behaviors to occur that are not generally considered to be acceptable. In each of these cases, specific behaviors occurred that should not have been tolerated. These behaviors appear to be warning flags that should alert adults, rather than lull them into a false sense of security (De Becker, 1999). Identifying how the adult community is groomed is relevant to further understanding the dynamics of child sexual abuse and is necessary to better protect children from abuse.

Child abuse is not an isolated event that occurs to only a very few children. Rather, it is minimally estimated to occur to about one out of every four girls and one out of every six boys (Finkelhor, 1979a), and all of society is impacted by the psychological damage the abuse creates (Briere, 1992; van der Kolk, 1994). The occurrence of sexual abuse has been extensively documented (Summit, 1989; Sgroi, 1985; Salter, 1988; Halliday, 1995; Abel et al., 1987; Salter, 1995). Additional research has also focused on the "grooming" process, whereby molesters win the confidence of children to maintain their silence while the abuse continues (Conte, Wolf, and Smith, 1989; Berliner and Conte, 1990; Elliott, Browne, and Kilcoyne, 1995).

As a result of that work, current prevention programs teach children about safe touching, saying "no" to the molester, and telling adults about the abuse (Harms et al., 1986; Trickett and Schellenbach, 1998). The primary focus of these prevention programs is teaching children to "say no, run, and tell." Although a video by the Committee for Children (1996) recommends parents screen who baby-sits their children, the focus of current programs nevertheless leaves a vacuum for adult responsibility in the detection and prevention of child sexual abuse.

The resultant implicit message, that children are responsible for their own safety, suggests adults in the community may be unable to protect them. In no other area of criminal justice does society place the burden of responsibility on children to protect themselves. Telling children to continue reporting the abuse until they are believed is a reminder to them of how incredible their "stories" will seem, and how little credibility they have by virtue of their social status. Typically, they will need to tell nine different adults before their story might even be heard (CARE Productions, 1985), requiring perseverance beyond what most adults would endure when addressing less emotionally complex concerns. Children are even less likely to be heard and found credible when they disclose abuse by those known and loved in their family or community, despite most molestations being initiated by "trusted" family and community members (Russell, 1983; Halliday, 1985; Briere, 1992). As a result, disclosures are often met with reactions of disbelief (Miller, 1990; Salter, 1995).

Although much has been studied about how molesters groom children, research has not focused on the dynamics of how these molesters also establish themselves in the adult community as being "above reproach," thereby ensuring continued safe access to children. This grooming of adults does occur, according to offender treatment specialists, molesters, and victim advocates (van Dam, 1996). As a result, adults often unwittingly become enthusiastic supporters of molesters, which communicates to children that any disclosures are unlikely to be believed, thereby inadvertently colluding with the molesters in undermining the children's willingness to talk. Understanding these dynamics can help create a different focus in the field of child sexual abuse prevention by giving adults the tools and knowledge to protect children more directly from child sexual abuse. This will put the onus of prevention and detection on the adult community, where it belongs.

Much as experienced burglars can best teach homeowners how to protect their homes, molesters practiced in grooming adults are the best educators on how to keep children safe. In structured interviews (van Dam, 1996), molesters described how they charmed adults to secure their access to children. Recognizing this grooming process will better help adults protect children from child sexual abuse. Identifying when such grooming occurs is only the first step. The second step is responding correctly to manage and discourage the behavior, and to stop giving such a person free access to children.

To do this, adults need to have a thorough understanding of the slippery terrain that inevitably surrounds child sexual abuse. Therefore, it is important to know what constitutes child sexual abuse, understand the harm it causes, and become familiar with the behaviors most typically exhibited by potential molesters. This is because successful molesters, and the community members enamored of them, will readily put a positive spin on what is happening, which succeeds precisely because of adult naïveté. Timely intervention will require a good understanding of child sexual abuse, knowing who molests, and recognizing how they do it.

Chapter 2

Knowing It Is a Problem:
The Need for Clarity

CLEAR DEFINITIONS

People's views on what constitutes child sexual abuse often differ, which may prevent them from responding appropriately and with the necessary certainty. This was exactly the case with the families whose children were molested by Mr. Clay. The parents, who believed their children, were initially told that he put his hands down their pants after school. The parents, however, were unclear about what this meant. As one parent remarked, "[W]e hadn't come out and called it sexual abuse because it was hands down the back of the pants, and it was referred to as inappropriate touching, and nobody was really too willing to label it sexual abuse." Because of their confusion, they initially took their concerns only to the principal, rather than to the police.

The principal's response to them, that "little boys that age can dream up some pretty wild stories" revealed his naïveté, which was further evidenced by his decision to discuss the matter with the alleged molester, Mr. Clay. In no criminal case is an understanding of events primarily determined by soliciting explanations from the accused person. Yet that is precisely how accusations against Mr. Clay were handled. After his discussion with Mr. Clay, the principal explained to the parents, "What we boiled it down to is some wild imaginations and the three boys being really close."

This failure to have clarity about what constitutes child sexual abuse did not end there. Since the parents were still disconcerted, they went to the school superintendent, who responded to them, "If allegations do not clearly indicate sexual abuse, a gray area exists."

A gray area implied nothing more should be done. The parents were subsequently further cowed by the teacher's union representative. He used their lack of clarity about what had taken place to bully them into believing that their allegations, which would tarnish Mr. Clay's reputation, would ensure that they would be sued for slander. This strategy succeeded precisely because they were unsure if what had happened to their children was really sexual abuse. Their uncertainty, especially in the face of clear opposition by powerful players—the principal, the superintendent, the school board, and, ultimately, the teacher's union representative—made them timid.

This lack of clarity in definitions is endemic to the field, so that even when professionals talk about child sexual abuse, they are not in agreement about what behavior meets the requirements. Russell (1983) confirms this phenomenon:

> There is no consensus among researchers and practitioners about what sex acts constitute sexual abuse, what age defines children, nor even when the concept of child sexual abuse is preferable to others such as sexual victimization, sexual exploitation, sexual assault, sexual misuse, child molestation, sexual maltreatment, or child rape. . . . Cases in which children are raped or otherwise sexually abused by their peers, younger children, or children less than five years older than themselves, are often discounted as instances of child sexual abuse. (p. 133)

Yet, in managing the protection of children, clarity is exactly what is required. Confusion about what constitutes child sexual abuse, and the subsequent lack of decisiveness about when to respond, only assists the molesters, for whom ambiguity and lack of clear responses are an asset. A thorough understanding of the terms will help identify what is taking place and how to respond to those events. Lack of clarity can lead to tolerating behavior that should not be supported and failing to take action when action should be taken, as well as creating hysteria when none is needed. Both failing to respond when an intervention would be helpful and interfering when no action is required are deleterious (Wylie, 1993).

In one school district, a fourth-grade teacher massaged students under their shirts. He explained that "this was an effective teaching technique learned when working with the mentally disabled." The community tolerated this behavior. Some considered it a personal quirk; others believed it was a teaching method. A number of children later reported the massage also went below the belt, which the teacher explained as "accidental slips" of the hand. The parents did not know what to do and so did nothing. But doing nothing inadvertently condoned child sexual abuse.

At another school, a young girl complained to a school nurse of pain in her genitalia. She explained that she had been riding a boy's bike and had fallen on the crossbar. The nurse called Child Protective Services, the girl was removed from her home, and it was assumed, despite her description of the injury, that she had, in fact, been sexually abused. She clearly and consistently described her injury, until she was finally examined by a doctor who found her injury to be consistent with her story. She was eventually returned to the family home. This crisis could have been avoided had there been a clear understanding of the topic.

Elsewhere a doctor surmised that his young patient must have been sexually abused because she was still wetting her bed at night. He had read lists of signs and symptoms to identify when a child has been sexually abused. He failed, however, to understand that such lists are only intended as a guideline to alert adults to the possibility of abuse when a cluster of symptoms is present. Evidence of any one of the symptoms, or even a number of them, is not automatically indicative of child sexual abuse. The mother was informed by her family doctor that her husband had been sexually molesting the child, which needlessly destroyed the marriage. Although the child had never been molested, the doctor's false diagnosis resulted in unnecessary harm to the child and her family.

GUIDING TREATMENT

This lack of clarity also prevents many clients from getting the treatment they need. In the case of Mr. Clay's victims, one mother seeking treatment for her son was told it was normal for boys to engage in homosexual play. Many therapy clients, even when directly asked if they have ever been sexually abused, frequently deny any such history, despite the fact that a trusted adult might have touched them on their genitalia, or required them to touch the adult's genitalia, or even engaged them in oral sexual contact. When these events are later revealed in therapy, and they are asked why they had previously denied ever being sexually abused, they often answer that "no sexual intercourse ever took place." In their minds, therefore, they had not been sexually abused (Briere, 1992). They assumed the question to mean, Had intercourse ever occurred? A clearer understanding and agreement on terminology would facilitate treatment for those whose sexual abuse contributed to their therapeutic needs.

GUIDING RESEARCH

Both the molestation and the person doing the molesting are variously defined in the literature (Sgroi, 1985; Finkelhor, 1984) and by the law (Revised Code of Washington [RCW], 1994). This further contributes to ambiguity, which results in many activities being ignored or dismissed as "a misunderstanding." This ambiguity creates a climate that inadvertently fosters tolerance of molesters and their crimes. It further ensures that each isolated instance will be treated as a one-time occurrence, rather than a pattern, and subsequently written off as an "error in judgment" or "a misunderstanding." This was the case with Robert Noyes, whose proclivities were well known by many professionals in numerous school districts. All of these adults failed to protect children precisely because they incorrectly believed each event to be a one-time error in judgment. As exemplified by the Noyes case, such an appearance of tolerance more accurately reflects both lack of knowledge about the dynamics of child sexual abuse and a general discomfort with the topic. This is exactly the right breeding ground to allow further abuse to flourish.

The psychological literature refers interchangeably to various definitions in documenting the prevalence of child sexual abuse. For instance, Russell (1984) and Badgley (1984) define child sexual abuse as any unwanted sexual touching. Sedney and Brooks (1984) refer to any "sexual experiences involving other people while they were growing up" (p. 215), while Finkelhor (1979a) includes intercourse, fondling, and exhibitionism. Sorrenti-Little (cited in Salter,

1988) refers to intercourse or fondling of the child's unclothed genitalia.

The majority of psychological studies limit sexual abuse to sexualized contact with a person five years older (Salter, 1988), but some do not include an age differential or differentiate between consenting sex play and sexual abuse. Since so little is understood about normal sexual development and peer involvement (Money, 1986), any sexual activities between peers is frequently assumed to be normal. This ignores those coercive interactions between peers which are abusive (Salter, 1988). These discrepancies further contribute to ambiguity in identifying and defining child sexual abuse, which understandably leaves adults confused, creating situations in which improprieties are simply ignored. This ambiguity also creates room to trivialize events. The offenders interviewed for this book, as well as those cited in other studies (Salter, 1988; Salter, 1995), used this ambiguity to minimize and exonerate their own behavior. The victims' families and the communities used this ambiguity to avoid addressing a difficult situation.

GUIDING RELATIONSHIPS

Equally worrisome are the cases in which this lack of knowledge prevents wholesome interactions that should be encouraged. Peter Alsop (1988) addresses this issue in song form to help guide professionals. The lyrics of a letter written by "the kids in grade two" to their teacher Mr. Brown are "you never touched us anywhere that was against the rule," wondering why Mr. Brown no longer "thumb wrestles" with them or "musses their hair." Such inhibited behavior reflects an overreaction to the issue of child touching.

Clearly, children need physical contact (McConnell, 1980), which should be regarded as a primary requirement for healthy emotional growth. Confusion about child sexual abuse may incorrectly impede opportunities for developmentally important physical contact. In one school, the principal developed elaborate schemes regarding allowable physical touch between kindergarten teachers and their students. This did nothing to deter the molesters, who disregarded all rules, but deprived small children of opportunities for much-needed support.

GUIDING INTERVENTIONS

Many of the molesters interviewed for this book acknowledged frequent early experiences where their molestations of children were identified and then ignored. Westley Allan Dodd, who eventually murdered a number of his victims, had come to the attention of the police and school authorities many times during his adolescence, but nothing was ever done. He reported that "no charges were ever filed, because I was a 'nice kid.' I did go to therapy for about two months, then quit." Another molester, named Jim, who worked as an after-school child care provider, stated that by the age of twenty-one he had already molested over 300 children. He described numerous instances at the ages of ten, eleven, and twelve, when parents walked into a room while he had his hands in their child's pants, or "one time I had my hand right on this kid's crotch when his mother walked in the room. He was four. I was twelve. I thought for sure, 'Uh oh. This is it.' She didn't do anything." He was asked to go home but was subsequently again allowed to play with this four-year-old "friend." He continued to have similar experiences, each making him bolder and more confident. Years later, in his after-school child care job, he was frequently seen by parents holding their ten- or eleven-year-old children on his lap, or wrestling with a group of youngsters on the floor. "No one ever said anything to me. I got away with it for years."

Such societal responses are, unfortunately, all too typical and reflect the need for an increased understanding of the dynamics of child sexual abuse. This was confirmed by convicted molesters Silva (1990) and Cook (1989), who wrote in detail about the power they obtained when their initial forays seemed invisible to the adults who clearly saw the inappropriate touching. In one community, a number of parents witnessed an adult's hand straying to their children's genital area during various tickling games. What was observed individually by parents was ignored as an "accidental slip" each time it occurred, so every event was treated as an isolated instance.

In Mr. Clay's case, the parents whose children eventually more explicitly reported having been touched on the penis and buttocks by Mr. Clay, recognized in hindsight that they had seen roughhousing play between the teacher and various boys in his classes that had made them uncomfortable, but they had ignored it. This was also true in the case of Mr. Smith. Only by viewing the behaviors in a larger context can questions of child sexual abuse arise. Mr. Smith's touching girls on their bottoms when helping them off the monkey bars, having children put their hands in his pockets to find candy, and ignoring requests to discontinue these behaviors were all viewed as isolated events.

Mr. Clay was constantly seen playing contact games with children: he wrestled with them in the gym, held them upside down in the hallway, and turned every game into a high contact sport. In the case of Robert Noyes, many school districts and therapists failed to properly address the issues of sexual abuse exactly because they viewed the circumstances they were aware of as isolated instances, rather than understanding each event as probably representing the tip of the iceberg. The widespread sexual assault of children is typically viewed as "the (first) best kept secret" (Rush, 1980). The failure to recognize each identified instance as, in all likelihood, representing a larger pattern is "the second largest societal blind spot," which "sex offenders themselves have little reason to emphasize" (Salter, 1995, p. 5).

This inability to see behavior in a larger context also allowed a father to remain ignorant of his son's pedophilia, despite accurately observing specific improprieties. The son (Silva, 1990) describes "horsing around" with a nine-year-old "friend" during a sleepover: "My father . . . called me aside to ask just what I, a twenty-six-year-old man, [was] doing with this kid" (p. 479). Although his father noted the behavior and recognized that a twenty-six-year-old man playing with a nine-year-old boy seemed odd, he did not have the framework to understand the problem. He subsequently ignored what he saw, which exemplifies this frequent failure to respond appropriately to what individually appear to be vaguely questionable behaviors.

In many cases, numerous incidents are commonly witnessed that seem somewhat inappropriate. For instance, parents report overhearing sexualized talk, seeing a hand "accidentally" touching their child's clothed genitalia, or witnessing a caress. Mr. Clay's colleague remembered her response to his roughhousing with children in the hallway long before she knew of any of the allegations. At the time she felt it was inappropriate, but because she did not have a context for understanding it, she did nothing.

Teachers reported seeing children shrink from Mr. Smith's touch, and finding it peculiar that he should have children look for candy by putting their hands in his pants pockets. Friends considered Mr. Martin's eagerness to bathe children as rather odd but trivialized it as just one of his idiosyncrasies. Instead of responding to specific events that seemed peculiar, in each case, witnesses reported trivializing the event, explaining it away, feeling helpless, or not knowing what to do, and they therefore ignored the entire event.

Molesters describe being empowered each time these visible slips are overlooked or ignored. "I think most folks are frightened of and intimidated by people who are right in their face doing something wrong. You know that's true. When you're trying to do something sneakily, you know to behave as though you're supposed to be there doin' that, right? The more confidence you project, the less others feel confidence to confront. Their callous confidence even makes you question yourself" (in Schlessinger, 1996, p. 60). This, in combination with the nature of what is witnessed, has many both disbelieving and ignoring what they see. This is variously referred to as a "shared negative hallucination" (Goodwin, 1985, p. 14) or nescience, "a willful refusal to see" (Summit, 1989, p. 419). Yet "of all the approaches you might take to enhance the safety of your child, do you suppose that ignorance about violence is an effective one?" (de Becker, 1999, p. 14).

Although many adults would have no difficulty intervening when they see other types of inappropriate behavior, observing seemingly ambiguous sexual activities often leaves adults feeling helpless, uncomfortable, and confused. A typical response to such ambiguity and discomfort is blocking it out altogether (Goleman, 1985; Summit, 1989). Effectively protecting children from sexual abuse requires the opposite reaction (Summit, 1989). It requires understanding the dynamics of child sexual abuse clearly enough to tackle an extremely complex and challenging dilemma. Ignoring disquieting information covertly endorses the behavior and has adults inadvertently colluding with the molester: "During the beginning of sexual abuse, deniers are unconscious co-conspirators" (de Becker, 1999, p. 15).

Since child sexual abuse has both a legal and a psychological impact, definitions may vary depending on the arena. In the legal community, definitions serve the purpose of defining the criminal behavior to aid in establishing guilt or innocence. The focus of this book is to terminate inappropriate behavior long before it reaches the extent required to meet legal definitions. Legal definitions will be provided in Appendix I to give the reader an understanding of what the law considers to be sexual abuse. More important for the purposes of this book is giving readers a framework that will allow them to act surely and appropriately before any clearly illegal behavior transpires. The psychological definition given here will provide such a framework.

In the psychological community, definitions primarily serve the purpose of guiding treatment planning. Psychological definitions can also be useful in helping adults to develop enough of an understanding of child sexual abuse to participate more actively in the prevention of abuse. Although legal and psychological definitions may vary somewhat, some overlap does occur (Ashley and Houston, 1990). For the purposes of this book, the following psychological definitions will be used when referring to child sexual abuse.

Psychological Definitions

A psychological definition of child sexual abuse does not need to meet the strict criteria required in a court of law. Rather, this definition is a guideline to help adults know what to do so they can graciously, directly, and appropriately address even minor transgressions.

Child sexual abuse involves *a violation of a trust relationship* between a molester and a child (Groth, 1979; Finkelhor, 1979a). It involves *secrecy* (Groth, 1979; Finkelhor, 1979a), and it involves *sexual activity* the molester knows to be unacceptable (Groth, 1979; Harms and van Dam, 1992). Child sexual abuse includes a continuum of activities, from talk to voyeurism to intercourse (Sgroi, 1985). By using these three criteria as a guideline, a number of

---

Sexual Abuse: A Working Definition

• Violation of a trust relationship *with* unequal power and/or advanced knowledge (and)
• The need for secrecy (and)
• Sexual activity

---

seemingly ambiguous activities can be determined to qualify or not qualify as sexual abuse.

For instance, two children with equal power and knowledge touching each other's genitalia without knowing to maintain secrecy are engaging in normal sexual play, and their behavior can be safely ignored. Sexual activity between two children would qualify as sexual abuse, however, if *power and coercion* were used. If one child is bigger, more aggressive, older, has *advanced knowledge,* or in any way *threatens* the other child, then the situation is one of abuse (van Dam, 1987; Harms and van Dam, 1992).

Other activities on this continuum can also be more easily identified as child sexual abuse. For instance, voyeurism, which is frequently ignored, correctly meets these criteria. In one small town, the high school football coach (who had advanced knowledge and power) created a peephole in a small closet to look into the shower room. He knew to keep this secret and later confessed to masturbating while watching players bathe, giving the activity a sexual nature. Although most team members were ignorant of their coach's behavior, his behavior meets the criteria for child sexual abuse. The athlete who accidentally discovered his coach engaged "in the act" experienced discomfort and humiliation, especially when his accusations were not believed and he was ridiculed. Twenty years later, this coach was charged and convicted after other students described the same behavior.

Therapy clients frequently report experiencing similar invasions into their privacy, involving peepholes drilled into bathroom and/or bedroom walls. Carruthers attributed the need for open bathroom and bedroom doors to problems with a settling foundation and used this as an initial opportunity to begin desensitizing her victim and blurring the boundaries. Using this definition of child sexual abuse correctly acknowledges such situations as sexually abusive. Many of these victims, even those never directly touched by the molester, were aware of the invasion of their privacy and fearful about other potential violations. Some people incorrectly believe such peeping to be relatively harmless (Kincaid, 1998), ignoring both that most individuals who peep also more directly molest (Salter, 1995), and the uncertain emotional climate such behavior creates.

Understanding what constitutes child sexual abuse helps adults correctly identify these and other improprieties as sexually abusive. This allows people to differentiate between appropriate and inappropriate touching, not tolerate ambiguous behavior, and comfortably terminate activities that seem questionable. This could have been possible in any of the following examples, had the participants possessed a clear framework from which to operate: One mother reported, "We never thought too much about it. Our daughter had a lot of tomboy friends and one of her friends' father wrestled with them. It wasn't until many years later that we found out he undressed them in the process of wrestling" (Sanford, 1980, p. 87). A number of the molesters interviewed for this book described variations on this theme of engaging in wrestling, roughhousing, and tickling games, even with young teenagers. Others described having thirteen-, fourteen-, and fifteen-year-old girls sitting on their laps while caressing their hair. In each case, adults were aware of these behaviors, but none of these molesters were ever told that the lap sitting, wrestling, roughhousing, tickling, or hair caressing should be stopped. In fact, Jim's experience (the after-school counselor previously described) of initially being told to go home and then having it be "like nothing happened" is much more common.

Most people who are interested in children are eager to cooperate with family or school standards and adhere to behavioral guidelines. In contrast, Mr. Smith ignored reasonable requests: He was told by more than one principal to stop helping girls off the monkey bars by holding their bottoms. He was asked to quit handing out candy and money to children on the school playground. He was instructed to attend birthday parties only at the invitation of parents. A responsible person would happily comply with such requests. Mr. Smith did not. Even if Mr. Smith's candy-giving games, with children putting their hands in his pants pockets, and his tickling games, and other behaviors are totally innocent, they desensitize children and adults to future encounters that might not be innocent.

A zero-tolerance policy for possibly ambiguous behavior would help everybody steer a safer course through a maze of unnecessary complexities. This would protect children from a continuum of sexually or potentially sexually abusive behavior and help adults know to end behavior typical of grooming. Tolerating such behavior helps to make children more vulnerable. As one child molester stated, "There were a lot of children I never got around to molesting, but I got them more ready for the next guy."

Setting clear boundaries sends the message to potential molesters that the adults will not tolerate inappropriate behavior and teaches children the parameters of appropriate interactions with others. It also directly communicates to children that adults will be in charge.

Sexual Molester Definitions

Not only is it important to understand what constitutes child sexual abuse, but the reader also needs to be aware of the terminology. In the case of Mr. Smith, a failure to understand this had parents erroneously believing that because he was not biologically related to the children, they were safe in his presence. "After all," as one parent pointed out, "everybody knows that sex offenders only abuse their own children." To this parent, Mr. Smith's behavior was not worrisome precisely because he was not related to the children in his care.

A number of terms are interchangeably used in the literature: Those who sexually molest children are variously referred to as sex offenders (RCW, 1994), pedophiles (Becker and Quinsey, 1993), or incest offenders (Herman, 1981). Pedophiles and incest offenders are sometimes differentiated into pedophiles who abuse outside the family and incest offenders who abuse their own children, as if these are separate and distinct populations (Salter, 1988). Many of these distinctions are questions of opportunities, rather than predilections, with research frequently revealing that those who were thought to be only incest offenders were instead "lazy" offenders, who also molested other children when presented with the opportunity to do so (Salter, 1995).

Some researchers believe pedophiles are sexually attracted only to children, while incest offenders are primarily interested in age-appropriate sexual relationships, with their sexual improprieties blamed on "dysfunctional" family functioning (James and Nasjleti, 1983; Taylor, 1984; de Young, 1988). Feierman (1990) defines incest as any sexual relationship with a blood relative, regardless of the age of both parties. A sexual interest in prepubescent children is called pedophilia, and a sexual interest in adolescents is called ephebophilia.

Other definitions differentiate by motivation. For instance, chronic repetitive offenders have a deviant arousal pattern, while episodic offenders are motivated by other nonsexual problems that lead to the sexual abuse (Salter, 1988). These distinctions of chronic, repetitive, and episodic parallel those of pedophile and incest offender. Groth (1979) also classifies offenders into two groups, using the terms fixated and regressed. Fixated offenders (pedophiles) are persistently sexually attracted to children, and primarily males. Their orientation begins in adolescence, and the crimes are premeditated. They are immature, have little sexual contact with age mates, and are generally not drug and alcohol involved. Regressed offenders are primarily attracted to peers. Their sexual involvement with children is impulsive and stress related. Using the earlier definitions, Groth's fixated offenders are chronic offenders with a repetitive pattern, or pedophiles. The regressed offenders are episodic, or incest offenders.

The research does not entirely support this differentiation of offenders into two distinct categories. Incest offenders do not simply abuse their own children because of sexual frustrations with their adult partners. They are frequently known to also abuse non-family members (Abel et al., 1981; Murphy et al., 1986; van Dam, 1996). Nor do pedophiles only abuse children. They are just as capable of having sexual interactions with age-appropriate partners (Ruedrich and Wilkinson, 1992). Silva (1990) confirms this in his autobiography when he describes being simultaneously sexually involved with two adult females and two male children:

Evelyn came to visit again. I explained that I would be on call one or two nights each week, but I actually was staying at Debby's house. Romantically, this was the wildest period of my life, as there frequently were days when I made love to Evelyn in the evening or morning before going to work, to Charles that afternoon, and then to Debby, his mother, that night. But clearly, I enjoyed myself most with Charles. David (who was six years old) and I were also involved in a minor way. (p. 481)

In studies with convicted offenders guaranteed confidentiality, these distinctions between pedophile and incest offender were further blurred, as each of the offenders was seen to have many more victims than those identified in court files. Thus, those convicted of incest admitted to a number of extrafamilial molestations (Abel, Mittelman, and Becker, 1985; Abel and Osborn, 1992). In another study, a plethysmograph was used to measure arousal in incest offenders. The controls showed more arousal to adult stimuli than to child stimuli, while the pedophiles showed equivalent levels of arousal to child and adult stimuli (Ruedrich and Wilkinson, 1992). This again suggests that the child sexual molester may be aroused to both adult and child stimuli, rather than only to child stimuli.

The distinction between pedophile and incest offender is further challenged by a number of other studies. Salter (1988) confirms that many of those charged and convicted for incest also have engaged in sexually abusing nonrelatives. This was true of many of the molesters interviewed for this book, as well as those interviewed in a number of other studies (Abel, Rouleau, and Cunningham-Rathner, 1986). Those who were identified as having only molested their own children often did not molest other children, primarily because of fear and/or lack of opportunity, rather than lack of desire, or they had molested other children but had not been convicted for those other molestations (Ruedrich and Wilkinson, 1992).

Any distinction between pedophiles who are only interested in having sex with children, as opposed to incest offenders who are primarily interested in peer relationships, is further confounded in that a number of molesters also describe fantasizing about sex with children, while engaging in sex with peers (Salter, 1988). Furthermore, it should be noted that these differential categories of sexual abuse have been developed in discussions with offenders. Solely relying on offenders to create definitions, however, is like asking foxes to rationalize their chicken-eating proclivities. It is no accident that one of the two categories (incest offender) not only minimizes the sexual behavior but also considers it to be a reaction to environmental stresses. This neatly allows the molester to avoid direct responsibility for the abuses and instead handily places the blame on others. Frequently heard explanations include "My wife was giving me the cold shoulder," or "I was asleep and rolled over thinking it was my wife. I had no idea it was my five-year-old daughter I was trying to have sex with."

The *Diagnostic and Statistical Manual of Mental Disorders,* Fourth Edition (DSM-IV) (American Psychiatric Association [APA], 1994), includes both categories in the definition of pedophilia: "Individuals may limit their activities to their own children, stepchildren, or relatives or may victimize children outside their families" (p. 528). The DSM-IV (APA, 1994) then requires the clinician making a diagnosis of pedophilia to use the categories of exclusive type (chronic, fixated, or pedophile) or nonexclusive type (regressed, episodic, or incest offender). Yet Abel and Osborn's (1992) work clearly demonstrates the futility of such classifications, as most sexual molesters engage in a variety of different sexual activities with children and operate both within and outside the family. The categories specified are determined by what the client admits to during an assessment, which will be limited, at best (Abel and Osborn, 1992).

But although the DSM-IV (APA, 1994) provides some useful clarity in defining pedophilia, it also creates confusion. In the DSM-III-R (Third Edition, Revised) (APA, 1987), the three diagnostic criteria for pedophilia included (A) sexual urges or fantasies involving children, (B) acting on these urges or being distressed by them, and (C) being sixteen years old and five years older than the victim. In the DSM-IV (APA, 1994), however, the B criterion has been changed to "The fantasies, sexual urges, or behaviors cause clinically significant distress or impairment in social, occupational, or other important areas of functioning" (p. 528). This slight change from the DSM-III-R (APA, 1987) would mean that, by definition, someone is a pedophile only if that person's sexual proclivities interfere with his or her level of functioning. Most offenders, both according to those interviewed for this book and according to other studies, consider the impairment in their functioning to result from being reported to the police. Before they were charged and convicted, their lives were "fine." Therefore, by definition, according to the DSM-IV (APA, 1994), a pedophile might be only someone whose sexual crimes have been reported. This is one more example of the confusion in the field.

Although it is recognized that both men and women sexually abuse children, the data on female offenders are still extremely limited (Wolfe, 1985; Halliday, 1985; Mayer, 1992; Elliott, 1993; Anderson and Struckman-Johnson, 1998; Chesney-Lind, 1997). Although it is known that women also sexually abuse children, most of the references and literature primarily cover data on male molesters. Fehrenbach and colleagues' (1986) study includes eight female offenders who all committed indecent liberties on children under age six. Russell's (1983) study includes eight females, 4 percent of all incestuous perpetrators in her study. Halliday (1995), with an annual average caseload of 350 offender interviews, states that awareness of the percentage of molestations by female offenders rose from three percent in the 1980s to 25 to 30 percent in the 1990s. Other data appear to confirm this, suggesting that as many as one-third of child sexual molesters are female.

The term child molester will be used in this book to encompass anyone whose sexual behavior meets the previously discussed psychological definition of child sexual abuse. The term child molester will refer to both males and females.

Chapter 3

Why It Is a Problem:
What Is the Harm?

It is important to accurately understand the impact child sexual abuse has on those children who are molested. Likewise, it is significant to consider the direct and indirect consequences society incurs by tolerating, ignoring, or failing to prevent the sexual victimization of children. Clearly the topic of child sexual abuse would not warrant much attention if the consequences of such contact were harmless or benign. This is exactly what child molesters would have people believe.

Some groups, such as the North American Man-Boy Love Association (NAMBLA) (founding member Thorstad, 1991), the Rene Guyon Society, and their allies (Brongersma, 1991; Li, 1991; Jones, 1991), openly promulgate the idea that sexual contact with children is wholesome. They use such slogans as "sex before eight or else it's too late" to further their cause. They consider themselves a sexual minority, which is why they believe they should be accorded civil rights regarding their sexual preference. They view their attraction to children as "wholesome," and as a "sexual orientation" rather than aberrant criminal behavior. Numerous authors have espoused variations on this point of view (Kincaid, 1998; Jones, 1991; Li, 1991), and the Internet child pornography traffic suggests this perspective to have a larger following than many would openly admit. For instance, in September 1998, simultaneous raids in thirty-two U.S. cities and eleven other countries were made on the "largest, most sophisticated online child pornography ring yet, called 'wOnderland'" (Associated Press, 1998, p. A4). Many prominent and successful professionals were caught actively participating in this extensive pyramid-style club that exchanged pictures among its members, with each of the 10,000 confiscated images representing "a permanent record of a child being abused" (Associated Press, 1998, p. A4). In Canada, the Supreme Court ruled possession of such pornography to be legal (Heakes, 1999). This decision was handed down even though these images represent illegal acts and research indicates that viewing such material is directly linked to an increased likelihood of enacting the fantasy behavior (Salter, 1995).

Other groups contribute to the emotionally reactive climate surrounding this topic by insisting all sexual contacts create an equally harmful and permanent impact on children. Such a perspective suggests that even random frottage by a stranger on a crowded subway, with no danger of further touching, may cause permanent trauma, and those who deny any problems created by such contact are masking their pain. Still others believe the harm related to sexual molestations primarily occurs from the cultural standards and mores of this society (Gardner, 1993; Kincaid, 1998). According to this perspective, it is not the molestation that is harmful, but society's response that causes the trauma. One molester pointed out that "the taboo against sex with children is Victorian-age hysteria whipped up by feminists who don't understand male sexuality." He states "all the harm is done by the taboo. If nobody is getting hurt there is nothing to worry about."

Just as failure to understand what constitutes child sexual abuse creates the kind of confusion that translates into inertia, failure to understand the impact of abuse on children also interferes with properly managing events preceding the molest. Poor understanding may stifle appropriate responses and interventions, which indirectly perpetuates the problem. Child molesters will minimize what happens or extol the advantages of their behavior. They look respectable and have prestige and support in the community. To question their tactics or stop this almost invisible behavior requires exceptional clarity and understanding to proceed.

This was exemplified by a number of the cases already discussed. For example, the parents who struggled to protect their sons from Mr. Clay, the second-grade teacher, noted that people minimized the abuse. They reported comments repeatedly made by the teachers, the school system, professionals, and their own friends: "It was just little boys," and "It only happened for four months. . . . You're making a big deal of it." They also heard, "It was just touching," as well as "Don't worry. Boys that age are predominantly homosexual in their activity anyway, and there is nothing to worry about." Such overwhelming negation of the impact of the abuse made it even more difficult and confusing for these parents to protect their children.

A similar pattern occurred with parents who protested Mr. Smith's violation of a number of school rules. In this case, no allegations of child sexual abuse arose, and no abuse may have occurred. However, those parents were rightly concerned that tolerance and approval regarding the violation of appropriate boundaries might, at the very least, put children at risk in other situations. They were against allowing behaviors that violated school rules and general safety standards. Yet they were chided by school personnel and the community for robbing children of the joy of a grandfatherly influence on the school grounds. Mr. Smith maintained this support even though teachers saw children put their hands in his pants pockets to retrieve candy. This occurred even after he had been told not to give candy to children on the school grounds. Despite the apparent enthusiasm he engendered, a few teachers also reported that many children shrank from his touch.

In the case of convicted sex offender Mary Kay Letourneau (Cloud, 1998), the police intercepted the thirty-six-year-old teacher with her twelve-year-old student, undressed and under a blanket, yet let her call the boy's mother to explain the situation. The mother was placated by the teacher, and the police allowed the boy, who was later "raped" by this teacher, to go home with her. A clearer understanding of this terrain and the impact of molestations on children would have provided the police with the clarity they needed not to send the victim home in the care of the perpetrator. All of these cases exemplify how the perpetrator's charm and competency lulled adults into failing to protect children. Increased clarity regarding the potential gravity of turning a blind eye to such abuse will help to mitigate the confusion and difficulty adults inevitably encounter in these situations.

It is important to clearly understand the potential impact of child sexual abuse so as not to be dissuaded from correctly intervening in complex and ambiguous situations. Such knowledge and clarity will help adults proceed correctly and clearly under circumstances that are guaranteed to feel confusing.

PSYCHOLOGICAL ISSUES

Both subtly and overtly, the price society pays for tolerating and/or ignoring child sexual abuse continues. The true cost to society is difficult to ascertain, as much of the research fails to identify the underlying common etiology created by child sexual abuse. Thus, many disorders, behavioral problems, and/or social dilemmas studied in isolation may more accurately also be attributable, in some part, to the effects of early childhood abuse (Steinem, 1983; Summit, 1989; van der Kolk, 1994). Other costs the society may pay for tolerating child sexual abuse include increased reliance on government services and subsequent need for intervention (Bagley and Ramsey, 1985; Salter, 1995; Schlank and Cohen, 1999; Quinsey et al., 1998) to protect individuals from continued violence. It should be noted that the true psychological price for tolerating child sexual abuse is not yet known. The following only minimally identifies some of the known sequelae.

Psychiatric Concerns Associated with Child Sexual Abuse

- Post-traumatic stress disorder
- Increased drug and alcohol abuse
- Obsessive-compulsive disorder
- Panic attacks and anxiety disorders
- Depression
- Personality disorders
- Increased utilization of health services
- Increased utilization of social services
- Sexual dysfunctions
- Suicidal ideation
- Greater risk for relationship and parenting problems

Child sexual abuse deprives children of the normal developmental tasks of childhood in a number of ways. Premature sexual contact prevents them from engaging in innocent peer exploration because of their advanced knowledge as a result of their own abuse (van Dam, 1987). If human sexual development parallels animal sexual development (Money, 1990), being deprived of the opportunity to engage in exploratory play with peers may interfere with the normal development of adult sexual behavior and relationships.

Also, sexual molestation requires secrecy. The child, through direct threats or more subtle coercion, is told to keep the sexual contact secret. Such secrecy interferes with intimacy (Lerner, 1993) because the energy invested in maintaining the secret prevents the closeness in personal relationships necessary to successful emotional growth (Clarke and Dawson, 1998). Maintaining the secret further isolates the child from freely interacting with others (Lerner, 1993). The ongoing effort required to ensure this information does not get leaked preoccupies the child's time and attention, which impedes attending to the necessary daily emotional and intellectual tasks that growing up entails.

In addition, the emotional reactivity that frequently results from the abuse, as well as the confusion and the isolation, often contributes to the alienation of the child, as others react to the misbehavior with anger, hostility, and distancing. Then, if the child reenacts the abuse through seductive and aggressive play, as is typically the case, the child may be further punished. If the molestation is later revealed, the very symptoms the child developed as a result of the abuse are often used to further victimize the child, by explaining that the child "asked for it" (Rush, 1980; Salter, 1995), thereby creating a catch-22 that places responsibility and blame on the child.

It has been well documented that some forms of sexual abuse are more damaging than others (Briere and Elliott, 1994). The psychological impact of any molestation will vary depending on individual circumstances, the invasiveness of the molestation, the duration of the abuse, the support for the child, and the treatment provided (van Dam, 1996). Obviously, the brief noncontact exposures experienced by so many victims of the molesters (Abel, Mittelman, and Becker, 1985) interviewed probably result in little or no psychological trauma. For instance, the child who was touched by a straying hand on a crowded train and did not feel trapped may not even recall the event.

Much of the psychological damage resulting from sexual abuse during childhood has been documented by comparing adult populations who were molested to those who were not. This creates an indirect picture of some of the possible long-term sequelae of child sexual abuse. More recent studies have also looked at the immediate impact of sexual assault on children (Briere and Elliott, 1994). Yet the true price of child sexual abuse may continue to remain underreported, as myriad symptoms fail to be attributed directly to the abuse. What typically happens is that the psychological effects of child sexual abuse, although pervasive, are difficult to identify and, when identified, may be ignored. Instead, each psychiatric disorder is viewed separately and treated as an isolated problem.

For instance, one psychiatrist working with adolescent psychiatric patients noted that disclosures of child sexual abuse were "coming out all over the ward. No matter what the problem is, runaway, delinquency, drugs, eating disorder, suicidal depression . . . they all start talking about their sexual abuse" (Summit, 1989, p. 413). The importance of this information was not pursued, as the psychiatrist proceeded to treat the diagnosed disorders, ignoring the relevance of the molestations to these psychiatric symptoms. As in the case just cited, patients with various psychiatric diagnoses have previously been noted to share a history of childhood sexual abuse, but only recently has the significance of this correlation been more closely examined (Summit, 1989; Briere, 1992; Briere and Elliott, 1994).

People who have been victimized as children are more likely to enter and remain in abusive situations. This can be explained by looking at Seligman's learned helplessness studies (McConnell, 1980). As with the child trapped in an abusive environment where the abuse is invisible to anyone else, the laboratory animals under study could not escape the painful stimuli. The unpleasant shocks they received occurred regardless of their behavior. Later, when the cages were opened and the animals were free to leave, they did not. This held true even when healthy animals were used to model escape behavior. Similarly, many victims remain in abusive situations long after escape is possible. Their response patterns parallel those studied by Seligman, as they have acquired the same helpless reactions noted in the research studies.

Child sexual abuse victims also experience depression in greater numbers than is otherwise found in the general population (Ratican, 1992; Breire and Elliott, 1994). Guilt and shame eat away at self-esteem. Keeping the secret about the abuse is part of the trauma and also contributes to lowered self-esteem and depression (Briere, 1992). In fact, depression may be the most frequently reported symptom (Browne and Finkelhor, 1986). Extensive evidence linking adult depression to childhood sexual abuse has been noted in the literature (Briere and Runtz, 1989). It appears that many adults who experience clinical depression had been sexually abused as children. Looking specifically at clinical samples of adults who were sexually abused, 92 percent reported mood disturbances, such as depression, guilt, and low self-esteem. In addition, these adults were more self-destructive and suicidal than their nonabused counterparts, or than depressed adults who did not have a history of child sexual abuse (Ratican, 1992).

Adult victims of child sexual abuse are also higher utilizers of health services (Kluft, 1990) and more likely to rely on welfare and other social service funding. In one study, 26 percent of all hospitalized adult women reported childhood sexual abuse and assault (Carmen, Rieker, and Mills, 1987). In another study, over 52 percent of all patients in a large mental health center were victims of childhood sexual abuse (Briere, 1984; Lanktree, Briere, and Zaide, 1991). Although depression is one of the most commonly reported psychological effects of childhood sexual abuse, a number of other psychiatric disorders are also considered to result from such abuse. Foremost among these are the anxiety and panic disorders, as well as obsessive-compulsive disorders (Briere and Elliott, 1994).

Self-injury, including suicide, is frequently linked to child sexual abuse. According to van der Kolk, Perry, and Herman (1991), 7 to 10 percent of psychiatric patients injure themselves deliberately, and 5 percent of those with personality disorders end their lives by suicide. Such self-injurious behavior is consistently linked with a childhood history of physical or sexual abuse. "Many patients report feeling numb and 'dead' prior to harming themselves. They often claim not to feel pain during self-injury and report a sense of relief afterwards" (van der Kolk, Perry, and Herman, 1991, p. 1665). This is consistent with primate studies that show self-mutilation as a reaction to extreme disruptions of parental caretaking (van der Kolk, 1991). Halliday's (1985) database of over 3,000 victims also indicates that cutting and self-mutilation occur frequently among victims.

The characterological disorders, as defined by the DSM-IV (APA, 1994) on Axis II, result from problems in childhood. A great number of those who develop these disorders are child sexual abuse victims (Kessler et al., 1994). Their inability to function puts them at increased risk for requiring hospitalizations (van der Kolk, 1988; van der Kolk and van der Hart, 1989). Many of the psychiatric conditions currently associated with childhood sexual abuse are similar to symptoms of hysteria first identified by Freud (Masson, 1984):

> The somatoform disorders in the DSM-III-R (APA, 1987) encompass some of the diagnostic categories that have evolved from the classic concept of hysteria. In DSM-III-R (APA, 1987) hysteria has been transformed into the somatoform disorders, the dissociative disorders (psychogenic amnesia, fugue, and multiple personality disorder), two of the personality disorders (histrionic and borderline personality disorders), and even posttraumatic stress disorder. (Loewenstein, 1990, p. 76)

Closer examination of these different psychiatric disorders reveals a high correlation between childhood sexual abuse and psychiatric disorders. Those diagnosed with borderline personality disorder frequently have histories of childhood sexual abuse. For instance, in one study,

> 81 percent of subjects with definite borderline personality disorder gave histories of major childhood trauma. Of these, 71 percent had been physically abused, 67 percent had been sexually abused, and 62 percent had witnessed domestic violence. Histories of trauma in early childhood (zero to six years) were found almost exclusively in patients with borderline personality disorder. These results suggest a strong correlation between borderline personality disorder and childhood trauma. (Herman, Perry, and van der Kolk, 1989, p. 491)

In another group of outpatients with borderline personality disorder, 60 percent claimed a history of childhood physical or sexual abuse (Herman, 1986). Patients in a different study reported high rates of self-destructive behavior, frequent suicide attempts, five or more episodes of self-inflicted injuries, and half had self-reported eating disorders of bulimia or anorexia. Over 77 percent of these patients reported a history of major childhood trauma. A history of child sexual abuse was most strongly related to all forms of self-destructive behavior in this population (van der Kolk, Perry, and Herman, 1991).

It is increasingly recognized that childhood sexual abuse produces complex posttraumatic syndromes involving chronic affect dysregulation, destructive behavior against self and others, learning disabilities, dissociative problems, somatization, and distortions in concepts about self and others. The field trials for DSM-IV (APA, 1994) showed that this conglomeration of symptoms tended to occur together, and the severity of the syndrome was proportional to the duration of the trauma and the age of the child when it began (van der Kolk, 1994). Recent experiments suggest that fear responses create electrical stimulation to the amygdala, resulting in cortical lesions that, once formed, become indelible. This suggests that "emotional memory may be forever" (van der Kolk, 1994, p. 261). These memories can then be activated by decreased inhibitory control through drugs and alcohol, nightmares, and strong environmental reminders. "Conceivably, traumatic memories then could emerge, not in the distorted fashion of ordinary recall but as affect states, somatic sensations, or visual images (i.e., nightmares or flashbacks) that are timeless and unmodified by further experience" (van der Kolk, 1994, p. 261).

Dissociative disorders have been linked to childhood experiences of sexual abuse. Studies suggest that dissociative capacities were spontaneously mobilized to help some victims cope with their assaults (Braun, 1990). The most extreme form of pathologic dissociation, multiple personality disorder (MPD) in the DSM-III-R (APA, 1987), relabeled dissociative identity disorder (DID) in the DSM-IV (APA, 1994), can be understood as a chronic form of post-traumatic stress disorder (Patten et al., 1989). These patients frequently have a history of childhood sexual abuse and physical violence (Putnam, 1985; Kluft, 1985).

Other studies compared sexually abused inpatients in a general hospital population with inpatients who had not been sexually abused. Differences between populations varied significantly. Those who had been sexually abused had sexual delusions, sexual preoccupation, histories of depressive symptoms, substance abuse, and major medical problems. Although they sought social contact more than others, the social contact was characterized by hyperarousal, agitation, disorganized thinking, and delusions. They were also more likely to threaten others (Beck and van der Kolk, 1987).

Other researchers link drug and alcohol abuse to sexual abuse histories (Burnam et al., 1988). Peters (1984) and Bagley and Ramsey (1985) also found increased substance use among child abuse victims. Burnam and colleagues (1988) studied a representative sample of 3,123 households in Los Angeles and noted significantly higher levels of affective disorder (major depression and manic episodes), drug abuse or dependence, and anxiety disorders (phobia, panic, obsessive-compulsive disorder) among those women who had been sexually abused.

Increased psychiatric problems and substance abuse histories are found among sexual abuse victims successfully integrated into the general population. Peters (1984), in a random sample of 119 Los Angeles households, found childhood sexual abuse associated with depression and alcoholism. Bagley and Ramsey (1985) surveyed 377 urban women in Canada in a random sample and found similar increases in depression, substance abuse, and anxiety among sexually abused women. Kilpatrick and colleagues (1985), in a survey of 2,000 South Carolina women, found a high prevalence of "nervous breakdowns" among women with a history of childhood sexual abuse.

Many sexual assault survivors develop sexual problems as a consequence of their assaults, and these problems do not appear to dissipate with the passage of time (Becker and Skinner, 1994). Depression, sexual dysfunction, anxiety, and substance abuse typically result from childhood sexual abuse. Although most victims of sexual assault do not seek professional services, those who do may have higher rates of psychopathology than members of the general population (Burnam et al., 1988). Histories of child sexual abuse are also prominent among prison inmates.

Other researchers concur that victims frequently do not seek counseling for their abuse but suffer the symptoms of trauma caused by the abuse (Becker and Kaplan, 1991). This continued silence, and failure to seek help, may compound the trauma of the abuse:

> This nightmarish isolation and sequential rejection reinforces what becomes for the victim the most painful reality of incest: "It's my fault. I brought it on myself. I'm so bad I invite trouble and make trouble for others. I'm not worth caring for. There's no place for me in the world of reasonable, decent people. I'll never be reasonable or decent. I'm crazy. I'm nothing but a whore." (Summit, 1982, p. 129)

Child sexual abuse victims are more likely to become prostitutes. Incest is highly correlated with running away from home, which can lead indirectly to prostitution (Westerlund, 1992). Studies by Silbert (1994) suggest that over two-thirds of prostitutes have a history of sexual abuse during childhood.

Although it is hoped that, today, most victims seeking help for their abuse would be believed, over twenty years ago, patients were further victimized by professionals who assumed their reports to be symptomatic of their psychiatric condition (Rush, 1980). Some writers continue to minimize the harm (Kincaid, 1998). A meta-analysis (Rind, Tromovitch, and Bauserman, 1998) of the effects of child sexual abuse on college students concluded that minimal harm was caused by child sexual abuse. College students however, should not be viewed as a representative sample. Although half of the general population may have attended college, as these researchers attest, those most affected by child sexual abuse typically do not. Furthermore, the family chaos that often accompanies those who have been abused is not unrelated to their abuse, but another sequela of such abuse. Factoring out these influences inappropriately helps to minimize further the effect of child sexual abuse.

Others view the molestations not as harmful sexually deviant behaviors but as a subcultural phenomenon (Greenberg, 1979) that has been previously accepted and should therefore be viewed in the continuum of normal human behavior (Rind, Tromovitch, and

Bauserman, 1998). More writers suggest that the sexual abuse of children, at the very least, results in long-term bitterness, hostility, and distrust of adults, as well as conflicts causing guilt, shame, and depression. Behavioral disorders, psychiatric illnesses, and disturbances in future behavior as parents are also cited as long-term effects of childhood sexual abuse (Greenberg, 1979).

Child sexual abuse is also associated with child-rearing problems when the children who were abused become parents. The cycle of child sexual abuse continues in a number of ways. Goodwin (1985) found that over 24 percent of abusive mothers had been incest victims. Halliday (1985) reported that a very high percentage of child sexual abuse victims had mothers who had been sexually abused. The mothers often gave the original molesters access to their children and were also more likely to marry men who molested. Over one-third of those who sexually molest children were themselves sexually abused as children.

Child sexual abuse, by its very nature, violates personal boundaries. Family system therapists (Corey, 1996; Jacobson and Gurman, 1995) describe therapy as helping individuals and families develop boundaries and learn to differentiate. Differentiation and individuation, in Western mainstream culture, are equated with mental health (Beavers and Hampson, 1990). The dynamics of child sexual abuse, which systematically blurs these boundaries, are antithetical to such mental health, involving a violation of these tenets of emotional well-being (Jacobson and Gurman, 1995). Kerr and Bowen (1988) believe that the ill effects of enmeshment worsen with each successive generation if intervention is not provided. This would suggest an increasing cyclical harm created by child sexual abuse.

Trauma that occurs to such a large percentage of the population would normally be considered of epidemic proportion. But just as each instance of child sexual abuse has been seen in isolation, so have the effects of the abuse been observed individually. Many psychiatrists (Summit, 1989) continue to view each case separately, thereby ignoring the common etiology of child sexual abuse reported by so many patients. Both van der Kolk (1994) and Briere (1992) suggest that a number of seemingly unrelated DSM-IV (APA, 1994) disorders all have in common an etiology of child sexual abuse.

Although the main, and most common, harm is psychological rather than physical (Finkelhor, 1984; Kluft, 1990), physical trauma and damage, including sexually transmitted diseases, pregnancy (Finkel, 1987), as well as anal fissures, may also occur. Occasional internal damage from the abuse can result in death (Rush, 1980).

MORAL ISSUES

Many molesters promote the idea that sexual contact between adults and children benefits children. This is similar to a therapist explaining that sexual intercourse with a client is therapeutically indicated (yet these therapeutic benefits only serve those clients whom the therapist finds sexually attractive). In the field of psychology, ethical guidelines clearly stipulate that sex with clients is not acceptable (Keith-Spiegel and Koocher, 1985). This is precisely because clients are seen to be in an emotionally vulnerable position by virtue of their seeking therapy:

> The vast majority of psychologists work in the context of relationships. Psychologists often hold an advantage of power over the people with whom they work, especially when they are psychotherapy clients or students. They occupy a position of trust and are expected to advocate for the welfare of those who depend on them. When psychologists place their own needs and goals above those of consumers or when they lose sight of the fiduciary nature of their professional relationships, exploitation, faulty professional judgment, and harm to consumers can result. (Keith-Spiegal and Koocher, 1985, p. 251)

The same dynamics of occupying a position of trust and being expected to advocate for the welfare of those who depend on them are true of all adults in their relationships with children. When adults consider sexual interactions with a child, they automatically enter into an exploitative relationship with the child, meeting their personal needs and agendas, rather than attending to the child's best interests. By definition, at that point, they are no longer able to advocate for the child.

A number of molesters argue that children can, and do, desire sex with adults and give consent to such activities. These statements simply reflect their already faulty judgment, resulting from attempting to meet their own needs rather than those of the child (Finkelhor, 1979b). A child cannot give consent for two reasons. First, the nature of the relationship between the more powerful adult and the powerless child ensures the child cannot respond independently. The child may appear to agree, but only because of the spin created by the adult, the adult's power, the adult's persuasive abilities, and the adult's control over all essential amenities.

Simply the way in which a situation is framed can even persuade adults to engage in behaviors they otherwise would not (Wade and Tavris, 1990). Children are even more vulnerable. Even in politics, with only adults involved, it has been recognized that ideas generated by the leaders are frequently endorsed by their advisers precisely because of the leaders' more powerful position (McConnell, 1980). It would be unreasonable to imagine children could behave independently when adults under less tightly controlled circumstances could not.

Children will support and even become seemingly enthusiastic about something simply by virtue of their position in the relationship. Or their enthusiasm may be the delusion of the adult whose judgment has been impaired by a sexual agenda. This is exemplified by molesters misinterpreting children's responsiveness as sexual invitations. Frequently heard is "She was coming on to me." This is exemplified in *Lolita,* with the first hundred pages devoted to the seeming collusion of the child in the seduction, whereas the second half of the book explores the molester's delusions of the child's lust and love. The child is revealed as being a prisoner in the home, seeking to escape (Rush, 1980).

Children cannot give free consent because of their powerless position. Second, because of their tender years and their lack of true understanding of sex, they cannot give informed consent. Piaget (McConnell, 1980) describes the various developmental stages of cognitive maturation that occur as humans grow. Young children, and those with developmental disabilities, are very concrete thinkers, incapable of the abstract reasoning required to give informed consent (Wade and Tavris, 1990; Vance, 1998), as their frontal lobes are not yet fully developed (Kolb and Whishaw, 1996). Thus, they are easily swayed and happily agree to situations they cannot fully

comprehend. This makes them incapable of meaningfully participating in financial decisions or agreeing to business terms. This is
so easily generally understood that children are not included in the
running of commerce and government. Yet when it comes to sexual
relationships, those who would never give financial decision-making
authority to a child argue that the same child can, and should, have
independent authority to give consent.

"For true consent to occur, two conditions must prevail. A person
must know what it is that he or she is consenting to, and a person
must be free to say yes or no" (Finkelhor, 1979b, p. 694). Neither
condition applies in the sexual relationship between any child and
an older, more knowledgeable and powerful adult. In addition to not
being able to freely say yes or no, children cannot be provided with
adequate information about sexual matters to give informed consent: They lack accurate details about sex and sexual relationships.
They do not have the emotional maturity to understand the social
mores or the various physical, social, and ethical concerns involved
in developing a sexual liaison. Their dependence on adult largess
and support further help to mitigate against being able to give true
consent.

Most important, sexual involvement with a child is a self-serving
act on the part of molesters, which, by definition, makes their judgment about the appropriateness of the activity unreliable. Should
psychologists demonstrate such lack of judgment with their clients,
then according to their ethical guidelines, they would be unsuited
for conducting their profession. These same guidelines can be applied to all adults who have an inherent responsibility for the care
and safekeeping of children.

CULTURAL ISSUES

Molesters argue that their proclivities reflect a minority sexual
orientation that should be tolerated in a culturally diverse society.
This argument, riding on the coattails of a society grappling with
racism and discrimination, has inappropriately gained momentum.
Multiculturalism, however, should not be confused with cultural relativism. Tolerance for difference and acceptance of alternative perspectives broaden and enrich everyone. Cultural relativism, on the

other hand, incorrectly uses the limitations of imposing a Western "mainstream" orientation on other groups as a way to justify unethical behavior. Such an emic, or narrow, orientation ignores the larger "etic perspective that emphasizes universals among human beings by using examinations and comparison of many cultures from a position outside those cultures" (Dana, 1993, p. 21).

The issues of child sexual abuse cannot be viewed merely from an emic perspective. In other words, just because a behavior has been tolerated by a culture does not make it acceptable.

Clearly, different cultural and historical groups have sanctioned adult-child sex, as noted in ancient Greek times, for instance. Greek poetry "abounds with men swooning for the 'tender flower of youth' and 'the thighs and delicious mouth' of pubescent boys" (Rush, 1980, p. 52), but, "oddly enough, we hear nothing from youths admiring the hairy thighs and bristling lips of their bearded lovers" (Rush, 1980, p. 52). Child-adult sexual relations are also sanctioned in current cultures (Masters, Johnson, and Kolodny, 1988) and generate a trade, with Western males traveling to Asian countries to have sex with children (Joseph, 1995) and, as those countries crack down on such practices, finding a haven in Latin American destinations (Reuters News Service, 1999). Increasingly more literature appears, both paving the way for such behavior (Rind, Tromovitch, and Bauserman, 1998) and promoting the acceptance and tolerance of such behavior (Jones, 1991; Li, 1991). Some authors cite victims extolling the benefits of their own experiences in defense of pedophilia. This can be compared to some slaves who may have claimed to prefer the security of slavery to freedom, which neither excuses nor condones slavery but, rather, further reflects the harm of slavery on the human spirit.

Philosophical arguments of ethical realism suggest that a standard, independent of culture, guides human behavior (Hergenhahn, 1992; Singer, 1991), and that such a standard of human nature is unchanging. Thereby, decisions about what is good and what is bad are determined by what contributes to making humans function properly (Hergenhahn, 1992; Singer, 1991), rather than by cultural norms or standards. Thus, the oppression of any group to benefit those who are more powerful is inherently wrong. Although ethical relativism, with its more utilitarian approach, has become generally accepted (Singer, 1991), it should not be confused with cultural relativism as an excuse for tolerating the oppression of others because another culture condones the practice.

By examining the history of the mutilation of women, changing social standards can be compared to a more universal ethical stance (Scully, 1980). Throughout the centuries, various forms of mutilation of women, from binding feet, to placing widows on their husbands' funeral pyres, to performing clitoridectomies, were routinely conducted and socially sanctioned (Scully, 1980). As with the Greek youths who never extolled the virtues of their sexual relations with adults (Rush, 1980), neither were the female victims enamored of these practices of mutilation. As women gained political status and power, the mutilations met with increased protest. Today, many of the generally sanctioned practices against women are no longer acceptable in Western "mainstream" culture but continue to be practiced in other societies where women's silence is ensured.

Child sexual abuse can be examined from a similar perspective. The sexual exploitation of children may be sanctioned by various cultures and is lauded by some groups within this culture (de Young, 1988; Brongersma, 1991) who are working to become accepted within the culture as another sexual minority, with all the social acceptance of any other minority. Tolerating such an emic perspective would ignore the more basic tenets of the rights and dignity of all humans, in preference for those more powerful and persuasive, and would be a travesty of the enrichment generated by cultural diversity:

> We cannot stand by idly and watch torture, disappearances, arbitrary arrest and detention, racism, anti-Semitism, repression of trade unions, and churches, debilitating poverty, illiteracy, and disease in the name of diversity or respect for cultural traditions. . . . To act as if internationally recognized human rights are an exotic Western luxury is to display not cultural sensitivity but indefensible moral elitism. (Donnelly, 1989, p. 235)

Neither should society tolerate the sexual abuse of children under the false guise of embracing diversity.

Chapter 4

Prevalence:
How Often Does It Happen?

Twenty years ago, no reference was made in most psychology programs to child sexual abuse. If it was discussed at all, it was mentioned in passing, as an aberration, even though a number of studies existed reporting incidence rates consistent with current data (Kinsey et al., 1948; Salter, 1988). Yet in 1955, Weinberg cited one case of incest per million persons per year in English-speaking countries, and in 1972, Ferracuti estimated between one and five cases per million persons throughout the world. In such a context, child sexual abuse clearly did not deserve much attention.

By 1969, however, numerous studies appeared suggesting that child sexual abuse occurred with disturbing frequency. The early studies in the 1940s by Kinsey and colleagues (1948), De Francis (1969), and later work by Finkelhor (1979a) became standard guidelines. Now it is generally accepted that at least approximately one out of every four women and one out of every six to ten men have been sexually abused during childhood (Finkelhor, 1979a; Finkel, 1984). These are considered conservative estimates. Other studies suggest a higher incidence. Russell's (1983) extensive study with 930 subjects from a cross section of the population indicates as many as one out of every three women has been sexually abused. Herman (1981), in a survey of ten studies conducted since 1940, concludes that anywhere from one-fifth to one-third of all women have been sexually abused. Black and DeBlassie (1993) summarize data on male victims and report that anywhere from 11 percent to 47 percent of sexual abuse victims are males (Singer, 1989; Wyatt and Powell, 1988).

Currently, one controversy in the field centers around the possibility that some allegations of child sexual abuse are, in fact, false memories (Crews, 1994a, b). This debate primarily surrounds those cases in which victims regain previously repressed memory, often as a result of therapy (Wylie, 1993; Schwarz and Gilligan, 1995), or those involving confessions obtained under questionable circumstances (Wright, 1994). Few disagree, however, either with the fact that child sexual abuse occurs or with the usual prevalence data reported (Loftus, 1993). In fact, one advocate promoting pedophilia believes the numbers to be much higher than any of those reviewed here:

> One should always keep in mind when examining these figures that they apply to only a minuscule sample of adult-minor sexual acts, which take place day in, day out in our society. Brongersma and des Sables, using quite different methods of calculation, independently arrived at an identical estimate: one unlawful sexual act with a minor in three thousand is discovered, tried and results in a sentence: the rest are "dark numbers." (Brongersma, 1991, p. 154)

Onset of abuse for most victims occurs prior to age sixteen (Finkel, 1984), with 48 percent of the victims being under the age of twelve (Saylor, 1979) and the average age of disclosure being eleven (De Francis, 1969). A study of 117 juvenile rape records in San Francisco revealed that 20.5 percent of the victims were six or younger (Copeland, 1976). Fehrenbach and colleagues' (1986) study also confirms that over 50 percent of the victims were under the age of six. According to some studies, the risk of being abused decreases significantly past the age of ten (Finkelhor, 1981; Russell, 1983; Badgley, 1984). Halliday (1985) states that if a child has not been sexually abused by the age of eight, the risk of abuse greatly decreases.

Clearly this is an enormous problem affecting a large percentage of the population at a very young age. It is also known that a great number of victims are abused by more than one offender (Halliday, 1985). Therefore, identifying the number of victims still does not reveal how many people molest. Although the data all indicate that child sexual abuse is a commonly occurring event, they still do not generate information about the percentage of the population who commit these acts. De Becker (1999) states that "the U.S. Department of

Justice estimates that on average, there is one child molester per square mile" (p. 16). How this can be ascertained is difficult to understand.

Offenders do not readily volunteer information about their activities (Becker and Quinsey, 1993), victims do not always disclose (Russell, 1983), and some allegations may be false (Crews, 1994a). As a result, there are no straightforward direct measures to determine prevalence. At best, the research data give an indirect measure of the extent of the problem. This measure either examines the percentage of known victims in the population (Russell, 1983; Badgley, 1984; Halliday, 1985), the number of known offenses committed by identified molesters (Abel, Mittelman, and Becker, 1985; Freeman-Longo and Wall, 1986), or even the possibility that a group of seemingly normal college students might consider such activities (Malamuth, 1981; Briere, 1992; Mayer, 1992).

To further confuse the situation, many molesters abuse a great number of children. Some of this information has been supplied by interviewing molesters. Although there is always concern about the accuracy of self-reported data, this is confounded since convicted child sexual molesters typically minimize their behavior and are unlikely to report activities for which they were not convicted (Abel, Mittleman, and Becker, 1985). In fact, as guarantees of the safeguarding of research data increases, the likelihood of previously undetected sexual crimes being reported increases as well (Kaplan et al., 1990). Some studies have revealed molesters to be extremely active. One study of 232 convicted child molesters guaranteed confidentially reported 55,250 attempted molestations and 38,727 completed molestations (Abel, Mittlelman, and Becker, 1985). If accurate, this translates into each molester averaging 106 completed molestations and another 111 attempted molestations. Freeman-Longo and Wall (1986) report even higher rates, with fifty-three offenders committing 25,757 sexual crimes, or an average of 470 molestations each. Remember that these figures refer to a variety of molesting behaviors. Even with such frequent activity, it is difficult to determine whether the high incidence of victimization is the result of only a few very active molesters in the population or is reflective of a large percentage of the population being sexual molesters.

Another way to examine the number of sexual molestations that occur is to look at prison populations. In Washington State, anywhere from one-fourth to one-third of all inmates are incarcerated for sexually related offenses (van Dam, 1996). Canadian numbers parallel this, with approximately 31 percent of all federal prisoners incarcerated because of sex offenses (Halliday-Sumner, 1997a). Adolescents also contribute to the high arrest records for sexual offenses, in that approximately 30 percent of arrests because of sexual abuse involve adolescents (Fehrenbach et al., 1986). This still does not reveal much about the percentage of the general population that might engage in such criminal activity, as it is unknown what percentage of molesters are never charged or convicted. In one study of molesters, "only one in 150 deviant episodes actually led to arrest" (Abel et al., 1987, p. 11), and Russell (1983) found that "fewer than five percent of the 647 child molestations reported in her study of adult females were ever reported to the police." This is consistent with insider data by offenders who brag that only "one unlawful sexual act with a minor in three thousand is discovered, tried and results in a sentence" (Brongersma, 1991, p. 154).

Studies of convicted molesters and examination of the percentage of prison populations devoted to sexual crimes still do not reveal the percentage of the general population involved in sexually molesting children. The incidence range revealed by a general population study of adolescents suggests that 10 percent of teens are involved in sexual offending (Ageton, 1983), and "almost half (47 percent) of adolescent males charged with indecent liberties with minors were baby-sitting at the time" (Arndt, 1991, p. 223). Polls taken of college students to determine their attitudes about women also shed a little light on this question (Malamuth, 1981; Craig, 1990). College males were asked about their willingness to use force and their beliefs about the appropriateness of sexual involvement under various circumstances. Malamuth (1981) discovered that approximately 35 percent of college males "indicated some likelihood of raping." In another study of undergraduate males, "21 percent described sexual attraction to at least some small children" (Briere, 1992, p. 94), and "a significant minority of university students at least partially endorsed statements such as 'Many children would like sex with an adult once they tried it'" (Briere, 1992, p. 94). In another study, "one in twenty-five men admitted having sexually misused a child" (Arndt, 1991, p. 212).

These studies suggest that possibly 21 to 35 percent of the male population do not consider some sex with children problematical and can imagine, under certain circumstances, engaging in such behavior. This, of course, still does not reveal the percentage of the population that actually molests children but gives an indirect snapshot of the percentage of the population that might consider doing so. In another study of men's erotic fantasies, 61.7 percent fantasized sexually initiating a young girl, 33 percent fantasized rape, and 3.2 percent fantasized sexually initiating a young boy (Crepault and Coulture, 1980).

In another study, 21 percent of male undergraduates reported sexual attraction to children, 9 percent fantasized sex with a child, 5 percent masturbated to fantasies of sex with children, and 7 percent indicated the likelihood of actual sexual involvement with a child if there were no deleterious consequences (Briere and Runtz, 1989). In another study of undergraduates, 3 percent reported a history of sexual contact with girls under twelve, 42 percent reported a history of voyeurism, 8 percent reported a history of making obscene phone calls, 35 percent reported engaging in frottage, two percent reported prior exhibitionism, 5 percent reported engaging in coercive sex, and a total of 65 percent reported some category of sexual misconduct. When questioned about their desire for specific sexual contact, 5 percent reported a desire to have sex with girls under twelve, 54 percent expressed a desire for voyeuristic experiences, and 7 percent mentioned a desire for exhibitionistic experiences (Templeman and Stinnett, 1991).

These studies suggest that a great number of seemingly "normal" males have some sexual molestation fantasies and a large percentage have actually engaged in various inappropriate sexual contacts. Reported widespread use of the Internet for transmitting child pornography (Associated Press, 1995; Elmer-Dewitt, 1995) is consistent with information suggesting that sexual interest in children may be widespread. Calvin Klein has met with controversy and commercial success by using scantily clad children to sell products. The ads were labeled "kiddie porn" (Ingrassia et al., 1995; Kincaid, 1998) as the poses became more explicit. Such images further reflect this sexualized interest in children. The current social climate that tolerates sexual fantasies involving children increases the likelihood of such behavior occurring (Schmitt, 1994).

Chapter 5

Characteristics of the Child Molester: Who Does It?

DEMOGRAPHICS

Until recently, the public generally only thought of "stranger danger" when worrying about the occurrence of child sexual abuse. A molester was assumed to be a single man who was easily identified by his "seedy" looks and unshaven appearance. He would lurk in shadows and grab children. He was called the "bogeyman" by some and a "pervert" by all. Other commonly held misconceived ideas were that the sex offender was visibly insane, mentally retarded, brutal, depraved, immoral, or oversexed. He was assumed to be a fiend and to spend his time reading or viewing pornography, and he was either an alcoholic or a drug addict (Cohen and Boucher, 1972). Such popular misconceptions contributed to the belief that the sex offender was somehow not an ordinary person, was easily distinguishable (Delin, 1978), and was always male.

It was believed that families could protect their children by teaching them not to "talk to strangers." Unfortunately, this was not the case then, nor is this the case now. Stranger danger does present a potential threat to children, but these strangers are not as easily identifiable as such myths would suggest. Furthermore, much of the research would relegate stranger danger to a smaller role. Here again, however, as in all facets of this field, various figures are cited on the number of molests that are perpetrated by strangers. This variation depends both on the focus of the research and the population under study. Attempts to understand these dynamics through studies that interviewed victims about their abuse differ from those which interviewed perpetrators about their sexual molesting.

It is generally agreed, however, that no one profile describes the sex offender (Salter, 1995). "Realistically, the sex offender may be a close relative, a friend, or acquaintance, rather than a stranger; an older person or a youth; wealthy or poor; a Caucasian or a person of color; gay or straight; literate or illiterate; able or disabled; religious or non-religious; a professional, white or blue collar, or unemployed worker; a person with an extensive criminal record or one with no offense history at all" (Lloyd, 1987, p. 56).

Molesters are a heterogeneous population (Drieblatt, 1982). In an elaborate study conducted by Abel and colleagues (1987), using 561 subjects recruited through various health agencies, probation departments, and the media, results indicated that, as a group, molesters were employed, had a high socioeconomic status, and were well educated, with over 40 percent having finished at least one year of college. They were fairly young, with a mean age of 31.5 years. Over one-fourth were married. Their ethnic backgrounds were primarily Caucasian (62.1 percent), with some African American (23.8 percent), and some Hispanic (11.2 percent). The group represented a broad spectrum of socioeconomic levels, with 64.6 percent fully employed and over 50 percent earning more than $25,000 annually (in 1970 dollars). Their religious orientations varied, with over 60 percent being Christian. As a group, their IQ (intelligence quotient) paralleled that of the general population (Groth et al., 1978). In a Steilacoom, Washington, group of 956 sex offenders, over one-third had an IQ in the average range, one-third in the bright average and superior range, and 10 percent in the very superior range of intellectual functioning. Over 70 percent had no previous history of alcohol abuse, most were in their twenties and thirties, and over 65 percent had no prior incarcerations (Saylor, 1979).

Sex offenders are not limited to any racial or ethnic groups (Saylor, 1979; van Dam, 1986). Although some molesters may use their ethnic heritage or cultural traditions to justify the behavior, the methods they use to charm adults and then groom children do not vary significantly. Providing services can present unique problems, but this is impacted more by isolation and lack of resources (Halliday-Sumner, 1997b).

Data on who the molesters are in relation to the victim vary depending on whether the information was obtained by interviewing victims or molesters. Although figures differ among studies, those differences can be attributed to the populations under study. Halliday's (1985) data came from women who joined Sexual Abuse Victims Anonymous (SAVA), a self-help group. Finkelhor's (1979a) data were obtained through questioning college populations. Russell's (1983) data were collected from random samples of the population.

The women who joined SAVA were there specifically to address psychological issues resulting from their abuse. Many, because of the help received from the support group, took the molesters to court (van Dam, Halliday, and Bates, 1985). These victims were self-selected because of the severity of their abuse. That abuse, by virtue of being more psychologically damaging, is more likely to have been committed by family members (Abel and Osborn, 1992). In Halliday's (1985) data on over 1,000 subjects, 13 percent of child sexual abuse cases involved strangers. Of the offenses, 57 percent were committed by family members and 28 percent were committed by friends. Approximately 21 percent of the molestations were done by the natural fathers, 12 percent by the stepfathers, 10 percent by brothers, and another 10 percent by uncles. Grandfathers committed 5 percent of the molestations, and family friends another 19 percent of the abuses. Of the molestations, 3 percent were committed by baby-sitters.

Children living in stepfamilies are more at risk of being sexually abused, according to SAVA (Halliday, 1985) data, but this is not because stepfathers are more likely to sexually molest than natural fathers. In fact, only 12 percent of the molests were by stepfathers, whereas almost double that amount, 21 percent, were committed by natural fathers. Rather, children living in stepfamilies have a greater number of extended family members and close family friends in their lives, by virtue of their involvement with both parents and those people who subsequently become involved with their parents in separate households. This added exposure to newly blended families possibly puts them at greater risk simply because, suddenly, many more people have easy access to them.

Finkelhor (1979a) used college students answering questionnaires about their childhood to collect his data. His results show that approximately 24 percent of the abuses were perpetrated by strangers. This is higher than Halliday's (1985) 13 percent. Of the women studied by Finkelhor (1978), 6 percent had been abused by an older child, primarily in a baby-sitting-type situation. This is also higher than Halliday's 3 percent who had been abused by baby-sitters.

Russell's (1983) study involved a random sample of 930 women. Her data are the most extensive in that they involve a large random sample of the population, rather than the college samples used by Finkelhor or the victim samples used by Halliday. In Russell's (1983) study, 24 percent of the molests involved fathers and step-fathers, with the more severe abuses perpetrated by stepfathers, while 26 percent of the molesters were uncles and 11 percent were total strangers. Russell's data showing that 11 percent of molests are perpetrated by strangers parallel Halliday's (1985) 13 percent.

Greenberg (1979) reports that between 19 and 32 percent of the molestations were perpetrated by parents, 18 percent by other family members, and 26 percent by friends and acquaintances. Gagnon (1965) indicated that 58 percent of molests were done by strangers, and 65 percent of the molests were done by strangers according to Landis (1956).

In a study of offender data by Abel and Osborn (1992), the numbers paint a surprisingly different picture of child molestation than does information gathered from victim treatment programs or victim reports. This study indicates that although more molests of children are conducted by nonfamily members, these molestations are briefer, involve less contact, and may, therefore, be less psychologically damaging. "Of the 38,671 victims of child molestation involving touching, 99.1% of all victims were victims of nonincest, whereas 0.9% of the total victims were family members who were molested numerous times" (p. 680), and less than 21 percent of all pedophilic acts were committed against victims related to the offender. These studies indicate that the molestations of family members, however, involve more contact and are of longer duration. Because these abuses have a greater impact on the victims, they are more likely to come to the attention of the treatment professionals and other reporting agencies. It would appear that the Halliday and Russell data primarily reflect the more severe offenses that were identified by molesters.

Data from studies that interviewed molesters would attest to an even higher rate of sexual abuse victimization, with a great many victims never reporting their abuse because of the brevity of the attack. This failure to report is consistent with Russell's (1983) data that only 2 percent of the intrafamilial and 6 percent of the extrafamilial molestations were ever reported. Reporting intrafamilial child sexual abuse is, understandably, even more complex than reporting extrafamilial child sexual abuse.

In another study, 29 percent of convicted molesters selected victims who were complete strangers (Salter, 1988). This is again a somewhat skewed perspective, as family members and friends are less likely to be charged and prosecuted (Groth et al., 1978). These data reveal two things: One, the molester does not lurk in dark alleys but lives in the child's home and is included in the child's social network. Two, the number of molestations is underreported, suggesting that the occurrence may be even more frequent than the usual 25 to 33 percent of female children and 15 percent of male children currently cited in the literature (Finkelhor, 1979a; Russell, 1983).

The type of molestation varies greatly. According to Saylor's (1979) data, 23 percent of convicted molesters have committed rape, 24 percent statutory rape, 33 percent indecent liberties, 3 percent indecent exposure, 6 percent incest, and 11 percent various other offenses, such as lewd behavior, contributing to the delinquency of a minor, etc. In another study, the most frequently occurring offense for male offenders was indecent liberties (59 percent), followed by rape (23 percent), exposure (11 percent), and other hands-off offenses (7 percent) (Fehrenbach et al., 1986). (See Appendix I for definitions of these various charges.)

The image of the "dirty old man" is also a misconception, as molesters are not necessarily old or always male. Although molesters continue to sexually abuse children throughout their lives, many begin their activities before adolescence, as repeatedly confirmed by those interviewed for this book. In Abel and colleagues' (1987) study, the mean age was 31.5 years. In Groth and colleagues' (1978) study, the majority of the subjects were under the age of thirty-five and a great number were still children themselves. Another sample of convicted child molesters reported that "they had committed their first sexual offenses between the ages of eight and eighteen years" (Fehrenbach et al., 1986, p. 226). In Saylor's (1979) study, the average age at first conviction was in the twenties.

Another misconception is that "Peeping Toms" are relatively harmless. Abel and colleagues (1987), Fehrenbach and colleagues (1986), and Elliott, Browne, and Kilcoyne (1995) report otherwise. Fehrenbach and colleagues (1986) note the "evidence of progression from nonviolent sex crimes during adolescence to more serious sexual assaults as adults" (p. 226). Wolfe (cited in van Dam, 1996) adds that some molesters sometimes also temporarily revert back to indirect contact crimes. This confirms that seemingly minor molestations should not be ignored. Excusing, denying, or interfering with the reporting of seemingly less invasive sexual abuse provides for those committing the noncontact offenses with opportunities to also commit direct contact molestations.

Fehrenbach and colleagues' (1986) study broke down the relationship between the perpetrator and the victim by type of sexual abuse. Only 2.3 percent of the younger victims (under age six) and 7 percent of the older victims were molested by strangers. These molestations were primarily self-exposure. All other cases involved either a relative or acquaintance. In almost 50 percent of the cases, the abuse occurred while the molester was "baby-sitting." These data differ from other data because his definition of baby-sitting includes father figures or family friends offering to care for the child while sending the mother off to run errands.

These studies all examined male sexual molesters. Although little is known about male molesters, even less is known about female molesters. It is often suggested that women who molest do so only at the request of their male partners (Finkelhor, 1979a). This is probably a myth, and a form of sexism that protects women from detection, as some women are known to offend entirely on their own (Mayer, 1992; Elliott, 1993). "When women are charged with forcing themselves on others, it is treated as a medical curiosity" (Abel, Rouleau, and Cunningham-Rathner, 1986, p. 1). Halliday (1985) suggests that female molesters, in addition to the sexual molestations, often engage in more vicious behavior than the male sexual molesters.

Since women are more typically assigned the task of child care and attendance to child hygiene, abuse is more easily masked as part of their caretaking role. Societal attitudes toward women make disclosures about female molesters even less likely. For instance, boys prematurely sexualized by an older female are traditionally considered "lucky." Those who tell get such responses as "What are you complaining about?" (Anderson and Struckman-Johnson, 1998). Younger children are simply not believed, or the evidence is ignored. In one court case, the judge convicted the mother of sexually abusing her two sons, then returned the boys to her custody, stating that "she didn't really mean anything by it" (Halliday, 1985). In Washington State, Mary Kay Letourneau became a media sensation, as the public grappled with the seeming incongruity of an attractive successful married teacher and mother of four charged with the sexual assault of her pupil, who was a sixth-grade student (Cloud, 1998). The boy's mother, evidencing the grooming by Ms. Letourneau, became her ally and advocate; she blessed the sexual relationship between her prepubescent son and this adult more than three times his age even though her son was robbed of his childhood and prematurely became the father of two infant daughters.

Because the male molesters who have been studied were so active, molesting hundreds of children on average (Abel and Osborn, 1992), it remains impossible at this time to determine what percentage of the population sexually molests children. Although the various studies leave room for disagreement, one can only conclude that molesters include trusted family and friends as well as less well-known assailants who may be respectable members of the community.

Psychopathy has been well studied (Meloy, 1988; Hare 1993), and has become more clinically quantifiable when using the symptom checklist developed by Hare (1991). Child sexual molesters automatically meet some of the criteria (such as lack of empathy, impulsive behavior, and poor behavioral control), but not necessarily enough to meet Hare's criteria for a diagnosis of psychopathy. They typically do not qualify primarily because the psychopath engages in myriad criminal activities, whereas many of the molesters, who carefully groom their victims and the families and commu-

6## 88   IDENTIFYING CHILD MOLESTERS

nities where their victims live, are otherwise law-abiding citizens (Salter, 1995; Hare, 1993).

Many observations from this literature are, nevertheless, relevant to understanding sexual molesters of children. Psychopaths are notoriously successful at gaining support and cooperation from people they plan to exploit. They accomplish this through a variety of techniques that also apply to the operating style of a number of child molesters. These methods are deliberately disorienting. For instance, "many people find it difficult to deal with the intense, emotionless or 'predatory' stare of the psychopaths. . . . Some people respond to the emotionless stare with considerable discomfort, almost as if they feel like potential prey in the presence of a predator" (Hare, 1993, p. 207). This same empty, intense stare is referred to by Meloy (1988) and mentioned or demonstrated by molesters interviewed for this book. Hare's (1993) advice to those targeted by the psychopath might be equally relevant for those targeted by molesters:

> The next time you find yourself dealing with an individual with nonverbal mannerisms or gimmicks whose riveting eye contact, dramatic hand movements, "stage scenery" and so on, tend to overwhelm you, close your eyes or look away and carefully listen to what the person is saying. (p. 208)

Hare (1993) adds the following warning: "The police and consumer advocates tell us that extra caution is called for whenever someone or something looks too good to be true" (p. 211). This will be important to keep in mind during later discussions of how molesters function. However, whereas psychopaths may commit sexual molestations as one of a number of criminal acts, the majority of sexual molestations are carried out by individuals with paraphilic tendencies as their only psychiatric diagnosis (Abel, Rouleau, and Cunningham-Rathner, 1986).

Chapter 6

The Grooming Process:
How Do They Do It?

The idea that reasonable, likable adults seek sexual contact with small children is so unacceptable to most people that they are blind to it, minimize it, excuse it, justify it, assume it to be caused by environmental stress, or blame the victim. Freud explained that patients fantasize these assaults (van Dam and Bates, 1986). Others blamed it on sexually unresponsive wives (Frude, 1982) or precociously seductive children. In "Wisconsin [a] judge sentenced a twenty-four-year-old man to three years' probation after he was found guilty of first-degree sexual assault on a five-year-old girl, commenting that, 'I am satisfied that we have an unusual sexually promiscuous young lady and that this man did not know enough to knock off her advances'" (Salter, 1995, p. 37).

Such explanations belie the facts: infants, toddlers, children, and adolescents are raped, assaulted, molested, and otherwise forced into sexual activity with adults. For this to occur, there must first be *sexual attraction to children.* Second, molesters must *justify the interest* in having sex with children to themselves, at which point they *groom the adult community* to gain access to children. Finally they must *groom children* to maintain security.

The Grooming Process
- Sexual attraction to children
- Justification of interest
- Grooming adults
- Grooming children

SEXUAL ATTRACTION TO CHILDREN

Various presented models explain the sexual abuse of children by adults. Frude (1982) summarizes some of these by presenting a five-step process that proceeds from sexual need, to attractive partner, to opportunity, to disinhibition, to sexual behavior. This theoretical approach subsumes that men have an innate sexual drive that must be satisfied, so that "we see predominantly heterophile men satisfying themselves from sheer necessity" (Brongersma, 1991, p. 148). The underlying assumption is that men may molest children if their wives do not meet their "normal" needs. According to Frude:

> There can be no doubt that the fathers who approach their daughters sexually are unsatisfied sexually in other relationships. Several authors have pointed to the frustration of other sexual outlets. Sexual relationships with the wife are often unsatisfactory, and Riemer, on the basis of a study with a large sample, claimed that 'With almost no exceptions the patient, shortly before the incestuous relationship begins, finds himself barred from sexual intercourse with his own wife.' Maisch found that a high proportion of his sample claimed that their wife was 'frigid' and Lustig suggested that the wives were sometimes sexually provocative, but ultimately denying. (1982, p. 213)

Another argument frequently expressed by pedophiles is that all men experience sexual arousal to young children, but most are in too much denial to heed these "natural" urges. This neatly creates a catch-22 for those who do not agree. Brongersma (1991) extols the virtues of eras when sex between men and boys was tolerated, encouraged, and exonerated. He concludes, "This shows that sexual attraction to youthful individuals of his own sex is present to a greater or lesser degree in every human male, and this makes it possible for every man to have sex with a handsome boy" (p. 148). To support this view, he cites another author, who states, "Surprising as it may seem, otherwise normal adult males who work with young boys can often, quite inexplicably, find themselves becoming sexually aroused" (p. 148). From this he concludes that "we should face the fact that quite normal men can be aroused sexually by young boys. That they are is not evidence of homosexuality, but may even be evidence of their humanness and sensitivity" (p. 148). Kincaid (1998) builds on this argument to conclude that all men have such desires and their protests are simply denials of natural truths. In support, he argues that terms such as "cute" simply mask these "self-evident" prurient interests.

Money (1990) suggests that sexual interest in children is explained using a biosocial learning theory, by describing appropriate pair bonding between caretaker and child as overlapping the sensual relationship of lovers or breeding partners: "In nature's design of things, the pair bonding of infancy serves a dual developmental role. As it does with other mammals, it ensures the survival of the individual, and as a precursor of later sexuoeretic pair bonding, it also ensures the survival of the species. Both manifestations of pair bonding are intimately related to the skin senses through the acts of holding, cuddling, hugging, rubbing, patting, rocking, and kissing" (p. 446).

Other theorists focus primarily on environmental cues to conclude that adult sexual arousal to children results from learning in childhood. Researchers used to assume that all child molesters had themselves been sexually abused as children, which may be true for those who also experienced pleasurable sensations during the abuse (Feierman, 1990). "Perverse fantasies and acts are the means by which an individual symbolically attempts to gain revenge for and mastery over a childhood sexual trauma. As a result of identification with the aggressor, the individual, through such activities, is capable of temporarily turning a passively endured childhood trauma into an actively controlled adult triumph" (p. 492). A number of molesters were themselves never sexually abused but witnessed sexual abuse of others by significant role models. Helpless to prevent the molestations, identification with the aggressor is postulated to occur, resulting in their engaging in child sexual abuse as adults.

Thirty-three percent of child molesters report a history of physical abuse in childhood (Awad and Saunders, 1991). Feierman (1990) suggests that such aversive events can become internalized. Money (1990) states that "for pedophilia to become permanently lodged in the lovemap, some pertinent mechanism has to operate during the course of development. Such a mechanism may be similar to the one that creates addictions" (p. 450). The opponent-process learning theory (Solomon, 1980) would suggest that an initially aversive event can be reversed and become addictive. The fear associated with the initial event can be accompanied by a brain-released flood of the body's own opiates, or endorphins (Money, 1990), and thereby create a subsequent addiction to the events associated with the release of endorphins. Cognitive mediators would make it possible for various responses to environmental events to become subsequently paired with sexual arousal (Money, 1990). Thus, the physical abuse during childhood could find expression in subsequent deviant sexual arousal.

Another behavioral explanation for sexual arousal to deviant stimuli is that stimuli paired with initial orgasms experienced during adolescence become triggers for future orgasmic responses. This pairing, through repeated experiences, becomes entrenched, resulting in the original stimuli becoming discriminative stimuli for future exposures. The adolescent who originally masturbates to orgasm while viewing pictures of young children may become locked into sexual arousal to young children (Sanford, 1980). Thus, initial sexualization through abuse, witnessing abuse, or private experimentation can create sexual arousal to those events. As a result, the preferred victim's age of the child molester can be a predictor of the molester's own earlier experiences, including victimization (Freund and Kuban, 1994). Not all molesters were sexually abused, but sexual arousal only to children more typically occurs to those who were abused in childhood. These molesters were also found to be more sexually active (Langevin, Wrighty, and Handy, 1989; Becker and Stein, 1991).

JUSTIFYING THE INTEREST

To overcome social inhibitions against engaging in sex with children, it becomes necessary to redefine reality or engage in what has been called *neutralization* (De Young, 1988). This is a four-step procedure.

Neutralization

- Denial of injury
- Denial of victimization
- Condemnation of dissension
- A more enlightened viewpoint

---

1. *Denial of injury:* Various pedophile organizations publish stories of the positive benefits of sex with children. The empirical literature regarding the harm of child sexual abuse is counteracted with anecdotal information, testimonials, and fantasy. Articles describe how

> children benefit from this behavior by chronicling the harms they experience when they are denied the opportunity to do so. Drug abuse, suicide, obesity, attacks on the weak and the elderly, and even sloth and indolence are listed by the [Rene Guyon] Society as injuries sustained by children who have been prohibited by society from engaging in sexual behavior with adults. (in de Young, 1988 p. 586)

Injury is further denied by publishing supposed letters from children attesting to the benefits they have experienced from sex with adults. This was published in a NAMBLA Bulletin:

> I am a boy of 13, and I hope you will read this letter. The spelling and stuff isn't too good. . . . I wish I was one of the kids (in the stories featured in the Bulletin) with someone to love me like that. (in de Young, 1988, p. 586)

2. *Denial of victimization:* "With this strategy, the victim is reconceptualized as having deserved or brought on the offending behavior" (de Young, 1988, p. 587). This means redescribing the children as being willing sexual partners who seek out the relationship. This is nothing more than "blaming the victim" to allow molesters to fool themselves into believing they are simply accommodating the needs and desires of the child. As part of this strategy, the various publications promoting pedophilia discuss issues of consent. NAMBLA states:

> If a child and adult want to have sex, they should be free to do so. Consent is the critical point . . . force and coercion are abhorrent to NAMBLA . . . which is strongly opposed to age of consent laws and other restrictions which deny adults and youth the full enjoyment of their bodies and control over their lives. (de Young, 1988, p. 587)

The Rene Guyon Society's motto is "sex before eight or else it's too late" (de Young, 1988). Their guidelines indicate that "a four-year-old child's anus is large enough to comfortably accommodate an adult male's penis" (de Young, 1988, p. 587), and the Childhood Sensuality Circle publication encourages families to "practice the masturbation of infants as well as the massage resulting in orgasm of very young children" (de Young, 1988, p. 587).

3. *Condemnation of dissension:* Thus, the magazines point out that

> protectors of children are the real perverts, the real child abusers, the real molesters, who take advantage of innocence and inexperience to spread the venom of guilt and fear. They damage a child's self-image and self-esteem in a way impossible for any loving relationship, no matter what the age difference. (de Young, 1988, p. 588)

4. *A more enlightened viewpoint:* The molester is working towards the sexual liberalization of children from the oppressive laws of a sexually repressed society. In the case of NAMBLA, the organization has allied itself with both the women's movement and the gay rights movement who are also "trying to free themselves from the prejudices of the larger society" (de Young, 1998, p. 589). The Childhood Sensuality Circle has similarly attempted to become more mainstream by lending their support to the sexual education movement in the schools, and against the use of school corporal punishment (de Young, 1988).

The appearance of these publications has been accompanied by a simultaneous erosion of sexual norms and standards. Many more people have fewer clear guidelines of appropriateness and fewer social controls (Finkelhor, 1982). There is an increased availability of pornography and child pornography. "In some pornography stores and in some areas as many as a quarter or a third of the book titles refer to incestuous sex or sex with underage children. So even the man who was slow to draw the conclusion on his own that the sexual revolution now permits sex with children might certainly get that message quickly from pornography" (Finkelhor, 1982, p. 99).

All of these factors lower the resistance for someone already sexually attracted to children to consider taking action. The role that drugs and alcohol then seem to play is that once the decision to molest a child has been made, drugs or alcohol might be involved, either to get the courage to act or to mask subsequent remorse or guilt. The widespread consensus is that drugs and alcohol, of themselves, do not lower the resistance (Groth, 1979).

Another way to justify the behavior is to normalize sexual arousal to children, with the proviso that those who do not admit to such interests are in denial. Brongersma (1991), in trying to justify abuse, insists that all males are sexually aroused by boys and only "exhibit such violently emotional hostility toward boy-lovers because they fear their own unarticulated pedophile impulses" (p. 153). Kincaid (1998) goes to great lengths to point this out by labeling what others call "cute" as an indirect admission of sexual arousal:

> We might try to manage without stark essentialist ideas of sexuality and sexual behavior, see what might be done by positing a range of erotic feelings within and toward children. Rather than assuming that such feelings exist in only two forms—not at all or out of control—perhaps we could learn something of their differences, manner of expression, and effects, allowing them a complex and dynamic relativity. It's important to be plain about this and not try to counter erotic attraction to children with nothing stronger than nostalgia and talk about how sweet children are. For one thing, nostalgia and sweetness are not antidotes to eroticism but ingredients for it; for another, they are trifles. I believe most adults in our culture feel some measure of erotic attraction to children and the childlike; I do not know how it could be otherwise. I propose that as long as these feelings are denied and projected as outrage, nothing will happen. (p. 24)

Kincaid (1998) describes a number of Hollywood movies as exemplifying the overt pedophilia supposedly enjoyed by everyone, with scripts that, from his perspective, demonstrate how every movie featuring child stars simply caters to the sexual interest in children prominent among all viewers. "Current films work obsessively with a single plot: a child, most often a boy, possessed either of no father or a bad one, is isolated, sexualized, and imperiled" (p. 115). This is why "Matthew Stadler, reporting hilariously on a weekend of North American Man-Boy Love Association meetings, found that their secret eroticism was simply network television, the Disney channel, and mainline films: 'I had found NAMBLA'S porn, and it was Hollywood'" (p. 115). From his perspective, NAMBLA was simply acknowledging the arousal generally experienced by all viewers of movies intended to tickle everyone's sexual interest in children.

Others publish that society should have a more "humane attitude" toward those who love children (Arndt, 1991, p. 213), suggesting that the "pedophile may do a service to the child who is neglected at home by satisfying that child's craving for physical contact." Arndt (1991) notes that Ullerstram "laments the fact that there is no way to supply pedophiles with children, but believes that these men should be allowed to fulfill their desires," while Righton "goes a bit further when he argues that in a warm relation with a pedophile, the boy benefits from the friendship and is probably not harmed by sexual activities" (p. 214).

GROOMING THE ADULT COMMUNITY

Many of the molesters interviewed for this book described with varying insight their methods of image management, and the thoughtfulness with which they presented themselves to the adult community. Those who were brighter, more educated, and more sophisticated simply targeted people more similar to themselves and sometimes took longer to establish a good social foundation before engaging in sexual overtures toward the children. This deliberate grooming of the adult community was consistently noted by interviewed molesters.

Cook (1989), a convicted child molester, describes the grooming process, noting that long before he would molest the child,

> I would obviously have met his family several times. . . . I would have been invited to supper at his home and would have charmed the hell out of his parent(s) and they would be pleased the way their son responded to me and so obviously liked me. I am clean cut, very intelligent and personable and

the parent(s) would feel that I was a "good" influence on their boy. (p. 7)

One blue-collar worker said:

> I was always trying to be a nice guy. For instance, my wife had a girlfriend calling up one night [while] we were sitting around the table eating supper. Her car had broke down. I got up from the supper table and went to get her car jumped. I had in the back of my mind, "I can probably have sex with her daughter. This might be worth it in the long run. I might be giving a little bit now, but what might I be getting in the end?" I could have said to her, "I can't right now, but maybe in a little while if you can't get it started."

Shortly after helping the mother get her car started, he began molesting her daughter but pointed out that "my victim's parents saw me as such a nice person. I just complimented the mother. Treated her nice. Real polite. They'd say, 'He's a real gentleman. He's so polite. He's so well mannered. He's decent. He doesn't look raggedy.'"

Another molester, who was a highly paid medical specialist, pointed out, "I was too good to be true. I was the perfect husband. My wife's friends were all jealous of her. I made very good money, and when I got home from work, I took over the child care and the housework." Not only did his wife live in the lap of luxury, but he always encouraged her to enjoy trips with her friends. "The minute I came home from work, I would take over so she could go out. I would clean house, cook meals, change diapers, and even do the night feedings. She really had it great. The only thing was, she didn't know what else I was doing."

Over 33 percent of offenders interviewed by Elliott, Browne, and Kilcoyne (1995) specifically went to a great deal of trouble to make themselves welcome in the victim's home prior to the abuse. One in five "claimed they had gained the trust of the victim's whole family in order to be able to abuse the child" (p. 585). "It took a long time, but I finally became part of the family. I just helped out when I could, dropped in unannounced, became friends with the father— I did anything I could so they'd think there was nothing unusual about me spending time with their son" (in Sanford, 1980, p. 86).

This "grooming" of adults is a well-organized, long-term activity, with considerable thought and planning going into the event (Sanford, 1980). Many molesters confirmed that they would spend anywhere from two to three years getting established in a new community before molesting any children. One man specifically used the bars as a place to make friends, choosing those who had difficulty parenting their children. He would get to know them, go on picnics, and become a friend:

> I was just a friend doing things a friend would do. Helping them move, going to baseball games with them. What I found myself doing was getting close to the kids, becoming more of a father figure or a mentor, doing things for them that the parents weren't doing because the parents were out getting drunk all the time. And, of course, it made it easy for me to baby-sit. They'd say, "Oh yeah. We can off-load the kids with Jimmy."

At picnics and other outings he would play with the children. "With the adults, as long as the kid is having a good time and is not in their hair, then that would be fine."

Another molester described how he "was always looked on as being the best Dad. I don't smoke, I don't drink, but I don't criticize people who do. I'm a hard-working type of person. I'm easy to get along with. I'm friendly, outgoing, helpful. I'm always willing to give a hand." To elaborate on his helpfulness, he added:

> My neighbor now, he has a bad back. I told him, "Don't ever pick anything up. When you see me outside, come get me." That's the way I am. I don't think there's anything wrong with that. I don't know how many times I've seen someone out doing something that really should have been a two-man job, and they're doing it by themselves. I'll see somebody out doing something like that and I'll give them a hand. In a lot of ways, it'll give them a false image. I'll give them a hand and then turn around and groom and molest their daughter. And that's the way I am.

A number of molesters even used the topic of child sexual abuse to ingratiate themselves with the family to show they could be trusted. One molester described, "I was being extra nice, friendly with her kids. I was making her feel safe having me around her kids. There was this bathroom incident, for instance. While I was going to the bathroom, several times the kids tried to get in. I said to her 'You really should keep a lock on the bathroom.'"

One woman described how her boyfriend's admission of being a sex offender made him seem safe:

> I'd been sexually molested when I was a kid, and what my boyfriend did, is he told me right up front "We can't see each other anymore unless you go to this group therapy thing because I'm a sex offender." I thought, "How safe can you get?" If he was going to molest my kids, he wouldn't have told me he was a sex offender. Right? I mean, this has got to be the safest guy on the block. You know exactly what you're dealing with. And he was so advanced. He was going to graduated therapy. He'd completed, but he used the word graduated. He told me he graduated from the therapy program but that I'd need to go so I could learn as much. Then I could chaperone and he could be around my kids.

Molesters target families using a variety of methods. Many select those families most susceptible to their charms. Socially isolated families with patriarchal structures seem to be more vulnerable. The isolation and family structure may play a role in facilitating abuse (Finkelhor, 1982). Divorce puts families more at risk for a variety of reasons. One reason being that single parents are in even greater need of baby-sitting services and less able to pay for them (Finkelhor, 1982). "Single parents may be particularly vulnerable . . . as many offenders seem to target single-parent families" (Elliott, Browne, and Kilcoyne, 1995, p. 592). Mr. Martin (see Chapter 1) married a succession of single mothers, rescuing them from poverty by providing them with a nice home, steady paycheck, and help and involvement in raising their children. Each marriage only deteriorated as those children outgrew his primary age of interest.

Work in the field of social psychology on image management can help shed light on techniques used by molesters in gaining adult support. Name recognition is a technique frequently used in advertising. Getting the customer to recognize the product name, no matter what the circumstances, will increase sales or product acceptance. This technique has also been well used by politicians and other public figures (Wade and Tavris, 1990). For instance, the negative publicity surrounding Michael Jackson's anti-Semitic song lyrics was thought to boost record sales. Actor Hugh Grant's public encounter with a prostitute and subsequent legal charges kept his name on the front page of the newspaper. As one showman said, "I don't care what the papers say about me, provided they say something" (Gale Research, 1995).

Other techniques also help gain adult acceptance. Mr. Smith (see Chapter 1) was well known to the community for his endless dedication to children. For those not yet familiar with him, he often initiated contact by arriving at a neighborhood home to participate in a child's birthday party. Parents typically reported being initially dumbfounded. Here was a total stranger, arriving uninvited to their child's birthday party, playing party games. The children all loved the activity, which seemed like a planned part of the party. Asking someone to leave under such circumstances is extremely difficult, which is why most people passively watch events unfold instead. This maneuver accomplishes a number of things and is known in social psychology as the "foot-in-the door technique" (Brehm and Kassin, 1993). The concept here is that once cooperation is elicited with a small request, it becomes easier to later gain cooperation on a larger request. The family would then have more difficulty denying future access directly as a result of having supported this initial contact.

The process is further explained by self-perception theory, which states that people infer their attitudes by their behavior. For instance, seeing themselves hosting Mr. Smith at their child's birthday party helps the parents establish the attitude that he must be acceptable (Brehm and Kassin, 1993). Furthermore, cognitive dissonance (Festinger, 1957) sets in because people like to assume their behavior and beliefs are consistent. Parents might believe they would never give a total stranger access to their child, but this is precisely what occurred with Mr. Smith's involvement at children's birthday parties. These parents subsequently accepted Mr. Smith to make their beliefs consistent with their behavior. Therefore, many of the parents who expressed initial discomfort with Mr. Smith's appearance at their home became his staunchest allies. Any other stance would have required an admission of having given a "total stranger" access to their children in their own home.

This initial contact with the child under the auspices of the family also sends a strong message to the child. Both Mr. Smith and the parents appeared to accept that he was an invited guest. Mr. Smith therefore had, in the eyes of the child, parental approval. He was not a stranger, but an invited friend. The parents also noted the situation and assumed their behavior reflected their beliefs. They accommodated their belief system to be consistent with their behavior (Brehm and Kassin, 1993). Mr. Smith became a family friend.

Succeeding in this initial small request is all a matter of timing and wording. Research shows that the framing and timing of an otherwise unreasonable request can elicit support if appearing to be reasonable (Langer, 1989). In this case, Mr. Smith told the parents he was an envoy from the school, knew the neighbors, and engaged in this behavior with all the children in the school. This was supposed to reframe the activity as something appreciated by everyone else. Timing this intrusion while the family was busy managing a birthday party, while framing it in the context of something everyone else allows, helped to normalize the event.

Studies on conformity confirm that publicly going against the norm is difficult for most people (Asch, 1956). It would have been rude to ask Mr. Smith to leave in the middle of such generosity. People are also trained to observe the niceties. The seemingly more socially appropriate response would involve saying something appreciative to Mr. Smith for his contribution to the birthday party. Saying something nice out loud helps to make it feel true (Rosenthal and Jacobson, 1968). Since he was not asked to leave, cognitive dissonance would have the parents assume that his presence was acceptable. The easiest way to reduce dissonance is to change one's attitude to be consistent with one's behavior (Brehm and Kassin, 1993).

Some families in the community did have initial concerns about Mr. Smith's behavior, but in the face of the overwhelming community support he received, they chose to keep quiet. This appearance of going along with the crowd, while not necessarily accepting the crowd's response, is not uncommon (Asch, 1956; Brehm and Kassin, 1993). Conformity studies indicate that few people will publicly disagree with a majority opinion (Snyder and Swann, 1978). This was especially true with the deafeningly enthusiastic public support enjoyed by Mr. Smith, against an only vague unease experienced by a few parents in isolation. In some cases, participants will change their view to conform to others. In many cases, however, participants will simply voice the more popular viewpoint, knowing it to be inconsistent with their own perception (Brehm and Kassin, 1993). A few parents were uncomfortable with Mr. Smith, could not clearly articulate their worries, and chose to keep their complaints quiet in the face of his overwhelming enthusiastic public support.

Once an attitude has been formed, it becomes well entrenched and extremely difficult to change. People seek information that confirms their belief system (Asch and Zukier, 1984). Parents stated that Mr. Smith was loved by children, who sought him out. Nevertheless, a number of people noted contradictory evidence. Under normal circumstances, this would be enough to suggest that Mr. Smith's presence in the school was unacceptable. Yet parents were unable to hear this evidence against Mr. Smith. The confirmation bias (Brehm and Kassin, 1993) describes how people maintain an initial stance by only accepting information that verifies existing beliefs. Furthermore, people then rationalize the maintenance of those beliefs by exaggerating both the benefits of that response and the inadequacies of the opposite response (Brehm and Kassin, 1993). Thus, many believed a few disgruntled parents were on a witch-hunt and deliberately maligning a wonderful man's character. They also considered Mr. Smith to be above reproach, despite his primary saintly quality being handing out money and candy to children.

Mr. Smith successfully gained the parents' support and approval of his interactions with their children. Once they allowed him into their homes and school, supported his candy- and money-giving activities, and publicly applauded him, three things happened: (1) they sent the message to their children that this man is a friend of the family; (2) they also sent the message that candy bribes are acceptable; and (3) they made it clear that any information to the contrary would not be heard. These responses allowed this activity to flourish outside the home, thereby making it possible for Mr. Smith to spend time with their children on the school grounds as well as in the community, with impunity.

Mr. Smith's behavior had been raised to saintliness. Implicit personality theory suggests that other traits are then assumed. It becomes accepted that he is, therefore, "above reproach," and the halo effect ensures that all his behaviors are seen in this positive light (Cooper, 1981). Belief perseverance then describes how people contrive to see things the same way despite new information to the contrary (Brehm and Kassin, 1993). Mr. Smith was an established figure in the community, and all questionable behavior was ignored. He became a "cause célèbre." Not only did everyone come to his defense, but those who suggested the possibility that the "emperor had no clothes" were accused of witch hunting, and the matter was thus settled.

Since the concerns about Mr. Smith's behavior were raised by various individuals in isolation a number of times, one can examine the principle of diffusion of responsibility to describe how people fail to act appropriately when they assume someone else to be in charge (Wegner and Schaeffer, 1978). In this case, each administration stood by and did nothing while Mr. Smith brought his activities to another school. Also, the school district, in the face of Mr. Smith's overwhelming popularity and support from the parent community, chose to use avoidance strategies in coping with this dilemma (Brehm and Kassin, 1993).

All of these techniques, studied by social psychologists, and effectively used in sales and image management, and applied by psychopaths (Hare, 1993; Meloy, 1988), are consistently used by molesters to successfully gain adult support. Mr. Smith's methods were typical of those used by many successful molesters. Utilizing research in social psychology to explore these dynamics creates a basis for trying to understand further how the sexual molester manages to gain adult support.

GROOMING THE CHILD

Much has already been studied about how molesters manage to groom children into sexual relationships, gaining their cooperation, participation, and silence (Halliday, 1985; Sanford, 1980; Sgroi, 1985; Butler, 1978). This grooming can typically be identified as inevitably following a five-step process, whereby the molester (1) first identifies a vulnerable child, (2) then engages that child in peerlike involvement, (3) desensitizes the child to touch, (4) isolates the child, and (5) makes the child feel responsible (Harms and van Dam, 1992). Understanding how children are groomed into a sexual molestation may be helpful but cannot by itself prevent molestations. "I don't think that any of my victims had a chance against me, once I made up my mind that they were my next friend [victim]" (Cook, 1989, p. 12).

Identify Vulnerable Children

One of the key ingredients in sexual molestation is that the child targeted for victimization is somehow vulnerable. "Offenders reported that they were attracted to children who seemed to lack confidence or had low self-esteem" (Elliott, Browne, and Kilcoyne, 1995, p. 584). This may be because of their extremely young age, their social circumstances, or their loneliness and need for attention. The children are specially targeted because, in many cases, the relationship "filled a significant deficit in the child's life, or disclosure posed a serious threat to the child's (perceived) situation" (Berliner and Conte, 1990, p. 35).

One convicted child molester, Joe Henry, testifying to the U.S. Senate in February 1985, explained how he gained cooperation from his many young victims:

> I showed them affection and the attention they thought they were not getting anywhere else. Almost without exception, every child I have molested was lonely and longing for attention. . . . Their desire to be loved, their trust of adults, their normal sexual playfulness and their inquisitive minds made them perfect victims. (West Vancouver Policemen's Association [WVPA], 1986, p. 131)

Similar information was revealed in studies on prevention strategies, as molesters described how they selected their victims. In a study by Conte, Wolf, and Smith (1989), various molesters stated the following:

> I would choose the youngest one, or the one whom I thought would not talk about it. . . . I would probably pick the one who

appeared more needy, the child hanging back from others or feeling picked on by brothers or sisters. . . . The one who liked to sit in my lap. . . . The one who likes attention and stroking. (p. 296)

Other responses to Conte, Wolf, and Smith (1989) further illustrate how many of the molesters selected a vulnerable child:

> friendly. . . . Showed me their panties. . . . The way the child would look at me, trustingly. . . . Someone who had been a victim before; quiet, withdrawn, compliant. . . . Someone who had not been a victim would be more non accepting of the sexual language or stepping over the boundaries of modesty . . . quieter, easier to manipulate, less likely to object or put up a fight. (p. 296)

Elliott, Browne, and Kilcoyne (1995) concluded that "overall, according to the offender's perceptions, the child who was most vulnerable had family problems, was alone, was nonconfident, curious, pretty, 'provocatively' dressed, trusting, and young or small" (p. 584).

This is consistent with other reports on how children are selected and targeted for molestation. For instance, Mr. Clay successfully chose his victims by screening those children who were least likely to report the activities and most willing to tolerate his authority. They were asked to help out after school or asked to stay after school to finish their work. Those who could not do so without parental permission were screened out. Those who were available were then caressed on the back, initially only over the shirt. If this met with no resistance, the caressing progressed to under the shirt. The child's response was evaluated by waiting to see what was reported to the parents. Parents inquiring about this behavior were told by Mr. Clay that he had simply been checking their child for signs of chicken pox. These children were then not targeted further. Children who accepted the stroking and did not report the activity to their parents were selected for more contact. The contact only very gradually escalated to include touching below the belt and, finally, genital contact.

A variety of circumstances make a child particularly vulnerable. Certainly infants, because of their tender years, are totally at a molester's mercy. Preverbal children are also more vulnerable. Many of the molesters targeted young children precisely for this reason: "That's why most of my victims were seven and below. Some were even three years old. . . . I went after the victims that had a low potential for telling someone" (Conte, Wolf, and Smith, 1989, p. 296). As children become more verbal, some develop skills, confidence, and assertiveness that make them somewhat less likely targets. Children who are not hungry for affection and attention, and those who are capable of safely disagreeing with adults, are less vulnerable since they are more risky targets for molestation precisely because these children are more likely to tell and be heard (Elliott, Browne, and Kilcoyne, 1995).

The vulnerable child, however, is more eager to please and has a greater need for adult attention:

> The offender relies on the child's wish to not displease him, even though to the child the request may have seemed unpleasant, distasteful, or even bizarre. In other words, the child's need and wish to please was exploited by the offender. In some instances, the child was assured that what was requested was perfectly normal and proper between them because of the relationship. (De Francis, 1969, p. 46)

Many of the molesters interviewed by Elliott, Browne, and Kilcoyne (1995) described this process as educational.

This targeting of a vulnerable child suggests that some children are at greater risk for molestation (Conte, Wolf, and Smith, 1989; Elliott, Browne, and Kilcoyne, 1995), and is one of the limitations of the prevention training programs currently in place. Expecting these children to report the abuse creates an ongoing dilemma, as the more vulnerable children often include those who lack parental support or may be less likely to be believed should they disclose. It should be noted that the psychological sequelae of child sexual abuse can also impact parenting abilities in adulthood (Schetky, 1990). Those who were themselves molested often have difficulty with assertiveness and do not know how to provide their children with the differentiation (Kerr and Bowen, 1988) so necessary for protection from abuse. It is no accident that 89 percent of women who were sexually abused themselves as children have children who become victims of sexual abuse as well (Halliday, 1985).

However, children are vulnerable for a variety of reasons. Many molesters specifically target children with single parents. "As most parents will quickly tell you, kids can be stressful under the most ideal conditions, but given the extra problems a single parent has to contend with, there are times when they just about reach the end of their tether" (WVPA, 1986, p. 37). One successful molester who was a respected member of the community targeted exactly these children. He frequently dropped in unannounced on the children and their mothers, until he became a regular figure in the household. Once so established, he baby-sat and took the children on special outings that included fishing trips and skiing adventures. The mothers were delighted with these special opportunities for their sons, which were when the molestations would occur. "His victims, who were boys ranging from 9 years to 12 years, were taken completely by surprise and had no idea how to react to this man's advances. Here was a man trusted and liked by everyone. How could they go to their parents and tell them what was going on?" (WVPA, 1986, p. 35).

Cook (1989) details his successful selection of young boys:

> Since it is a given that the boy is interested in adult men anyway, it is a simple matter to take advantage of that. Most boys, by the time they are eight, have asserted enough independence at home that they do not receive the same amount of attention from their parents that they did when younger. Also, by this age there are generally siblings to split parental attention, and often this is a period when both parents work to pay mortgages, etc. Despite this desire for independence, the boys also still want to be loved, noticed, and valued. If a significant adult, even one they don't yet know, notices them, they are very aware of that. My most basic and successful grooming technique is "eye contact" accompanied by a friendly, interested look. (p. 3)

Cook (1989) further articulates how every child needs to be valued, loved, and cherished:

> If they don't get these feelings reinforced at home, they will look elsewhere. I have also noticed that even well-adjusted, well-loved boys are still susceptible to molesting. They are just not as easy to victimize as a boy who is really needy. The older boys are much more difficult to reach, but once they fall, they fall hard. (p. 11)

Peerlike Involvement

Once the vulnerable child is targeted, the molester starts breaking down any further defenses by becoming an ally. The intense interaction with the child often resembles the type of involvement one would expect from a peer, rather than from an adult. Examples of this are consistently reported by both molesters and their victims. Silva (1990), in his interactions with children, described behavior one would expect from another child, rather than from an adult. Even when he was in his late twenties, he invited young children to his house for a sleepover. He also met his "friends" at the video arcades and other hangouts.

One comment commonly heard from molesters is that they "really like to play with children." Many molesters have elaborated on this theme with such comments as "I get down on their level and play." Cook (1989) reiterated this in describing his grooming of older boys: "A lot of this [relationship] was accomplished verbally by discussing things with him, but not talking down to him. I treated the boy as a valid equal, a friend, with rights to opinions, etc." (p. 10).

Another indicator of this peerlike involvement is when the molester is more involved with children than with their peers. "A telling sign of a teen-age boy who might be tempted to exploit children sexually is a lack of contact with his peers. If the boy's willingness to help out with small children isn't balanced with an interest in peer activities and relationships, there might be reason to be concerned" (Sanford, 1980, p. 91). Elliott, Browne, and Kilcoyne's (1995) study confirmed that many of the molesters were more interested in the children than in the adults. Interviewed molesters consistently detailed their ability to play with children on a child's level, and many preferred the company of children to the company of adults. Adults frequently made this same observation, stating, "He's more like another kid himself," not understanding its potential significance. Mr. Smith was described by many as "having the playfulness of a twelve-year-old" because of the peerlike quality of his play with children.

Most molesters described "being on a child's wavelength." Those who abused small children played games with them and anticipated their needs. Those focused on older children described siding with them in arguments, talking with them about sexual matters like a friend, and generally behaving like a teenager. One man pointed out, "I'm really focused on kids. I like kids. I think like them. I'm on their wavelength. . . . When a kid is in the room, my focus is on the kid. I'm more interested in the kids than in the adults. . . . I'm a kid." Another one agreed, "I'm just a big kid myself." This theme was reiterated by most molesters. "I'm just a kid myself. I play with the kids on the kids' level. I talk to the kids. I'd spend more time with the kids than with the grown-ups. I'd end up with all the kids at the parties. I'm on their wavelength."

Even the sexual behavior many molesters engage in is often more childlike than adult:

> Regardless of the offender's choice of victim, the sexual activity he engages the child in is relatively immature. His choice of sexual expression correlates more to the age of the child rather than to his age. Exposing genitals, stroking, and touching are common interactions between victim and offender. As the victim grows older or the relationship progresses, mutual masturbation or oral-genital contact might be introduced. Intercourse or some form of penetration may be attempted with older victims or in violent cases, but for the most part, the immature sexual activity is easily disguised as a "game" or "playing." (Sanford, 1980, p. 87)

Victimized children also report this peerlike interaction. In one study, interviewed victims reported such things as "He was like my buddy instead of my stepfather." Another victim described, "We were really good friends, best friends" (Berliner and Conte, 1990, p. 33). Silva (1990) describes his sexual proclivities as "loving" children. He stated, "A special gift for dealing with young people was something I shared with and may have inherited from my mother" (p. 465). He went on to say that as he got older "it was clear to me that I loved children, especially boys, and was happiest when I was in their company" (p. 473).

Desensitize to Touch

After developing a close relationship with the child, the molester will typically begin blurring the boundaries between appropriate and inappropriate touch. Every molester interviewed described engaging in tickling games and roughhousing with children. Much of this is visible to adults. One teacher who worked with Mr. Clay (see Chapter 1) had noted how physical he always was with the children. He routinely would "pick up a kid, turn him upside down, pick him up by the legs." Whenever she talked to him in the hallway, he would always "grab a child who was walking by and put his arms over the child's shoulders. And he'd just talk to me . . . while he'd be pushing his arms back and forth in front of the child." She had seen this constant physical touching and remembered that "I didn't think it was appropriate." Elliott, Browne, and Kilcoyne (1995) described molesters initiating the molestation with seemingly accidental touch. Both the molesters and the child victims report various techniques used to normalize increasingly inappropriate touching.

Cook (1989) details some elaborate strategies for creating opportunities to blur these physical boundaries and also shows how calculating every move becomes:

> Some of the little tricks that always work with younger boys are things like always sitting in a sofa, or a chair with big, soft arms if possible. I would sit with my legs well out and my feet flat on the floor. My arms would always be in an "open" position. The younger kids have not developed a "personal space" yet, and when talking with me, will move in very close. If they are showing me something, particularly on paper, it is easy to hold the object in such a way that the child will move in between my legs or even perch on my knee very early on. If the boy sat on my lap, or very close-in, leaning against me, I would put my arm around him loosely. As this became a part

of our relationship, I would advance to two arms around him, and hold him closer and tighter. During walks, or appropriate moments, I would pick him up and swing him around or tickle him which would naturally progress into a hug or just being briefly carried. I would carry him on my back or shoulders as well, all these things establishing body contact and the habit of body contact. . . . I would brush my cheek against his hair and sometimes lightly kiss his hair or temple. Good-byes would progress from waves, to brief hugs, to kisses on the cheek, to kisses on the mouth in very short order. (p. 4)

Nore (van Dam, 1996) describes the typical physical touching seen in her investigations of teachers, which might include an arm over the shoulder or caressing of hair. Those molesters who were more focused on adolescent girls also described these types of touches, which included "holding her hands, arms over her shoulder, slumped over."

In each case described, the molester desensitizes the child to more and more inappropriate touch. "The majority of offenders coerced children by carefully testing the child's reactions by bringing up sexual matters or having sexual materials around, and by subtly increasing sexual touching" (Elliott, Browne, and Kilcoyne, 1995, p. 585). This was done in a variety of ways. The initial touch was often less directly sexual and yet succeeded in blurring the boundaries of appropriateness in touching. One child reported "he'd keep searching his pockets, and wanted us to fish for him, my nine-year-old sister and me, and we would fish for him in his pockets. He had real long pants pockets. He used to have treats for us like that" (Berliner and Conte, 1990, p. 34). This groping in the pants pockets was the initial overture for what was to become sexualized contact. The child, groping in the molester's pants pockets, inevitably came into contact with the molester's erect penis. Mr. Smith also used this technique.

Many of the children did not realize that the contact was sexually abusive until they were older. "I didn't know there was anything wrong with it, because I didn't know it was abuse until later. I thought he was showing me affection" (Berliner and Conte, 1990, p. 34). Another victim stated, "It took me forever to figure out what was going on. He called it 'roughhousing' and wanted to do it every time he was alone with me. In summer camp, that happened to be a lot of times. When I got older, I realized he was having erections when he rolled all over me (Sanford, 1980, p. 87).

Most of the molesters readily described their tendencies to engage children in physical play. One said, "I was always handling the kids." Another even added, "The danger was exciting. Could I trick people and do it right in front of them? I'd carry the girl on my back, piggyback, and have my finger in her vagina right in front of her parents." Another stated, "My victims got me to carry them on my back, piggyback, and in the process of doing so my hands were on their vaginas. They were fine. They never said nothing. My second victim wanted this piggyback ride also. As far as grabbing her vagina, as I did the first one, this other one took a few hours to get this grooming to the situation. And then back and forth, up and down the hallway, and all the time I'm holding them with my finger in their vagina and playing with them."

Isolate

Isolating the child from opportunities to disclose helps ensure secrecy. This can be done in a variety of ways. Many times, molesters simply tell the child, "This is our little secret," or something similar, to indicate that this information should not be shared with anyone else (Sanford, 1980). Isolation is also a natural by-product if the molester spends an inordinate amount of time with the child (Cook, 1989). The deception involved in maintaining secrecy also inevitably creates a sense of isolation (Lerner, 1993). If the victim initially lies about the sexual abuse, the lie helps to further isolate the child:

> It is easy to tell a lie, but it is almost impossible to tell only one. The first lie may need to be protected by others as well. Concealing something important takes attention and emotional energy that could otherwise serve more creative ends. When we must "watch ourselves" even when we do so automatically and seemingly effortlessly, the process dissipates our energy and erodes our integrity. (Lerner, 1993, p. 29)

Make Victim Feel Responsible

Molesters have myriad ways to make children feel responsible for the abuse. Groth (1979) describes how the molester might begin by providing the child with educational information about sex that the victim cannot obtain at home. When the lesson then transgresses from information to abuse, the victim assumes the blame for having engaged in the initial activity, which was also forbidden. Victims often assume their own behavior to be responsible for the abuse, unaware of the gradual grooming that has taken place, certain their silence and compliance implies guilt:

> Remember, in the child's mind they think they are as guilty as I am. They think other little boys and girls don't do this, so they must not be good children. They are overwhelmed with shame much of the time, and simply comply with the wishes of the adult. (WVPA, 1986, p. 135)

Child molesters help to encourage this. So when the contact turns into abuse, "Do they cry or fight off my advances? Usually not" (WVPA, 1986, p. 135).

Chapter 7

The Social Climate
That Helps Foster It:
Turning a Blind Eye

ATTITUDES TOWARD CHILDREN

In some respects, American society fails to make its children a priority (DeAngelis, 1995; Coontz, 1992):

> Time is a problem. Studies show the average couple talks to each other twenty-nine minutes per week; the average mother talks seven minutes a day to her teenager, while the average father talks only five minutes. Supervision is a problem. The small, tight-knit communities that helped families rear children are increasingly extinct. Instead television is the baby-sitter in many homes. (Pipher, 1994, p. 80)

Families are under increased stress that further helps to isolate children from parents (Pipher, 1996). In many households, both parents work and the children are sent to day care. Most elementary schools in the country have before- and after-school care available. Children are dropped off at school around 7:00 a.m. and picked up around 6:00 p.m. These busy parents, overburdened with work and the day-to-day routines of managing their lives, spend evenings and weekends completing the tasks of running a home and managing a family. This leaves limited time for the children. The children go from baby-sitter to teacher, and then to the television (Meloy, 1988).

As the community support systems of extended families have diminished, nothing substantial has replaced them (Coontz, 1992).

Tired parents are understandably eager to get respite from their children. This is done in a variety of ways, including utilizing available in-store baby-sitting services while running errands, leaving children at home unattended, using television as a baby-sitter, or even leaving children in the video store to play video games while shopping (Marriott, 1995). "In this last half of the twentieth century, families are under siege. Parents are more likely to be overworked, overcommitted, tired and poor. They are less likely to have outside support" (Pipher, 1994, p. 80).

A number of molesters utilize this opportunity to their advantage. In Elliott, Browne, and Kilcoyne's (1995) study, over 48 percent of the molesters interviewed obtained access to their victims through baby-sitting, an easy opportunity because of the parents' need for help. They recommended that parents recognize the danger to their children resulting from their own need to have a break. They stressed that "single parent families are a good target for pedophilia. The mothers are stressed, overworked, and are grateful for someone taking one of the children out for a while" (p. 590). Molesters in the WVPA (1986) study also described using the parents' need for a break to their advantage.

Being stressed and overworked is, however, not the sole domain of single parents. Two-parent families are also overburdened, making them equally vulnerable to offers of assistance. One molester described how he would spend over six months becoming acquainted with the family whose children he wanted to molest. Then, as a known and trusted family friend, he would conveniently make himself available to baby-sit the children so the parents could have a much-needed break. This method is such a cliché that it has been described in various publications:

> As most parents will quickly tell you, kids can be stressful. . . .
> It is at this time that the child abuser will appear on the scene.
> He may be an apartment manager, a friendly neighbor, or be
> employed at a local store the mum frequents. Over a period of
> time he will have taken the time to get to know the family and
> the children's names. When the opportunity arises he will offer
> to "baby-sit" the kids when some emergency comes up, or
> perhaps suggest to mum that she needs a break and why doesn't

she go shopping or just have a "quiet time" to herself while he looks after the little girl or boy. He may suggest that he will take the kids to the park or for an ice cream. (WVPA, 1986, p. 37)

Cook (1989) referred to using this availability of children because of the parents' busy schedules to his advantage, enabling him to sexually molest children: "I might even have filled in as a baby-sitter for the boy and his siblings" (p. 7). This helped make the parents grateful to him for his assistance and, thus, made the child more easily available to him.

ATTITUDES TOWARD WOMEN

Attitudes toward women also contribute to setting the stage for tolerating a number of behaviors that approximate child sexual abuse, and for providing a camouflage screen for those who molest. By creating a subservient role for women in society, and tolerating sexualized talk about women, it becomes more difficult to clearly identify and stop potential transgressions.

A number of molesters blamed this objectification of women by society as the cause of their aberrant sexual proclivities. One said, "Dad was open with talking about women sexually. He used to talk about women's breasts, their ass. I was taught by everyone around me [to] look at them as sexual objects." Only recently has he begun to develop a relationship with his wife. "We talk. I consider her my best friend now."

This objectification of women, and acceptance of them as property, creates an environment that masks, protects, and even tolerates abuse. This is reflected in a court ruling in which the judge stated that "rules are like women, they are made to be violated" (Halliday, 1995, p. 6). Women are blamed for failing to be sexually available to their husbands, who therefore "have" to choose other sexual outlets (Rush, 1980), making women responsible for men's sexual behavior.

Women seeking equal rights, considered by some to be the cause of the decline in American society through the deterioration of the family, further "forces" men to molest. In fact, some people argue that the decline in marriage rates is a reflection of women turning away from their proper place in society. This presumably threatens the stability of Western civilization because the single man "is disposed to criminality, drugs, and violence. He is irresponsible about his debts, alcoholic, accident prone, and venereally diseased. Unless he can marry, he is often destined to a Hobbesian life—solitary, poor, nasty, brutish, and short" (Coontz, 1992, p. 42). From this perspective, when these single men do marry, their women are responsible for managing and fulfilling their sexual appetites, nurturing them, and being respectable, while simultaneously being innocent and naive (Rush, 1980).

This lack of equality between the sexes makes children more vulnerable to sexual abuse (Groth, 1979). Girls still have a complicated role (Brown and Gilligan, 1992), requiring that they learn to cater to their men's needs. Plummer (1991) refers to this as the Ophelia Syndrome, based on Shakespeare's play *Hamlet.* Polonius reduces Ophelia to the status of a baby. "He clamors to be a parent to other adults and exhorts them to become children to his word. Ophelia is worse than naive. She is chronically ignorant, chronically dependent, and chronically submissive" (Plummer, 1991, p. 25). Pipher (1994) claims that girls learn this response pattern by junior high school, when many lose their momentum and start to behave in a manner they assume is expected of them.

Many girls who were self-confident and capable in elementary school become dependent and reliant on males by high school (Pipher, 1994). They are taught to focus on their appearance to make themselves attractive and available to males. This includes attaining the anorexic Barbie figure first taught to them through childhood play with Barbie dolls, then further extolled by the media. Many girls diet and purge to attain this impossible goal and experience lowered self-esteem when they fail (Pipher, 1994). Other habits also exemplify how adult females work to maintain a prepubescent appearance:

> The shaving of leg hair by nubile females is an example of culturally transmitted reproductive neotanization. The wearing of garments that uplift the breasts and flatten the abdomen, the using of facial creams to retard the development of skin wrinkles, and the coloring of hair to hide its gray color are all examples of

culturally transmitted nubility perpetuation. (Feierman, 1990, p. 555)

Eibel-Eibesfeldt (1990) likens this infantalizing to the animal world, where "kissfeeding" is typically a parental ritual to provide food to the infant. Humans have adapted this ritual to the custom of kissing. "The motor pattern in kissing clearly portrays its origin from kissfeeding, with one partner playing the accepting part by opening the mouth in a babyish fashion and the other partner performing tongue movements as if to pass food" (p. 156). He argues that rituals such as this further help to associate sexual relationships between males and females to relationships more traditionally associated between adults and the children.

In other words, in a number of ways,

> [m]en are socialized to see their appropriate sexual partners as persons who are younger and smaller than themselves, while women are socialized to see their appropriate sexual partners as being older and larger. It is less of a contortion for a man to find a child sexually attractive, because it is merely an extension of the gradient along which his appetites are already focused. (Finkelhor, 1982, p. 101)

Feminists suggest that infantalizing women is a way of keeping them in their place as "inferior, weaker, smaller, and dumber" (Schoemer and Chang, 1995, p. 58). It also helps blur the boundaries between women and children as sexual objects. Fashion trends perpetuate this as well. A fashion trend described in the popular press is "cute," and the more childlike the better (Schoemer and Chang, 1995). "Cute has to do with not wanting to grow up. A lot of young women today are anxious about making their way in the real world. If you're feeling threatened and you don't want to grow up and take responsibility, you want to look like a little girl and stay a little girl as long as possible" (Lurie, quoted in Schoemer and Chang, 1995, p. 57). This trend of "cute" further exacerbates the concept of childishness as sexually arousing.

Whereas adult women dress to look younger, the very young dress to look older. Teenagers look like adults, and little girls' fashions are sometimes created to accentuate their shapes as sexual (Kincaid,

1998). The fashion styles for children are frequently miniature imitations of the grown-ups' counterparts (Rush, 1980), with little girls' bikinis and bathing suits cut high in the legs, etc. One of the molesters, who sexually abused six- to eight-year-old girls, stated, "I was buying pornography . . . there was a league of pornography with pictures of women with shaved pubic hairs, hair in braids, young slim bodies, which is basically an approximation of a child." He did not need to buy "kiddie porn," as the pornography he bought was a good facsimile.

Psychological research (Bandura, 1986) establishes that humans reenact modeled behavior. The role modeling from movies and television teaches men to view women as sexualized objects. They see women and children degraded and dehumanized. For such interactions to also be associated with sex incorrectly teaches the male community that violence, power, and control should be linked with sexual arousal (Brownmiller, 1975; Steinem, 1983). This relationship between sex and violence is entrenched in the language: "Sexual phrases are the most common synonyms for conquering and humiliation (being had, being screwed, getting fucked)." Whereas "the sexually aggressive woman is a slut or a nymphomaniac, the sexually aggressive man is just normal" (Steinem, 1983, p. 220). This language helps to establish women as sexualized objects and justifies their subsequent treatment, as language creates consciousness (Whorf, 1941). Thus, these expressions pave the way for both normalizing and tolerating violence, while simultaneously pairing the violence with sexual arousal.

Pornography further contributes to dehumanizing women and children. It is viewed by some as a healthy outlet to redirect sexual aggression that would otherwise be aimed at women and/or children (Walsh, 1987). It might more accurately, however, be considered a training opportunity, with each masturbatory act more deeply pairing sexual arousal to fantasized material, which not only victimizes women and children but robs men of opportunities for intimacy, closeness, and love (Lerner, 1993; Steinem, 1983). Utilization of pornography should not be seen as an outlet to prevent the sexual violence from occurring (Green, 1987) because it alleviates a biological need. Many of the molesters interviewed for this book endorsed fixated sexual arousal that was reinforced by continuous masturbation. In their cases, masturbating to pornography did not satiate energy that might otherwise have been directed at women and children. Rather, it developed their appetite, lowered their resistance, and allowed them, finally, to reenact the continuously rehearsed fantasies.

Viewing women as sexual property caused one seemingly respectable, 1990s, professional adult male to whistle and make lewd comments to an attractive teenager, only to discover when she turned to look at him that she was his daughter (personal interview). In an earlier era, this same tendency was experienced by "a father, who after requesting the sexual use of a 12-year-old, found his own daughter whom he had earlier sent off to school, bound, gagged, and stripped awaiting him on a bed" (Rush, 1980, p. 71).

This objectification of female children as sexual property has ancient roots. Accordingly, the sexual use of property was only problematical if the owner of the property had been financially harmed (Rush, 1980). In early Christian and Judeo law, such harm was considered invisible while the child was extremely young, making sexual assaults on very young children acceptable (Rush, 1980). Assaults on older children required some form of remuneration to the owner (Rush, 1980).

Tolerating the perception of women as sexual objects reflects attitudes toward sex that help blur the boundaries of appropriateness. Society accepts that men have sexual needs which must be met. If these needs cannot be met with appropriate partners, many assume they must be met elsewhere. "Men are socialized to be able to focus their sexual interest around sexual acts isolated from the context of a relationship" (Finkelhor, 1982, p. 101). But, again, there is a double bind. On the one hand, it is expected that men must release their sexual needs through whatever outlet is available. On the other hand, their socialization deprives them of being able to seek nurturing and affection. They, therefore, must express these needs through sex as well:

> Men are not given many legitimate opportunities to practice nurturing and to express dependency needs except through sex. So when men need affection and are feeling dependent, they are much more likely to look for fulfillment in a sexual

form, even if this is with an inappropriate partner. (Finkelhor, 1982, p. 101)

Such a social climate helps to mask the occurrence of child sexual abuse, while ensuring that many of the protectors of children remain helpless.

SOCIETAL DENIAL

The topic of child sexual abuse is not new. A number of times, in recent history, researchers have discussed and described the dynamics of sexual abuse (Jenkins, 1998). Yet each time, for various reasons, a veil of silence returned. During Freud's time, for instance, in the late 1800s, French medical doctors published articles about the occurrence of child sexual abuse as perceptive as any written in the late 1900s (Masson, 1984).

When Freud first postulated his theories after studying with those French medical doctors in the late 1800s, he suggested that the hysteria and neurosis he observed in the women he treated was the direct result of their sexual abuse (Rush, 1980; Masson, 1984). This met with silence from his peers and pressure from his confidant Wilhelm Fliess to retract such an "absurd" notion. Interestingly enough, Wilhelm Fliess's son later became a psychiatrist and reported his father had been sexually abusing him at that time (Masson, 1984).

Freud altered his theory to suggest that children fantasized sex with their opposite-sex parent—the now famous Oedipus and Electra complexes. This placed the blame directly on the child victim and "has been the biggest obstacle to the serious study and promotion of the problem of child sex victimization" (Finkelhor, 1979a, p. 9), thus effectively ending the research on child sexual abuse for many years (Rush, 1980; Masson, 1984). Subsequently, children who described incidents of sexual abuse were accused of being unable to differentiate fact from fantasy, while those who denied the occurrence of any sexual abuse were admonished by their psychotherapists for being unable to acknowledge their fantasies (Rush, 1980; Masson, 1984; van Dam and Bates, 1986).

In the United States, Terman's (1938) studies and Hamilton's (1929) work revealed child sexual abuse incidence rates consistent with those published today. Hamilton (1929) found that 37 percent of females and 27 percent of males had been sexually abused. Later, other data (Kinsey et al., 1948; Gagnon, 1965) again revealed that child sexual abuse occurred to about 25 percent of the population. The social scientists of that era, however, feared public dissemination of such data would generate a hue and cry that would interfere with their social agenda of greater relaxation of sexual mores. As a result, such researchers as Kinsey ignored the data, and university programs continued to teach students that incest only occurred in about one out of one million cases (Salter, 1988).

Kinsey, whose own research revealed incidence rates of 24 percent, nevertheless maintained that incest was found to be more in the imagination of therapists than in the lives of their patients (Kinsey et al., 1948). Kinsey further stated that even though his own studies revealed 80 percent of the victims "reported being upset or frightened by the experience, there was no logical reason why children should be disturbed by sexual abuse" (quoted in Salter, 1988, p. 23).

Summit (1989) refers to this phenomenon as nescience: "The word for deliberate, beatific ignorance is nescience. In our historic failure to grasp the importance of sexual abuse and our reluctance to embrace it now, we might acknowledge that we are not naively innocent. We seem to be willfully ignorant, nescient" (p. 418). He tells the following story to exemplify how the professional community continues to ignore the impact of sexual abuse on children:

A colleague phoned . . . for help in preparing for a television interview. As a child psychiatrist specializing in the inpatient treatment of adolescent disorders he had been asked to discuss the effects of child sexual abuse. He conceded that he knew little about the subject. "It's a funny thing, though," he said. "It's coming out all over the ward. No matter what the problem is, runaway, delinquency, drugs, eating disorder, suicidal depression, just as many boys as girls, they all start talking about their sexual abuse. They won't admit it at first, but after about a week on the ward it's right there, eight times out of ten." The author prompted a reflection on the neglected importance of sexual abuse, only to hear a reversal. "But you know, once you really get to know their background, you find that sexual abuse is the least of their problems. They have so many other things going against them, there's no telling what messed them up." (p. 413)

By observing an event to be incidental or even irrelevant to issues under investigation, it can continue to be dismissed time after time. This occurred with Mr. Smith, when each observation of inappropriate handling and boundary violation was seen as an isolated instance, which could then be minimized or ignored. Those who worked with Robert Noyes (see Chapter 1) also assumed the abuse they knew about to have been yet another case of a single slipup. The principal who heard multiple complaints against Mr. Clay also handled each complaint as a new concern. Goleman (1985) describes the term *lacunas* to indicate how the widely held beliefs of an era can prevent recognition and acknowledgment of events taking place. Drug and alcohol therapists refer to this as denial (Bates, 1994), while parenting experts (Clarke and Dawson, 1998) use the term *discounting*.

In the case of child sexual abuse, nescience, denial, lacunas, and discounting allow the evidence to be ignored or the event to be trivialized. Kinsey and colleagues (1948) stated that the abuse itself is insignificant, and Gardner (1993) extends this further by stating that teaching children about safe touching and telling is the "hysterical" response that is sexually abusive.

Societal responses to reports of child sexual abuse often also include blaming the victim. In this case, the event, although acknowledged as possibly having occurred, is considered to be the fault of the child. Blaming the victim is a common phenomenon well identified by social psychologists (Brehm and Kassin, 1993) studying accident and crime victims. This becomes more intense, however, when the assaults are of a sexual nature because, in addition to a propensity to blame the victim, society also has preexisting attitudes toward gender roles and sexuality that exacerbate the blaming (Rush, 1980).

As a result, female victims are often blamed for the sexual abuse because of their dress, their manner, or their very existence. A group of high school boys who raped a ten-year-old girl were exonerated by their parents with such comments as "boys will be boys" and given a hero's welcome by the school. "One father said that his son was 'all man,'" and added, "there wouldn't be enough jails in America if boys were imprisoned for doing what he has done" (Pipher, 1994, p. 70). The ten-year-old girl was called a "slut," which allowed the boys to feel that she had deserved the assault (Pipher, 1994). Some movies reflect the cultural belief that all women want sex, even when they say they do not. Scenes are depicted as romantic when the woman's resistance is overcome with force and she subsequently happily succumbs to the male, reinforcing society's belief that "No" really means "Yes" (Rush, 1980), thus setting the stage for further victimization (De Becker, 1999).

A Canadian judge further reflected that attitude when he acquitted a man of sexual assault because "no may mean maybe" (Halliday, 1995, p. 5). A nine-year-old was also held responsible by the Chicago Board of Education for her sexual assault by a twelve-year-old boy that occurred in the presence of the classroom teacher (Associated Press, 1995). This attitude of blaming the female victim is further reflected in a court sentence in which the judge exonerated the charged molester because "any man entering a room full of 14-year-old girls is like putting your hand in a bag full of weasels" (Halliday, 1995, p. 6). In the professional literature, "Virkkunen found a pedophilic act was primarily incited by a 'provocative' or 'participating' victim on an offender who was a 'timid person'" (cited in Salter, 1988, p. 31). Revitch and Weiss reflect this same victim blaming, stating that "the child victim is aggressive and seductive and often induces the adult offender to commit the offense" (cited in Salter, 1988, p. 29).

The current climate for youngsters continues to be worrisome. Attitudes toward women as sexual objects result in school environments in which girls are frequently sexually harassed by both teachers and students (Pipher, 1994). The media and popular song lyrics further contribute to the misogyny, creating an atmosphere that tolerates, or even approves of, sexually assaultive behavior. Rap music of the 1990s even more explicitly glorified these sentiments. This social climate contributes to the creation of offenders, paves the way for the offense, and inhibits detection of the offender.

This tolerance for sexual aggression tacitly condones behaviors that should be opportunities to provide early interventions and treatment. For instance, a number of child molesters report experiences of being caught sexually molesting children early in their deviant history. Graham Cook (1989) writes:

> I was originally charged [at age 18] with indecent assault; which was reduced to contributing to the delinquency of a minor. I made one court appearance and received a $250.00 fine. My parents sent me to our family doctor, an Englishman, who felt that the whole thing was "just going through a stage" and he referred me to a psychiatrist under protest. The psychiatrist saw me three times and his solution was "get a girl-friend." (p. 4)

This reflects the commonly accepted misconception that any healthy male needs sexual outlets, and that sex with underage children is therefore unavoidable and only occurs because no age-appropriate partners are available. Such attitudes only serve to play into the hands of molesters, who are quickly empowered with the knowledge that they "can get away with it." Robert Noyes, the British Columbia teacher convicted of sexually abusing hundreds of boys, had been known to be molesting children by a number of school districts throughout the province. Over a twenty-year period he was transferred from district to district, as his sexual proclivities came to the attention of each particular system. Many professionals treated him for his sexual proclivities, and yet his behavior continued to be tolerated and met with silence and secrecy. It took a small child, who reported directly to the police rather than to school authorities, to finally bring Noyes's illegal behavior to an end.

The professionals, who were obligated by law to report the suspected abuse, all remained silent, thereby tacitly supporting the molestations through their failure to protect the children. Each viewed the behaviors he or she knew about as an aberration caused by inadequacies in others. Thus, each specific molestation occurred because "His wife failed to be available for him" or because "He was under a great deal of stress." Other explanations included "He didn't mean anything by it" as well as "It never really hurt anyone." Some of the professionals who saw him felt that "it would be a shame to damage such a fine man's reputation." Such reasoning plays into the hands of the molesters, whose denial regarding the meaning of their behavior helps protect them from having to acknowledge or admit to the reality of what they are doing to children.

MOLESTER DENIAL

To commit sexual offenses against children, the molester must overcome internal inhibitions (Finkelhor, 1984), which is done by Orwellian Newspeak. This occurs when the activities are reinterpreted in a different and seemingly more acceptable context. Such reinterpretations of reality range from denying the event, calling it social work, blaming the victim, or describing the abuse as an accident, to considering the problem to be with the rest of society. Many of the molesters, after developing some insight through treatment, refer to this as "grooming themselves."

The molesters' denial mechanisms in many ways parallel society's denial. Often they admit to the behavior but blame the victim. Russell (1984) describes three rapists who said their victim "was only getting what she deserved for walking on the street without a man at night" (p. 153). One molester told Salter (1988) that "this behavior isn't immoral you know, it's just illegal" (p. 99). Many molesters reported that "if she's old enough to bleed, she's old enough to breed." Others placed the responsibility on the victim by describing how she "was really well-built," or believing that the girl's attire and stature was to blame "because she was wearing a revealing nightgown." A judge told a reporter that in most sexual assault cases, the assaults "occur when the woman is drunk and passed out. The man comes along, sees a pair of hips, and helps himself" (Halliday, 1995, p. 4).

Other molesters believe that their behavior is inevitable because "She was coming on to me," or "She was running around nude and she really wanted it." Explanations also include comments such as "This kid had been hanging all over me. She comes on with a lot of the guys in the neighborhood—what could I do? For a ten-year-old, she really knew it all" (in Sanford, 1980, p. 88). Interestingly enough, these rationales are also given when the victim is three years old. Some judges accept this reasoning, agreeing that a three-year-old victim is to blame for being sexually provocative and "coming on" to the adult (Halliday, 1995). In these cases, the molesters believe that each child's behavior is sexual, and that they are helpless in the face of such pressure.

Some molesters admit to the abuse and claim it was a simple mistake: "It only happened once. I said I'd never do it again, so I don't know what the big deal with the police is" (in Sanford, 1980, p. 88). These stories are often accepted by a number of adults in the community. For instance, one molester told a judge, "I just rolled over and tried to make love to the wrong girl," and was acquitted (Bavelas, Chovil, and Coates, 1993, p. 1), a line repeated verbatim by many of the molesters interviewed for this book.

Molesters also proudly proclaim their sexual involvement with children to be therapeutic. Writing in seemingly professional journals, they equate child sexual abuse to good social work. Brongersma (1991) refers to

> several examples of social workers achieving miracles with apparently incorrigible young delinquents—not by preaching to them but by sleeping with them. Affection demonstrated by sexual arousal upon contact with the boy's body, by obvious pleasure taken in giving pleasure to the boy, did far more good than years in reformatories. . . . I personally know of cases brought before [a certain judge]. In one, a boy who had been arrested several times for shoplifting, who had been a terror at home and a failure in school, suddenly turned over a new leaf, gave up crime, started getting good marks at school and became a national champion in his favorite sport. All of this occurred after a boy-lover had been asked officially to take care of him . . . likewise, in Berlin a test program was instituted in which young delinquents were put under the supervision of boy-lovers. The results were totally successful, but unfortunately the fear of public reaction soon closed the program down. (p. 160)

Molesters will use such terminology as "making love," which is also misleading and suggests a consensual affectionate act. Even using the term *sexual* in these cases helps create confusion. For instance, "If sex is stolen rather than willingly shared, then in a world in which sex was understood to be a truly consensual activity, stolen sex would not be sex. Yet the law obliges us to label what has been stolen as sexual" (Boyle, 1985, p. 104). This language problem allows judgments against molesters to be lenient because "at least there was no external violence committed upon her," thereby implying that the "accused simply had sex with the complainant" (Coates, Bavelas, and Gibson, 1994, p. 194). In criminal records, this is also exemplified with such modifiers as "no harm was caused to the victim." This is further exemplified in court cases. In one case, for instance, "a man pled guilty to sexually assaulting a young girl and boy. The judge remarked that the 'indecent assault against the young girl is less serious because it involved no violence'. . . again having the language facilitate the minimization of the event" (Coates, Bavelas, and Gibson, 1994, p. 194).

Carnes (1983) likens the molester's behavior to an addiction and describes how the "addictive system starts with a belief system containing faulty assumptions, myths, and values which support impaired thinking" (p. 16). In the case of child sexual abuse, as already mentioned, much of the impaired thinking echoes societal attitudes and beliefs to some extent. Many molesters also blame their wives, saying such things as "She wouldn't have sex with me anymore; she was unresponsive; she was cold." The sexual abuse of children to them is a logical response to their situation, since they believe their sexual needs must be met one way or another. Because this mirrors generally held beliefs that "boys will be boys," that the male sexual appetite must be satisfied, and that any subsequent molestation reflects family dysfunction, the responsibility for the abuse is placed on the child and/or the wife. Thus, the molester blaming the victim and the wife fits in neatly with society's prejudices.

In the professional literature, this same blaming occurs. Kempe and Kempe (1984) consider the wife responsible in many cases: "These men are often described as passive-aggressive personalities who frequently have wives who are dominant-dependent and demanding but ungiving within the marital relationship" (p. 30). They further state that the wife's failure to provide nurturing and intimacy to both her husband and her daughter drive them into an incestuous relationship: "For example, incest often occurs in a family in which not only the father receives little affection and sexual intimacy from his wife but in which the daughter may also receive little affection, nurture, or even attention from her mother" (p. 192).

Caplan (1993) describes this double bind created solely for mothers, "where mothers will be damned no matter what they do." For instance, they are supposed to be "endless givers of nurturance," which simultaneously means "that they drain the emotional energy of those around them" (p. 96). In the case of child sexual abuse, the mothers are responsible for the sexual abuse of their children because they were sexually unavailable to their spouses. In addition to being unavailable, they also are accused of deliberately setting up their child for the abuse. As Salter (1988) states, "there is nowhere in the literature the kind of animosity shown toward offenders that has repeatedly been expressed toward the victims and their mothers" (p. 34).

Yet although marital dysfunction is the most frequently cited cause for mothers being responsible for sexual abuse (Salter, 1988), such lack of access to sex does not explain the behaviors of child molesters (Groth, 1979):

> In fact, the sexual encounters with children co-existed with sexual contacts with adults. For example, in the incest cases, we found that the men were having sexual relations with their daughters or sons in addition to, rather than instead of, sexual relations with their wives. Those offenders who confined their sexual activity to children did so through choice. There was no one for whom no other opportunity for sexual gratification existed. (p. 146)

Nevertheless, molesters continue to name their wives' unavailability as the reason for having sex with children. This not only ignores their sexual proclivities toward children but represents reasoning that is too often accepted in many segments of society. Molesters blame their assaults on the victim too, which is also an explanation accepted by others. Family therapists Minuchin and Fishman (1981) describe a case in which "the father has been (sexually) abusing his child, but the wife has clearly been colluding, and by now the boy is a willing participant in the total process" (p. 101). This reasoning blames the wife and the child for the assault. Slovenko (1971) describes a 1923 court ruling that also reflects such victim blaming:

> This wretched girl was young in years but old in sin and shame. A number of callow youths of otherwise blameless lives so far as this record shows, fell under her seductive influence . . . she was a mere "cistern for foul toads to know and gender in." Why should the boys misled by her be sacrificed? (p. 158)

Various therapists and researchers have also demonstrated an affinity with the molester's view of the blame. Revitch and Weiss (1962) stated that "the majority of pedophiles are harmless individuals and their victims are usually known to be aggressive and seductive children" (p. 78). Gagnon (1965) described most incidents of child molestation as collaborative, since the victim "might have, in fact, been more provocative in the offense than the bare bones of the descriptions might allow" (p. 180). Weiss and colleagues (1955) felt the sexual assaults could best be understood by examining the victims' personality and believed most victims to have "participating" personalities. These personality traits were then described to cover most of the behaviors typically associated as evidence of the abuse. Mohr, Turner, and Jerry (1964) considered the child "a willing participant if not the instigator of a sexual act with an adult" (p. 34). Lukianowicz (1972) further used the subsequent propensity for victimized children to be sexually promiscuous with older men as evidence of their responsibility in the initial assaults, rather than evidence of the effect of such abuse on the developing personality. Virkkunen (1975) stated, "without doubt, the child victim's own behavior often plays a considerable part in initiating and maintaining a pedophiliac crime" (p. 130).

Much of the research that reflects this perspective was obtained by interviewing child molesters. Unfortunately, this creates an alliance with the informant. Corroborating information from others was not obtained. Yet accepting information from molesters as independently reliable is fraught with difficulty, as it can be assumed that they will minimize, deny, and blame. This is a dilemma in both offender research and treatment programs.

In addition to blaming the wife and the victim, molesters minimize and rationalize their activities. One molester explained to the judge that a group of eight-year-old girls had asked him what a condom was. To best answer their question, he found it necessary to demonstrate. He further explained to the judge that to show them what a condom looked like required an erection, which he produced only to contribute to their education. He believed his activity to be educational and helpful (Halliday, 1985).

Groth (1979) considers appropriate sex education one of the best forms of protection parents can provide their children because it inoculates them from exactly this type of behavior. This was echoed by the advice of a number of molesters in Elliott, Browne, and Kilcoyne's (1995) study, who all confirmed the importance of parents teaching children about sex, different parts of the body, and right and wrong touches. "I used it to my advantage by teaching the child myself" (p. 590). The initial sex education provided by the molester quickly exceeds accepted boundaries of appropriateness.

Molester denial is clearly exemplified in Silva's (1990) writings. After detailing, for over twenty-one pages, a great number of intense sexual liaisons with eight- to thirteen-year-old children, he expresses shock and outrage at his conviction. He explains that his arrest occurred as a result of his "benevolent" interaction with "a cute eight-year-old boy":

We played in my room in the hospital. In good, clean fun, I threw him in the air several times. He became frightened, although I did not realize it, and went into the hallway, and when he did not return soon, I went looking for him. I found him in the hospital security office. When I opened the door, he pointed and said, "There's the man who tried to hurt me!" Of course, I had done no such thing, and nothing sexual had occurred between us. Nevertheless, Tommy's mother was phoned, and a policeman was called to investigate. He spoke with Tommy and then told the boy's mother that her son did not appear to have been interfered with. Mother denied wanting to press any charges, but my name was taken.

A few days later, a detective who read the report recognized my name from the report Charles [a previous victim] had made years earlier, and he went to interview Tommy. This time, false allegations were suggested to the boy, and then they were made against me. Still, there were no allegations that clothes had been removed. But on the basis of these two flimsy reports separated by years, a warrant for my arrest was issued. A full-scale witch-hunt was launched, and I was arrested, again and again. Relevant here is my behavior even after my arrest. I was facing multiple, horribly inflated charges, but I was unwilling to stay away from kids completely, especially when it might be years before I would ever get to be with them again. . . . Overwhelmed by what was happening, having no one to confide in, and foolishly trusting that my lawyer was vigorously preparing my defense, I wasted much time, using video games as an escape. At the arcade, I became friendly with a 14-year-old who seemed younger than his age and then, later, independently met his eight-year-old brother Bobbie.

Bobbie was outside alone late one night and, during our conversation, mentioned that he had not eaten. So I invited him to have a hamburger. When we returned to the arcade after half an hour, the security guard asked me to step into the office. As it happened, a third brother had seen Bobbie enter my car and had called their parents, who had called the police. The police had called the security guard. Bobbie and I did not know about these calls, and we were puzzled to see the police and his parents arrive. When he told everyone that everything was fine, the police just warned me and left.

I continued to run into Bobbie and his brothers in the area of the arcade. Our friendship grew after that shaky start, and I got to know Bobbie's whole family. They were poor and had no car. I took Bobbie many places, now with his parents' permission, and sometimes took his brothers, too, like the time I took them all to an anti-apartheid demonstration in an effort to instill in them a sense of social responsibility. I also took them to parks and movies. I frequently took Bobbie to my house, where we enjoyed lying together watching television. He even spent the night several times, sleeping in my arms while I had orgasms from the mere physical contact. He was a fairly bright boy to whom I supplied books to read, and I could never understand why he was in special education. He was taking well to the attention I showed him. (p. 487)

Silva (1990) considers this explanation a defense of his integrity. He demonstrates his belief that the charges against him are trumped up, while simultaneously delineating detailed sexual encounters and arousal to little children. Yet, in his defense, he further states, "I have never hurt a child. On the contrary, I have loved children in a way that covered every aspect of the human-love spectrum. Yet, now I reflect that perhaps there is such a thing as loving too much" (p. 487).

He ends his treatise with the observation that "it is remarkable in my opinion that an individual can be imprisoned for such a long period—for a first offense, no less—and looted of life simply for trying to add to its fullness" (Silva, 1990, p. 487). Silva's self-defense hovers between denying any sexual involvement, and outrage at being convicted, and believing his involvement with children was something that was developmentally good for them.

According to a number of professionals, some offenders continue to deny the crime altogether (Ward, Hudson, and Marshall, 1995; Roys, 1995). This is also seen among the prison population. The defenses start to sound like clichés: "I could not have done it. . . . I have a bad back. . . . I work all the time. . . . My diabetes prevents me from getting erections anymore." The molesters also describe how the victim fabricated the story: "She made it all up. . . . She's obviously been abused by someone else. . . . She's the one who has been sexually abusing others." In each of their cases, the reason for the false conviction and subsequent prison sentence was because "I had poor legal representation. . . . I didn't understand the system. . . . Everyone was swayed by the victim's innocent act."

This response from molesters and their powerful allies contributes to letting child sexual abuse flourish undetected. In addition to the type of denial and minimization already discussed, there is also, among some molesters, another type of denial. This is the belief that sexualizing children is a healthy practice that benefits them. They consider their proclivities to be a "sexual orientation" and, through such organizations as North American Man-Boy Love Association (NAMBLA), the Rene Guyon Society, and the Childhood Sexuality Circle, have lobbied for legislative changes. They have marched in gay pride parades, representing themselves as another discriminated against and misunderstood sexual minority. Although they promote this behavior, they nevertheless keep their identities secret. "John Miller, the WNBC-TV correspondent who broke the story, said last week: 'We thought these guys were people who lurk around outside schools. What we found was, they lurk around inside the schools'" (Leo, 1993, p. 37). One high school science teacher is on the "NAMBLA steering committee and the editorial board of the NAMBLA Bulletin, which has offered advice on how to entice a child into sex—'leave a pornographic magazine someplace where he's sure to find it'" (Leo, 1993, p. 37).

These molesters have been successful in politicizing their viewpoint through a number of organizations including Pedophile Information Exchange (PIE), Norwegian Pedophile Group, Amnesty for Child Sexuality, Wergrupp Pedophilie, and Studiegroep Pedofilie, all of which have been actively lobbying for the abolition of laws against "consensual" sexual acts between adults and minors (de Young, 1988). This links to Kinsey's time when the sexual abuse data were withheld because of the feared public backlash concerning sexual mores. However, successfully relaxing the sexual mores, without examining the dynamics of sexual abuse, has created a wedge of opportunity to tolerate behavior that should not be tolerated. NAMBLA is also a member of the International Lesbian and Gay Association, which has called on members "to treat all sexual minorities with respect, including pedophiles," and has allowed NAMBLA to march in gay pride parades in New York and San Francisco as another oppressed sexual minority (Leo, 1993).

NAMBLA also argues that laws against man-boy sex should be thrown out on the basis of age discrimination. A Canadian judge indirectly supported this perspective when she threw a case out of court for exactly those reasons. She acquitted a thirty-seven-year-old of sexual abuse charges against a thirteen-year-old boy on the basis of age discrimination, stating that the adult should be treated as any other peer playing doctor. She also ruled that the victim gave consent based on the offender's say-so and agreed with the defense attorney, who stated that young children have full knowledge and capacity to consent to sexual activities (Lee, 1985).

Chapter 8

Visible Grooming

It is time for adults to recognize potentially risky behaviors in order to intervene appropriately long before any abuse can even occur. This requires relying on minimally visible criteria, which is why it is crucial to become familiar with the relevant visible behavioral clues. These identifiers provide a framework for differentiating those who are reliable from those who probably should not be trusted. Recognizing the profile will put the correct spin on behavior that would otherwise be seen as "too good to be true." Remember that this profile of behaviors is based on information culled from the experts—acknowledged sexual molesters of children. This is not relying on information from those who may have been falsely accused, or from those whose behavior was misinterpreted or misunderstood. Instead, admitted molesters in various stages of treatment clearly described how they went about the business of obtaining access to children, and maintaining security to ensure continued opportunities to molest. This information generated a screening framework to help adults resume the direct responsibility of protecting children from child sexual abuse.

Like an iceberg, with only its tip showing while most of it remains invisible, molesters are not obviously identifiable. No physical characteristics set them apart, and no psychological profile can identify them (Salter, 1995), although most of the over 300 molesters interviewed for this book were surprisingly boyish-looking. Yet the need to prevent molesters from having unsupervised access to children necessitates knowing who might potentially molest.

As already mentioned, current "prevention" methods primarily rely on having children report when they are molested. This places the onus of responsibility on children and is aimed at secondary prevention (Levine and Perkins, 1987), namely stopping already occurring abuse from continuing or escalating. In study after study, the focus continues to be on teaching children to protect themselves (Trickett and Schellenbach, 1998; Daro, 1998; Rispens, Aleman, and Goudena, 1997), rather than expecting adults to take responsibility. Such activity incorrectly lulls adults into the false belief that they are already protecting children from sexual abuse. Newspaper articles echo this complacency by touting that "it's up to adults to protect children by teaching children to recognize sexual abuse" (Nolan, 1999 p. B1), rather than also addressing the need for more direct adult intervention. Since the task of protecting children from being sexually abused is so difficult that adults have been unable to manage it, surely children should not be expected to do so.

CURRENT PREVENTION STRATEGIES

A number of programs have been developed to help protect children from sexual abuse by teaching them what to do when such abuse occurs. These programs are offered to young children and serve two purposes: first, to get those children who are already being abused to report the abuse and second, to protect children from future abuse by teaching them to say "No" to anyone who should try to molest them. Such programs suggest to children that reporting abuse will successfully end it, and that saying "No" is sufficient, placing yet another burden of responsibility and guilt on those children who failed to say "No," or for whom saying "No" did not end the abuse.

The main message in these safety programs, theater productions, storybooks, and songs (Alsop, 1988) about "good touch, bad touch" is for children to say "NO" very loudly should someone try to touch them in "a bad way." The Care Kit (CARE Productions, 1985), developed in British Columbia, and the "Talk About Touching" (Harms et al., 1986) materials, developed in Washington State, are among the more elaborate curricula for use in schools with essentially the same message. Teachers use well-developed lesson plans for each grade level, with pictures generating class discussion about various issues of safety, including personal safety. The programs include material on "private parts," that these parts might appropriately need to be touched for hygiene and health reasons, and what children should do when they feel uncomfortable with the touching. Various other teaching materials with a similar message have also been developed (Trickett and Schellenbach, 1998).

No research yet exists on the effect these programs have on the psychosocial development of children (Trickett and Schellenbach, 1998; Rispens, Aleman, and Goudena, 1997). A number of professionals vociferously believe that teaching children awareness of child sexual abuse is sexually abusive (Gardner, 1993; Kincaid, 1998). Proponents compare it to teaching children to look both ways before crossing the street, which does not create excessive fear about roads and traffic (Halliday, 1995). Long and elaborate explanations of what "roadkill" looks like are not included in simple traffic safety lessons, yet these lessons successfully teach children how to cross the street safely. The same applies to other safety issues as well. Such programs are unlikely to be especially traumatic for children, while providing necessary skills training.

Unfortunately, as one mother learned, educating children about "bad" touching does not guarantee that they will tell when it does happen to them:

> The reason my daughter was running away, I found out later, was that my husband was molesting and raping her all that time, which was the furthest thing from my mind. When my kids were little, but old enough to understand, I would tell them, "If anyone ever touches you or anything, like touches you in your privates or whatever, you tell me." I would just talk to my kids that way because I knew what happened to me when I was little.

The daughter who had learned these lessons from her mother said, however, that her father

> used to tell me, "If you tell I'll kill myself." Imagine what it feels like being twelve years old and thinking that's what he will really do. Then, when he thinks I'm getting close to telling my mom because she's putting too much pressure on me, and she's coming down on me, saying, "I ain't never done nothing to hurt you. Why do you keep running away?" He's standing

right behind her looking at me. That's enough to drive you crazy when you're twelve years old.

For a number of children, however, knowledge about child sexual abuse may protect them from being molested. One of the molesters interviewed for this book had already successfully abused hundreds of children by the time he was arrested at age twenty-one. In detailing his molestations, he described how those children who had been taught personal safety were poor targets. They told him "No." It was a child who had been through such a safety course, who said "No" and then told his parents, that led to this man's arrest and conviction. Had the program been more generally available to schoolchildren while he had been actively molesting children, he feels someone would have "blown the whistle" on him earlier, which would have stopped him sooner. It was also a child educated about sexual abuse who accurately ascertained that Robert Noyes was sexually abusing other children in the classroom and called the police, thereby initiating the investigation that finally led to his conviction (see Chapter 1).

These training programs generally do an excellent job of introducing the topic to children and providing them with some skills training in saying "No" and telling adults. Children are also told to keep telling until they are believed. Unfortunately, the children who apply these lessons do not necessarily experience the success they are taught to expect. Typically, when they report inappropriate touching, they are not believed, told to quit making up stories, and generally ignored (CARE Productions, 1985). One girl, "Sue," who experienced this recalled, "I can remember one day in the van telling my mom what my dad did, and I don't even know if she remembers." Her mother had no recollection of having ever been told. The daughter added:

It was even past telling my mom because I told elementary school teachers, I told all my friends' parents. When I would have to go to the doctor when I was little I would tell the nurse and I would tell the doctor. To me, it was seriously probably twenty or more people who I told, but somehow or other my family was in this world of "lala" and everybody else was sucked into it. So by the time I was in fifth grade, I didn't say anything about it again.

Similarly, Donna Bouchard did tell a number of times about being abused by teacher Margaret Carruthers, to no avail (see Chapter 1). While still in her teens, she was told by one adult, "I promise that this will never happen again," which she assumed to mean that he knew about it but did nothing. Another adult responded by telling her that "this was not the first time she'd heard of Margaret Carruthers' abusive behavior," but again nothing was done.

Telling about the abuse even once is difficult, with such obstacles to disclosing as shame and embarrassment; fear of retaliation by the molester, against the victim or the victim's family; worry about being ridiculed or blamed or sued; and concern about the effect of such information on the family (Halliday-Sumner, 1997a). It is difficult enough for children to tell once. Each time they are not heard, believed, or understood decreases the likelihood they will try again. Sue finally gave up after having told twenty people to no avail. She never told again. "No one believed me. It couldn't happen in this family." Years later, when she was at a high school retreat, however, "I just mentioned something I thought was real insignificant, and bam, I didn't go home after that retreat. I never went home again after that."

Putting the onus of detection and protection on children also sends a covert message to children that they are responsible for their own safety, which implies that adults are unable or unwilling to protect them. Current safety-training programs primarily occur without parental involvement in a context in which parents remain largely unaware of the dynamics of child sexual abuse. Whereas the parents may not receive the education their children get, many molesters know about these programs and utilize them to their advantage. In fact, a number of the molesters interviewed for this book even taught the safety curriculum to their students. One of them stated, "I knew exactly what to say and what not to say," which he used to his advantage. The curriculum in the school where Mr. Smith volunteered also included a safety program. But, while the children were learning the lessons taught in the curriculum, they also saw that parents and teachers alike adored Mr. Smith. The vociferous support of his involvement with children given by the school, parents, and community precluded the likelihood that children would report their own experiences of improprieties (should any occur).

In no other area of child safety do adults put the onus of responsibility on children. Children are expected to look both ways before crossing the street, but adults take on the task of establishing traffic laws and ensuring that they are enforced. When traffic laws are violated, the adult community assumes responsibility for ending those violations. Yet, in the case of child sexual abuse, adults unthinkingly and unintentionally abdicate responsibility and even seem blind to improprieties that should alert them. Then, when children or their supporters describe such problems, the adult community will typically blame the messenger and strongly defend the accused. This generally creates an atmosphere antithetical to the curriculum taught to children, one that benefits child sexual molesters, who use this climate to their advantage to continue molesting with impunity. The prevention training currently available for children should be supplemented with plans for providing adults in the community with the information and skills to protect children more directly from ever being sexually abused.

VISIBLE GROOMING OF ADULTS

Some argue that having adults assume that everyone's behavior could be considered suspect results in a loss of spontaneity and trust that they are loathe to endorse. Interestingly enough, this does not prevent these same people from engaging in other routinely accepted and regularly used safety practices: they lock their doors at night, wear seat belts whenever they ride in a car, use helmets when riding a bicycle, draw up legal contracts, write wills, and have safety deposit boxes. This behavior does not preclude them from having rich, meaningful, close relationships. In fact, many of these tools help improve relationships precisely because they protect everyone.

Establishing an environment in which children are safe from sexual abuse should be no different from expecting them to be safe from other types of physical, psychological, or economic harm. When adults require children to wear seat belts, they are not considered alarmist, nor would reasonable adults allow a child to ride with friends who failed to follow this requirement. The recommendations in this book are no different. In other words, those with opportunities to interact with children and whose behavior does not meet acceptable safety standards should be denied access to children.

Over 300 molesters interviewed in the course of researching this book have all described engaging in variations of similar types of grooming behavior toward guardians of children. Obviously, any one of those behaviors in isolation may be perfectly harmless. Yet, again and again, the pattern of behavior these molesters described was repeated, making such behaviors, when found in combination, much less acceptable than they might first appear. Even though it may be possible that a perfectly naive, considerate, and innocent individual might engage in all these behaviors, the propensity of evidence indicates otherwise. This framework creates parameters for safety just as a helmet protects against calamities that hopefully will never occur. Not everyone who meets some of the criteria listed here is a molester. Rather, these criteria provide a filter for screening out people whose behavior signals that they are unnecessarily risky to have around children. If certain individuals are suggested by these criteria, then closer scrutiny of those people would be indicated. Individuals whose behavior fits the descriptions in the following paragraphs may have ulterior motives for becoming involved with children, and such involvement deserves closer scrutiny and more thorough supervision.

It is not recommended that this information be used to label people as molesters or even as suspected child molesters. Readers should use this information to consider the possibility and then gauge the risk based on how many factors are present. They should then more closely and clearly supervise access to children with those individuals whose behavior places them in the high-risk category. Although it would be unwise to leave children alone with those who exhibit several of the described risk factors, it does not require that such people be labeled as pedophiles.

Most of the interviewed molesters were seen by their circle of acquaintances as being extremely *charming*, which may alternately be viewed as being extensively involved in image management. The majority of them were unbelievably *helpful*. Clearly, many people who are charming and/or helpful have little interest in children and certainly do not go out of their way to initiate and maintain contact with children. Charm or helpfulness alone would not raise any warning flags. The profile becomes worrisome only when such individuals also engage in *peerlike play* with children, *prefer the company* of children to peers, like to *roughhouse and tickle,* and miraculously manage to obtain *insider status.* These categories are more thoroughly described in the following pages.

Any list alone cannot be used to differentiate those who might molest from those who would not. Although any one of these markers in isolation is not significant, the helpfulness or charm in combination with any one of the other behaviors should be enough to make one wary. People whose behavior fits this profile should have their contact with children very closely monitored and supervised at all times. Many people go to great lengths to be charming but do not have much contact with children. Their behavior would not be cause for alarm. Other people are exceptionally helpful but, again, have little interest in, or involvement with, children.

People frequently describe how difficult it is to confront, contain, or stop behavior by those who meet the described profile. When such an individual *fails to honor clear boundaries* or responds to such attempts by *going on the offensive,* that alone should suffice to exclude that person from having further access to children. This does not require legal action, nor does one need to prove anything. It is simply a prudent screening process to assess individuals entrusted with the care of children, to separate those whose behavior makes them suspect.

A closer, more detailed look at these key factors that should be viewed as warning signs is warranted.

Charming

Molesters can be unbelievably charming, which makes disclosures from children seem even less credible when they do occur. This is a superficial charm focused on looking good in the community. The more prestigious molesters develop a pristine image by engaging in community service activities, to be seen as pillars of the community. Even those who are less prominent would be seen as socially gifted. As one wife pointed out in describing her child-

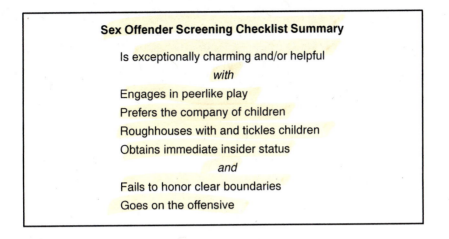

Sex Offender Screening Checklist Summary

Is exceptionally charming and/or helpful

with

Engages in peerlike play

Prefers the company of children

Roughhouses with and tickles children

Obtains immediate insider status

and

Fails to honor clear boundaries

Goes on the offensive

molesting husband, "He'd get along with people. He had friends, but it was superficial. Nothing lasting."

Numerous examples have been provided throughout this book attesting to this charm that generates incredible popularity: Mr. Clay was a well-liked teacher who kept the allegiance of most of his colleagues even after numerous allegations had forced his resignation. His therapist assured the concerned parents that he would remain in treatment until he was "cured," a level of support therapists do not typically provide, and a treatment goal they cannot promise. Robert Noyes's physician also became more directly involved than doctors typically do when he called two mothers to ask them not to report Robert Noyes to the police. This physician also wrote letters to the school board on behalf of his patient. Mr. Smith received standing ovations for his volunteer work with children, even though hundreds of other volunteers dedicated their time without such public accolades.

A hostage taker named Sheldon was "wanted on at least 35 child molestation and assault charges in Florida" (Nolan, 1998, p. A1). Yet he turned his hostages into allies, as at gunpoint they "developed a camaraderie . . . drank soda and beer and ate peanuts while police tried to talk Sheldon into releasing the men" (p. A1). After their release, the hostages described him as a delightfully charming man.

Prison inmates incarcerated for molesting children usually have numerous letters of support from prominent citizens written to the judge, attesting to their fine character, attributing the behavior to an error in judgment, and denigrating the victim. Even the parents of victims often continue to support the molester, exonerate his behavior, and write to him in prison, despite confessions confirming the abuse (Salter, 1995).

An eighteen-year-old molester has hundreds of younger children in his thrall. He has a ready, engaging smile for everyone he sees, as well as a friendly word, and parents and teachers sing his praises. Everywhere he goes he looks like the Pied Piper, as children are keen to talk to him, play a pickup game of basketball with him, wrestle in the swimming pool, or see him at their school functions. He remembers the kids by name, has a warm hug for each of them, and looks too good to be true. Everyone loves him. His friends marvel at how charming and likable he is all the time.

Adult molesters who have developed insight into their own prior behavior after years of treatment describe that ability to charm and endear adults: "I would talk to the parents, get them to like me, then happen to let slip that I was available to baby-sit. They thought they were getting a great deal." A thirty-year-old molester discussed this need to be constantly "on," both to obtain better access to more victims and to ensure continued security: "My smile is my entree. I'm like a salesman, but I'm never off work." Another molester pointed out that these smiles do not include the eyes, which is similar to Hare's (1993) description of the psychopath.

This charm is a carefully orchestrated approach. One molester in treatment noted that "when my style of friendliness wasn't working with an adult, I changed gears. I'd get serious. I would do whatever it took to get them to like me." Salter (1995) cites an offender who confirms this image management as well:

> In the meantime, you're grooming the family. You portray yourself as a church leader or a music teacher, or whatever it takes to make that family think you're okay. You show that child, you show the parents that you're really interested in that kid. And you just trick the family into believing that you are

the most trustworthy person in the world. Every one of my victims, their families just totally offered, they thought that there was nobody for their kids than me and they trusted me wholeheartedly with their children. (p. 80)

This popularity goes beyond any identifiable contributions. Mr. Smith was hailed as a hero in numerous schools where he volunteered, receiving thunderous applause and many awards; yet most of his efforts were directed at playing with children in the halls and on the playground. Hundreds of other volunteers quietly contributed to helping children develop reading or math skills, yet Mr. Smith, whose contributions had little substance, obtained enthusiastic loyalty and support from the adult community.

The Freyd family's prominent case also exemplifies this public face created for an essentially private matter. The two parents launched the False Memory Syndrome Foundation (FMSF) (Doe, 1992), to counteract their daughter's personal decision not to provide her presumably sexually abusive father with access to his grandchildren. They claimed that her memories of having been sexually abused by him were false, while his denials were accurate (Doe, 1992). This despite his reportedly being in an alcoholic blackout during most of her childhood (Freyd, 1994), and the inappropriately sexualized atmosphere of the home being confirmed by an uncle in the U.S. Senate (Freyd, 1995).

The parents' incestuous marriage (they were raised together as sister and brother) (Doe, 1992), at the very least, would suggest blurred boundaries regarding sexual proprieties. Interestingly enough, the parents inspired a vociferously loyal following disproportionate to the facts of their case. They also gained the support of numerous prestigious professionals, who serve on their scientific advisory board, and who publish prolifically on behalf of "falsely" accused child molesters, but fail to make their membership on this board public. Thus, Crews, Loftus, Gardner, and Ofshe (Pope, 1995) —all publish seemingly scientific studies and neutral articles that find victims and their allies to be histrionic, lying, or on a witch-hunt, yet they fail to mention their own status on the FMSF scientific advisory panel. Failure to mention affiliation with the FMSF would be similar to scientists working for the tobacco industry finding nicotine to be harmless without mentioning their funding source. Loftus (1991), who prolifically publishes that recovered memories are fabricated, nevertheless, ironically, gives credence to her own sudden recollection of a previously forgotten memory of abuse at the hands of a baby-sitter.

Hundreds of molesters describe how likable they are, which is confirmed by the public recognition and professional honors they receive for contributions made to their profession or the community. Among those interviewed for this book, a number of teachers were voted "Teacher of the Year" prior to their conviction (van Dam, 1996), were sought after and highly regarded by parents and students (Cloud, 1998), and were considered exceptionally likable (Meloy, 1988). Even judges found them credible despite overwhelming evidence to the contrary. One judge believed in a child molester's innocence precisely because the molester was very religious:

> I think the oath taken by the accused before testifying would have even more than the usual significance and would include an awareness in him that he was promising before God to tell the truth. To convict the accused I would have to, in effect, find that he intentionally lied under oath. (Halliday-Sumner, 1997c, p. 71)

This despite the fact that judges are trained to expect defendants to lie in their courtrooms. Three years later, this man was convicted on new charges and given a twenty-year sentence.

Molesters commonly continue to receive ardent enthusiastic community support even after their convictions. This knee-jerk community reaction is a cliché: One local newspaper article stated, "Sex offenders often are highly regarded citizens defended in the face of overwhelming evidence" (Whitemire and Hale, 1995, p. A2). One offender in that article was described as having "such winning ways it took him [only] five months to get his therapist to write the court suggesting [he] be allowed to coach youth soccer."

Another molester was "a kindergarten teacher considered such a great guy and a credit to his community [that] although the accused acknowledged molesting two students as they slept, the judge was deluged with letters . . . including one from [a senator] urging leniency" (Whitemire and Hale, 1995, p. A2). One molester interviewed for this book proudly stated, "I get access to children because I am so likable, and I can read people and know what they want to hear."

Despite incarcerations, numerous molesters under study also gained the loyalty and support of competent professional women, who married them after they were convicted and while they were in prison. These new wives then sent money to prison in support of their husbands, wrote letters on their behalf, and made plans to get together with these men upon their release, making other living arrangements for their children to ensure court approval of their new husbands' return home. Many convicted molesters had jobs waiting for them upon their release, often with the very employers whose children they had molested. Despite their convictions, they continued to enjoy the loyalty of employers, colleagues, and community members.

This popular support was also noted in the case of Noyes, who successfully charmed a number of powerful allies from his prison cell. One such supporter maintained "frequent telephone and mail contact with Robert Noyes and his wife" and argues that Noyes was "designated a 'dangerous offender' on the basis of political considerations rather than any objective features of his offense pattern." He is the victim, as the media prevent the public from recognizing the "deep, internal changes [he has made] around his ability to handle *biological preferences* [emphasis added] which he did not choose." According to this fan, the public should correctly understand that Noyes is "a very open person [who is] far more transparent and honest than most people," and who should be welcomed back into society "as an exemplar." This professional accepted the reframing provided by Noyes that he was a victim of his biology. In case after case, the offender is exonerated and the victim is demonized.

This typically noted rallying around molesters demonstrates how much people like them. One molester, who had sexually abused the daughters of all his friends, said, "It was weird. They [his friends] knew all the time, but I was such a good friend that they didn't want to believe it. Instead they said, 'Let's keep a closer eye on our kids and let him lead his life,' which they did," while he continued to molest their daughters.

Helpful

A specific strategy that child sexual molesters rely upon is being exceptionally helpful. They are hypervigilant to surroundings relevant to their agenda—children. Like a heroin addict continuously working on obtaining the next "fix," child molesters are constantly "on task." This makes them very productive and attentive to those gatekeepers who provide access to children. They are keenly attuned to every relevant social nuance, which gives them an uncanny knack for anticipating the needs of the adults responsible for children. Many of the molesters reported this exceptional helpfulness: knowing what others need and being available with offers to help out, by baby-sitting, driving, doing repair work, and myriad other tasks that daily inconvenience busy adults, often before the adults have even identified the need. This helpfulness always appears one-sided, as none of those who were exceptionally helpful ever asked for favors in return. In many ways, their thoughtfulness was too good to be true.

For instance, one molester noted that "the wife loses out if a neighbor calls and needs something. I'm a handyman. I can fix anything. I like to help people, but I don't want any help from anybody else. I don't accept it." Another said, "I was always doing something for her [his victim's] mother. She needed her car worked on, she needed a couple of dollars, she always needed something, and I was always, 'Yeah, okay.'" In each of these situations, the molester required or wanted nothing in return.

One molester who felt he was exceptionally generous and helpful, never asking for anything in return, considered this a marker that adults should notice: "Someone that's overly friendly, that goes out of his way and doesn't ask for the same thing back. That's a clue." As Hare (1993) stated, "the police and consumer advocates tell us that extra caution is called for whenever someone or something looks too good to be true" (p. 211).

One molester said, "I do things for the adults. I help them out. I tell them about how wonderful their kids are." He was always welcome at social gatherings because of his helpful attitude and attentiveness to children. "I anticipate their needs before their parents, who are right there. . . . The little girl might say, 'Dad, I need some help with this.' Her dad doesn't hear her because he's busy talking to someone, but I'm right there for her. I know that her parents really appreciate this because it lets them go on visiting with their friends."

Molesters consistently confirmed that they actively and successfully manipulated adults to their advantage. "When I'm on the job the first thing I do is size you up. I look for an angle, figure out what you need, and give it to you" (Hare, 1993, p. 147). In the case of molesters who want access to children, figuring out and delivering on what adults want is straightforward. "Then it's payback time, with interest. I tighten the screws" (Hare, 1993, p. 147). In the case of the molesters, payback time is sexual contact with children. As one molester pointed out, leaving the dinner table to help his wife's friend change a car tire, "I had it in the back of my mind that I liked her daughter." In other words, the helpfulness is not part of an obviously reciprocal relationship.

Peerlike Play

Molesters play with kids at their level. People frequently describe the "kidlike quality" about a molester's interactions with children. Wives will comment "It's like being married to another kid." Although they might lament at how irresponsible their spouses are, they incorrectly view this childlike play as a strength and as evidence of their husbands' skills as fathers. Mr. Smith's relatives proudly described this man in his seventies as "being like a twelve-year-old kid." With Mr. Clay, his tendency to play with the kids was also seen as one of his strengths.

One molester described his approach:

> Most of my victims were young teen-agers. I'd be understanding. I'd say, "I know how you feel." Just agreeing with them. Coming down to their level. At that age it makes them feel good about themselves if an older man is listening to them, paying attention, paying them compliments, telling them they're pretty. I mean, it's another thing when you're being an adult and you're talking to them like an adult and bringing them up to your level. To me, that's not as scary as the guy going down to their level. To me, that's scary because I know that's what I used to

do. I'd say, "Oh, what kind of music do you like?" I'd listen to their music, listen to their interests, do whatever they wanted to do.

Nonmolesting adults playing with children typically maintain an adult orientation when the need arises. Although they may be down on all fours building sand castles with the children, they will respond when adult intervention is necessary. They may stop or redirect hurtful or dangerous behavior; if the children start throwing sand, they will not join in and also throw sand, nor will they initiate hurtful taunting or potentially dangerous activity. In other words, even though they might be playing with children, they maintain their role as adults when necessary. Not so the molesters. They play with the children on their level, which means that they do not necessarily provide adult direction and assistance when the need arises. Rather, they go along with whatever the children want to do. For many of the molesters interviewed, this tendency to interact with children as peers reflected their own arrested development. They were themselves still operating at the emotional level of a child. Hence they were more at ease in the presence of children than in the presence of adults. Yet because of their advanced age and experience, they could use that immaturity and naïveté successfully to manipulate youngsters to do their bidding. Mr. Martin exemplified this. He liked children, and the touching games he engaged in with them were very similar to the peerlike sexual exploration that would be considered normal between two four-year-olds:

> I didn't know much about sex. I wasn't taught anything when I was a child. I wasn't allowed to bathe with other children. I didn't do nothin' wrong. I was just looking at what boys look like and what girls look like. It was just touching. There was no harm in it.

According to the Bouchard family, Margaret Carruthers "had few, if any, adult friends." She associated only with teens. Bouchard described how powerful that was:

> She treated me like a person, an equal, whereas others (especially teachers, parents) were treating me like a child. She wanted me

to call her Marg, or "Mugs." She hated it if I called her Miss Carruthers. . . . She'd call me "D." She would often marvel at how mature I was for my age (like I was thirteen or fourteen going on thirty), that it was no wonder other kids didn't understand me because they were just that—kids. She knew how to get down to my level even though she was a teacher and I was her student. She made me feel special, as though I was worth spending time with. As I've said, that was very powerful. She was interested in what I had to say and really seemed to listen. She'd say she understood, she'd "been there," and she knew what I needed. She could see herself in me when she was my age, etc.

A coach and minister who was a sex offender reported:

I would say to any adult, and I did this, any adult that moves down to a child's level to become their buddy, about just what they're involved in, their silly little romances and whatever, that to me is an abnormal thing for an adult. When an adult does that, I think that's a danger sign they need to watch. That should not be of interest to the adult. (Salter, 1995, p. 74)

Prefer the Company of Children

Many molesters have fewer interactions with peers than they do with children. A number described actively baby-sitting throughout their teens and even early twenties. Some continued to baby-sit throughout their adult lives. They were constantly in demand, with a string of customers keeping them busy seven nights a week. Most parents complain that favorite teenage baby-sitters become less available by the time they are fifteen or sixteen, as their social commitments, sports, and academics begin to take up more of their time. Not so the molesters. They continue to be available, preferring baby-sitting over socializing with peers. Many describe not having same-age friends: "I spent all of my time with younger children." One molester, who had assisted during a school outing, began calling a number of the children he met during that outing, with invitations to go with him to the movies. Many children, in three different schools where he volunteered, considered him a best friend and, as

a result, enthusiastically followed him. It should have seemed remarkable that an eighteen-year-old boy preferred the company of
twelve-year-olds to that of his peers.

This pattern of preferring the company of youngsters continues
throughout molesters' lives and is looked on as a strength and asset
by those who are naive about child molesters. Molesters congregate
with the children during parties, which allows the other adults the
freedom to relax and enjoy themselves in adult company. Molesters
describe always having an eye on the children, even while socializing with the adults. This is a natural response pattern for parents
with young children, so someone relieving them of the responsibility temporarily allows them to enjoy adult company. Child molesters using this approach endure adult company to get to the children.

Roughhousing and Tickling

Each of the molesters roughhoused and tickled children in the
presence of adults. This served the purpose of desensitizing the
children to touch and also helped to confer adult approval on subsequent interactions, since the children knew that the earlier activities
had met with acceptance by the adults. One of the molesters interviewed for this book elaborated:

> There'd be a lot of physical contact. A lot of lap sitting. I had
> kids sitting on my lap all the time, boys that I was grooming.
> Boys of all ages, from five to twelve, would be sitting on my
> lap. . . . There was plenty of physical contact. And there was lots
> of roughhousing. It looks innocent. It looks like fun. It probably
> looks like fun to the parents. It looks like we're just having fun,
> and it's easy to move from what might appear to be appropriate
> contact to inappropriate contact. . . . It was pretty common for
> lots of people to puppy pile. Lots of physical contact. Kids on the
> shoulders, kids on the back, lounging around, laying your head
> on the kid like a pillow. I would have my head on their lap, their
> stomach, or right on their genitals.

Another molester confirmed the importance of roughhousing, adding:

> I wouldn't touch them sexually. I would tickle them or wrestle with them while the parents were there. No one ever said anything about it. It started out when the kids were little, and there wasn't nothing sexual in that, but when they hit adolescence, it became sexual. But the parents were used to seeing me wrestle around with their kids and horseplaying with them, and so it didn't seem that much out of the ordinary. When the parents weren't around and I was horseplaying, I'd grab at their breasts, tickle between their thighs, the vagina area, feeling them out, checking them out. How far can I go? Will they tell? I kind of worked that into horseplay. Each step was a little bit further up the ladder.

In many cases, the tickling and roughhousing games also included inappropriate touch in full view of adults. Some of the molesters found this added danger to be particularly exhilarating: "The danger was exciting. Could I trick people and do it right in front of them? I'd carry the girl on my back and have my finger in her vagina right in front of her parents." Others described their feeling of empowerment because they could engage in such activities and know nothing would be said. Mr. Smith helped girls off the monkey bars by holding their bottoms and had children putting their hands in his pants pockets. Even though he was occasionally asked to stop, he never did, and nothing further was ever said.

Mr. Clay was constantly handling his students. His colleague noted that he would grab children in the hallways at school to hold them upside down. Mr. Smith was also continuously in physical contact with children. Fred (see the introduction) incorporated this into all of his activities with children too. One molester considered tickling and roughhousing to be such a significant indicator that he felt adults should develop a zero-tolerance policy regarding such contact. "A lot of these people [child molesters] act like they were real nice persons, until their second personality comes out of the closet. It's a precaution. It's like, nowadays, when you walk out of a mall, you carry your purse under your arm with your keys ready to get in your car. Not that you've ever been mugged." He suggested that adults take a similar precaution by not tolerating tickling games and roughhousing.

Insider Status

Unlike most people, who require time to proceed through stages of familiarity to become an accepted member of the group, many of these molesters gained immediate insider status. Mr. Smith exemplified this principle extremely well. One of his strategies was to arrive at children's birthday parties unannounced and uninvited. This is typically an intensely busy time, when the adults are preoccupied with many tasks, such as keeping the children entertained, organizing the food, and generally planning how to survive the two- to three-hour period, while ensuring everyone has a good time. Some parents manage these events more gracefully than others, but most find the task overwhelming. One father, for instance, described the frustration of discovering that within two minutes the children had completed the activities he assumed would keep them engaged for one hour. The cake and ice cream, which he anticipated would get them through another thirty minutes, took ten minutes. What was he going to do for the next one hour and forty-nine minutes before pickup time?

Mr. Smith's arrival happened when parents were extremely busy and preoccupied. He had an easy familiarity with the children and immediately started playing games with them that kept them squealing and laughing. They formed lines around him, jumping up and down with glee, and waiting for their turn. With a small handful of candies he kept them busy and happy for a long time.

What parent will wade into a group of happy children to confront the very stranger who is both rescuing them from their dilemma and being such a big hit with the children? Even though many adults described initially feeling a little awkward about the situation, they came to view it as harmless enough, since it all took place within their presence.

Afterward, Mr. Smith chatted with the parents. He was friendly, articulate, and knew everybody in the neighborhood and at the school. Most adults were incapable of being ungracious to the man at this point, so they interacted with him. They subsequently used their own behavior to gauge the situation and therefore decided he must be a "wonderful man." The children now saw him as someone their parents knew and liked, which made Mr. Smith a "resource we're all very lucky to have."

Fails to Honor Clear Boundaries

Mr. Smith was repeatedly asked to stop certain behaviors: One school administrator asked him to stop helping girls off the monkey bars by holding their bottoms. The administration at another school asked him to stop attending children's birthday parties without an invitation from the parents. He ignored this request and continued his practice of dropping in on parties. Nothing further was ever said. Yet another school administrator told him to stop giving children candy on the playground, which he also ignored, and, again, nothing further was ever said.

It can be reasonably argued that any one of the practices just described could reflect individual style, cultural milieu, and other idiosyncrasies not specific to a child sexual molester. Some people believe that handing out candy is a normal act of generosity, and something typically done by Mr. Smith's generation. For others, tickling and roughhousing with children takes them back to their childhood, and they believe that adults who can relax and enjoy the playfulness of childhood should be commended. Such people enrich children's lives by providing wholesome opportunities to interact. Clearly, someone who engages in only one of these behaviors may do so quite innocently.

However, when somebody exhibits a combination of markers, the profile may be less innocent. When a person fails to respond to reasonable requests to stop the behavior, a line is certainly crossed. Even a cultural difference does not excuse failure to comply with acceptable rules. Mr. Smith ignored basic school rules. Most people would be asked to stop volunteering if they could not abide by these rules. Mr. Smith simply ignored the requests. Such blatant disregard stymies most people, who have trouble making this type of request even once.

Mr. Martin continued to interact with children after having been twice convicted of child sexual abuse and each time court-ordered to have no further contact with children. Even though at the time of his third release the courts again told him to have no contact with children, he was already planning his next encounter: "My little grandson will be so glad to see me."

Going On the Offensive

In case after case, those who objected to some of the behavior found themselves on the defensive. Parents whose children described being molested by a female teenage baby-sitter were told by the police that girls do not sexually abuse children, and that any further attempt by the parents to pursue a police investigation would result in a libel suit. The parents who complained to the principal and school superintendent about Mr. Clay, the second-grade teacher they believed had molested their children, were scoffed at, told nothing happened, and then intimidated by powerful forces every step of the way to "stop interfering with this man's life." The parents who complained to the school about Mr. Smith's practice of giving candy to children on the playground and coming to birthday parties uninvited were accused of "being on a witch-hunt." In each of these cases, had the initial concern been expressed about someone who had not gone to such lengths to "look good," the situation would have been directly addressed without the instant counterattacks.

The Bouchards experienced this in a number of ways: Donna noted that "when Marg [Carruthers] was arrested, my mom, who was also employed at Debden School as a special education and speech aide, was virtually ostracized by and from her colleagues." Donna, who was employed as a teacher when the case was tried, also reported experiencing this hostility:

The teaching staff was quick to hide behind their Code of Ethics and display outrage at the charges. However, their collegial responsibility did not seem to extend to me, also a member of the Saskatchewan Teachers' Federation and a teacher with several years' experience by then. The small town was seemingly in shock at the news of Marg's arrest. Some questioned members of my family with "Why is Donna doing this to us? This is really bad for the town of Debden." People who normally greeted me were hard-pressed to even nod their head in passing. I felt like an outcast in my own community. Some community members were telling people that I "was doing this for revenge; I should just forgive and forget." Others wondered why I had waited so long. No one understood the magnitude of the situation, the length of the investigation, the extent of the abuse. Nor was I free to clear up misunderstandings, as the prosecutor and RCMP [Royal Canadian Mounted Police] had forbidden me from speaking of my involvement prior to criminal proceedings. I continued to live under a shroud of shame and silence.

By the time the preliminary hearing commenced in May of 1998, I was wishing I had never agreed to cooperate. In my self-righteousness I had thought that I had to do something to protect the students and future junior/senior high students in particular from Margaret Carruthers, something the administration at the school seemed reluctant to do. The preliminary hearing was held in Debden, in the basement of the town hall. Three days had been set aside—over those few days, people trickled in and out, but there was always a member of the school board in attendance, which I was glad to see. It showed that they finally wanted the facts in the case. I was on the stand for two and a half days and was appalled at how I was treated by defense counsel—a man who was retained by the STF (my union) to defend Carruthers. I wondered if it shamed him at all to know that I was a teacher too. By the end of the third day, he claimed he needed more time with me, so it was slated to reconvene in August of 1998. I again wished I could die. However, it was after those few days that people of my hometown began to send cards expressing their support, and I realized that some of them understood what had happened to me. Courage can be a very lonely place to be, but through those cards, I began to feel less of an outcast.

When the preliminary hearing resumed in August of 1998, lawyers (whom I had retained at my own expense) petitioned the court to have the publication ban on my identity as the victim in the case lifted. I had never wanted the ban imposed, but it had been done so just the same when Marg was arrested in 1997. The judge refused to lift it, saying that it would impede the accused's right to a fair trial. I again felt the crushing weight of the power differential—that her rights were somehow more important than mine. It wouldn't be until December 1998 (weeks prior to the Queen's Bench Trial) that the ban was lifted. While Marg's legal fees were paid for by the STF, mine came out of my own pocket, despite the fact that one of the reasons why I wanted the ban lifted was to clear my own professional name as a teacher, since the original prosecutor's daughter had gone to the school where I worked and said that I was being prosecuted for sexual assault in a case her dad was working on.

The response the Bouchards initially encountered is repeated everywhere. In fact, many people who try to stop sexual molestation typically report similar experiences. When complaints are lodged against individuals who fit the profile under study, others' attempts to investigate or pursue those concerns are thwarted, their own characters are assassinated, and they experience firsthand what is typically called "the circling of the wagons," in defense of the alleged perpetrator.

Chapter 9

Setting Boundaries
to Help Prevent
Child Sexual Abuse

If stopping sex offenders from molesting children were easy, then this book would not be needed. The skills, charm, and audacity they exhibit fly against the usual social standards and niceties, playing directly into most people's discomfort with both conflict and this topic. These molesters have developed a knack for getting their way with impunity because of people's unease with this topic, their unwillingness to believe whatever cues are visible, and their assumption that most people do not deliberately deceive. This has accorded molesters the ultimate power and protection that they use to advantage. Identifying the potential molester, as described in Chapter 8, is only the first step. When someone's behavior fits the profile, it is necessary to intervene to protect children. In light of how difficult adults have found this task to be, it is preposterous to consider that it has primarily been foisted on children to manage. Taking on the task of curtailing molesters' access to children will be challenging.

INTERVENING WITH A POTENTIAL
CHILD MOLESTER

The very behaviors identified in Chapter 8 that should alert adults to the potential danger also generate responses to preempt possible abuse. Rather than passively tolerating those behaviors, adults can more actively intervene by using the following guidelines.

Overview of Intervening with a Potential Molester

1. Listen to the content. Do not be mesmerized by the delivery.
2. If something looks too good to be true, the price tag is hidden.
3. Children need adult involvement, guidance, direction—not a big playmate.
4. Look out for adults who primarily interact with children, not peers.
5. Do not tolerate wrestling, tickling, massaging, and touching games.
6. Worry when someone is instantly accorded family/insider status.
7. Run when "NO" is ignored.
8. Stand firm. Do not be intimidated.

Charming

Listen to the content. Do not be mesmerized by the delivery.

To be inoculated against the self-serving charm of the sex offender, it will be necessary to understand it and differentiate it from other more socially meaningful skills. The charm under discussion is like cotton candy—it has no substance. It is entirely self-serving and oriented, in this case, to provide the molester with unimpeded access to children. It is the task of all adults to learn to differentiate between those who are genuinely delightful and those who present a veneer of charm to impress or flatter. The presentation is cunningly individually tailored to provide the person being groomed with the perfect flattery. One woman felt that description exactly fit her husband, whom she later discovered to be a child molester. He "would tell me things before we were married. He was white, and he would tell me, 'Your dark skin is beautiful.' In the black culture, if you're dark you're not that good, and if you're lighter you're better. Hearing that he liked my dark skin kind of helped me feel better." In other words, he knew to tell her exactly what she wanted to hear.

Robert De Niro, in the movie *This Boy's Life* (1993), portrays a seemingly charming man who is romancing Ellen Barkin's character. He is slick, without substance, and immediately drops all of the smarmy genteel mannerisms after the wedding. His presentation parallels the experiences of many women who found out too late that their Romeo had a darker side (Browne, 1987). "Think of charm as a verb, not as a trait. It has a motive—to control by attraction. If you tell yourself 'This person is trying to charm me,' as opposed to 'This person is charming,' you can see around it. Most often you'll see nothing sinister, but other times you'll be glad you looked" (de Becker, 1999, p. 67).

The charm may have varying appearances. The presentation might be more passive to allow others to impose their own perceptions onto a seemingly blank slate. Peter Sellers demonstrated this in the silent, dignified individual he portrayed in the movie *Being There* (1979). His stoic silence masks the character's mental retardation, which results in everyone projecting their own expectations onto him. His silence is seen as strength and political brilliance, catapulting him into national prominence. In both De Niro's and Sellers's roles, the characters are devious only in that those with whom they associated saw what they wanted rather than what was visibly there.

Molesters provide a similarly broad range of ways in which they charm, from overly obsequious to extremely low-key and quiet. The more skilled ones have the chameleon-like ability to provide whatever approach will work best, making it the task of adults not to be so easily deceived. One mother pointed out how her husband knew precisely what to say when they were courting:

> I was in a really miserable state. I was living at my mother's house, having just left my second husband. I had three children to raise. One of the first things he said to me when we just began seeing each other was, "I don't want to have sex with you. I just want to help you. I want to be in your life and I want to make things easier for you and your children." Those words really clicked with me. It was like he was thinking about me.

This prevented her from attending to the numerous cues that could have alerted her: "I only later found out that he was a very selfish person."

"Offenders often take great pride in how clever they were to manipulate everyone" (Salter, 1995, p. 38). As one of the molesters pointed out:

> When a person like myself wants to obtain access to a child, you don't just go up and get the child and sexually molest the

child. There's a process of obtaining the child's friendship, and in my case, also obtaining the family's friendship and their trust. When you get their trust, that's when the child becomes vulnerable and you can molest the child. (Salter, 1995, p. 38)

Think of the techniques used in sales, where there is also an agenda, in this case making money, rather than molesting a child. The techniques a salesperson might use to engage the customer are similar to some of the strategies used by molesters:

People who sell things for a living have a rotten reputation, but I like them. They look you in the eye, use your name a lot, hold your shoulder while they talk to you, and laugh really hard at your jokes. They take you out to expensive restaurants and when the waiter asks them if they want a drink they don't say, "Just water, please." They ask you where you've been to college and what your kids do after school. They suggest through facial expressions and body language that they would like to marry you. In other words, salespeople treat you exactly the way you wish everyone would treat you—the way you deserve to be treated. Their only tiny flaw is that they don't mean any of it: they're just trying to make a sale. But isn't that a trivial defect, all things considered? Doesn't the insincerity of salespeople seem like a negligible shortcoming in comparison with the incalculably opulent richness of their devotion? (Owen, 1999, p. 52)

These techniques are all goal oriented. In the case of the molester, the goal is to obtain sexual opportunities with children. The process of trust building fools people to such an extent that they welcome the potential molester into their midst, ignore numerous innuendos and allegations that arise, and continue to support the molester, while discounting the child and discrediting the child's allies. This is exactly what happens precisely because the alleged molesters are so well liked that otherwise reasonable people cannot believe the allegations. In the case of Mr. Clay, the psychologist, the school principal, and most of the staff who taught with him considered the allegations "not credible," leaving the families of those four boys to feel as victimized by the community as their boys had felt victimized by their teacher.

The charm is noteworthy for its audacity. In Mr. Clay's case, he lied to his colleagues. The mother who taught with Mr. Clay continued to support him throughout the year that various allegations were being made precisely because he convincingly assured her of his innocence. "He looked me right in the eye and said 'I swear to God I didn't do anything to those little boys.'"

The charm also generates popularity that is primarily based on perceived enthusiasm, rather than on substance. In Mr. Clay's case, supporters liked him so much primarily because he attended children's athletic events, made the gym available to children before school, and was generally friendly. One mother was especially happy for her son to have a male role model in the classroom:

> My son really liked Mr. Clay. My son's dad left when he started kindergarten. When I knew he was going to have a male teacher, I thought "Great." This fellow is very much into sports, and my son excelled in that. I thought that would be really good, and I knew he really liked him.

Another mother described him favorably as well:

> My impression of Mr. Clay was that, physically, I found him a very gentle person, but his appearance is somewhat effeminate. He has a little bit of a baby face. He's very young appearing and quite shy, the kind of guy who goes red quite easily when you talk to him. We were very pleased with him.

This overwhelming support ignored his professional competence. Problems that arose were attributed to his inexperience. Nevertheless, when specific comments were made about his teaching methods, rather than his apparent attentiveness to children and involvement with their sports, problems did surface. Despite his popularity, a number of parents worried about his competence as a teacher, which a colleague attributed to his being a beginning teacher, even though he had been teaching for six years. For instance, one mother pointed out:

> I was displeased with the fact that Mr. Clay didn't pick up on my son's reading problem. Mr. Clay was putting it down to my

son acting up in the classroom, whereas I was putting it down to the fact that he is a very proud child. If he can't read, he'll pretend he can, and if it means acting up to hide the fact that he can't read, he'll do it. If I can spot that as a parent, why didn't the teacher spot it?

Another mother noted that at the first open house in October, long before any of the allegations arose, Mr. Clay complained to her about her son's work:

Out of the blue Mr. Clay asked me if my husband was a slow talker. He said that since I wasn't a slow talker, my husband must be a slow talker, and that would explain my son's being such a slow reader. Mr. Clay showed me how my son would read. He held his head down; he mumbled the words very slowly. I felt he was mocking my son. I came home in tears that night. I was shocked. Everything he had to say about my son was negative. In the meantime, we had these complaints from my son. He was being confused and didn't understand what Mr. Clay expected of him. He'd tell my son to do one thing, my son would start doing it, and Mr. Clay would tell him to stand on the mat in front of the classroom. My son would be in tears about this at night because he couldn't get his work done and he'd have to stay after school.

One father said:

My son complained about that too, so I made an appointment to see Mr. Clay after school. My first impression was, I don't like people that shake hands like that, just with their fingertips. So, anyway, I sat there and went through this, about my son being called up onto the carpet and having to stand there and then not being able to get his homework done. And Mr. Clay says, "Oh no. No. That's not the case at all. They do something, and then we have the whole class come up here and I read them a story." I talked to him for fifteen minutes. I left, I came home, I told my wife, "That guy is a fruitcake. I will never go to that man again. Never." That was my impression of him right away, from day one, and it has never changed.

The routine of confusing the children was done to prevent them from getting their work done, which meant they had to stay after school. This was the time when most of the alleged sexual contact occurred. The aura of enthusiasm and popularity that surrounded him cloaked a different undercurrent. Although the parents assumed their children liked him, this was not entirely accurate. For instance, the teacher whose son was molested by him learned only later that her son did not like him. Another mother said:

> After grade two, the summer before my son was going into grade three, we had all the kids in the van, and they were talking about their teachers. Then someone mentioned Mr. Clay, and there was dead silence in the back of the van. Finally, one little girl said, "Well, I know I don't like him. He talks like a lady." And all the kids kind of giggled. It's hard to explain how kids talk about something, but they went on and on about the way that he talked like a lady and they hoped they wouldn't have him for a teacher.

Mr. Clay maintained tremendous popular support, yet the basis for this popularity was hard to pin down. Primarily, parents and colleagues were impressed at the involvement he had with his students, as demonstrated by his attendance at their various athletic events. Despite the fact that he was not a new teacher, colleagues attributed any problems with teaching to his naïveté. Margaret Carruthers also demonstrated this seeming commitment to her students, in that she was always available to help the ones she took under her wing.

A chameleon-like charm allows discrepancies to be ignored or glossed over and is used by molesters to successfully convince the adult community to ignore unsettling facts, suspend disbelief, and give them unimpeded access to children, despite disquieting clues. Mr. Clay continued teaching, without a proper official investigation, for over a year after the first allegations were made to the school. In the case of teacher Mary Kay Letourneau (see Chapter 5), even though the police found her half-naked under a blanket with a twelve-year-old student in the back of a parked van late at night, they overlooked the significance of what they saw and sent them both home together (Cloud, 1998). Police stopped Mr. Cook (see

Chapters 5 and 6) to investigate child abuse charges. He admitted his guilt, but they failed to interview the young boy who was with him at the time, leaving the young boy, "who was my primary victim," to go home with Mr. Cook (1989).

During face-to-face interviews, convicted molesters appear dynamic, attractive, interesting, and appealing, which can distract one from noting discrepancies and addressing problems. This is exactly how the police were able to send both Letourneau and Cook home with their victims. Yet most of the over 300 molesters interviewed looked surprisingly nondescript when seen from a distance in the waiting room. From afar, everything about them is often unobtrusive, yet throughout a direct interaction they are hypervigilant, using every available cue to develop rapport: "When I'm with you I'm gonna shine you on." With few exceptions, the presentation they create suggests they are narcissists and closet narcissists.

The Closet Narcissist

> *Watch out for the charmer who has no empathy.*

This common thread seen among the over 300 interviewed sex molesters is what Masterson (1988) calls the closet narcissist, previously identified as the regressive narcissist (Glickauf-Hughes and Wells, 1995). Narcissistic personality disorder is loosely based on the Greek god Narcissus who fell in love with his reflection in a pool. The characteristics of a narcissist are identified by psychologists using the DSM-IV (APA, 1994) definition, to include individuals who have little empathy, are interpersonally exploitative, have a sense of entitlement, and believe others adore and worship them. Narcissists

> present an unusual degree of self-reference in their interactions with other people, a great need to be loved and admired by others, and a curious apparent contradiction between a very inflated concept of themselves and an inordinate need for tribute from others. Their emotional life is shallow. They experience little empathy for the feelings of others, they obtain very little enjoyment from life other than from the tributes they receive from others or from their own grandiose fantasies, and

they feel restless and bored when external glitter wears off and no new sources feed their self-regard. They envy others, tend to idealize some people from whom they expect narcissistic supplies, and to depreciate and treat with contempt those from whom they do not expect anything (often their former idols). In general, their relationships with other people are clearly exploitative and sometimes parasitic. It is as if they feel they have the right to control and possess others and to exploit them without guilt feelings—and behind a surface which very often is charming and engaging, one senses coldness and ruthlessness. (Kernberg, quoted in Millon, 1996, p. 396)

Closet narcissists feel the same sense of entitlement as narcissists but meet these needs primarily through their associations with others, ostensibly basking in the reflected glory of these associations. This means they express their sense of entitlement and belief that others worship and adore them less obtrusively, increasing the likelihood that those graced by their presence can be made to feel special. The lack of empathy and interpersonal exploitativeness of the narcissist still exists but is subtler.

The hypervigilance has them discerning subtle clues to hook their audience, then using the intensity, smiles, and invasive inquisitiveness to lure the prey into the web. This always involves blurring boundaries, compromising small principles, and getting a foot in the door to become involved in a collaborative relationship.

The best way to inoculate against this charm is to listen with eyes closed. Turn away if necessary, look down if need be, but listen to what is said. Without the mesmerizing benefit of the engaging body language, the charm will lose its power (Hare, 1993). A failure to be charmed by molesters will quickly terminate the relationship, as one's status no longer remains special, and the opportunity to exploit diminishes.

Helpful

If something looks too good to be true, the price tag is hidden. DO NOT ACCEPT HELP FROM THOSE WHO SEEMINGLY WANT NOTHING IN RETURN.

The best way to be protected against the helpfulness of the sex offender is not to be too desperate for help. Build a support system with people who help one another. Expect to trade services. Worry when someone wants to help constantly, and seemingly expects nothing in return.

A single mother of three explained how she "chose to be really dependent on him time after time." During the courtship stage, "when anything would happen, lo and behold, he was there with everything I needed done in order to help me out of yet another bad situation. He appeared to be such an unselfish person." She later discovered how wrong she was. Being stretched too thin makes one more vulnerable, which makes it easier to succumb to the assistance so easily provided by a potential molester.

Thoughtfulness, consideration, and helpfulness should not automatically be viewed with alarm. Philanthropists and friendly neighbors have always been appreciated, and during times of crisis, individuals readily accept available assistance without being able to reciprocate. Such charity is not, however, the basis for an enduring connection, as friendship requires a more reciprocal relationship. The molesters under study were not developing friendships, nor were they interested in getting anything apparent in return. In short, their efforts were simply too good to be true. As the mother of three discovered after she married him, "He really wasn't an unselfish person. He was a selfish person." Again and again, molesters described offering free baby-sitting services, helping with remodeling jobs, providing car tune-ups, mowing lawns, while never asking for anything in return. In each case, they already had clear ideas of exactly how they wanted to receive payback. The predatory criminal consciously does everything possible to create this presentation:

"He was so nice" is a comment I often hear from people describing the man who, moments or months after his niceness, victimized them. We must learn and then teach our children that niceness does not equal goodness. Niceness is a decision, a strategy of social interaction. People seeking to control others almost always present the image of a nice person at the beginning. (de Becker, 1999, p. 67)

Having allowed someone to be so nice, and thereby accepted innumerable favors from that person is another way of having boundaries blurred. This creates an unspoken debt, with unidentified pressure that makes it more difficult to subsequently set clear boundaries concerning unrelated awkward or even visibly inappropriate behavior. After two years of letting the neighbor keep her car running, one mother pointed out how hard it was to stop him from just dropping in. She did not like that he would come over and pour himself a cup of coffee out of her coffee pot. The first time this happened, he had just worked on her car, so she did not stop him. In fact, she offered to make him a sandwich as well, which he declined. The next time he walked in, she did not say anything either, which both gave him permission to continue and simultaneously allowed him to begin to blur the boundaries in their relationship. Clearly, it is more difficult to establish and maintain clear boundaries after someone has been so helpful. Furthermore, once a small boundary violation has been tolerated, then it becomes more difficult to say anything when other boundaries become blurred. This foot-in-the-door technique is exactly the same method molesters use with children after they have successfully used it to win over the adults.

The molesters interviewed for this book demonstrated this hypervigilance, with attentiveness to subtle cues that would allow them, in even limited interactions, to appear helpful. One molester, while explaining his ability to target children, stated, "I can look in their eyes and know which children to target. I can read people like a book." He described how he used that ability to tell people what they wanted to hear and to know exactly what services to offer. Other molesters concurred that they used this skill to woo the guardians of the children they molested.

Some of the molesters under study were thought by many to be "lazy and self-centered," making their occasional helpfulness with the children even more suspect. One grandfather "never lifted a finger to help with anything," yet he was always quick to offer to bathe the grandchildren. Mr. Martin's baby-sitting services invariably centered around giving the children their baths. No matter what the circumstances, when the children were with him, they inevitably needed a bath. One successful molester, who mesmerized an entire resort community, miraculously had everything available that anyone might ever need. Sooner or later, every adult in the community ended up on his doorstep to borrow some indispensable item only he seemed to have. While the adult was busy using the borrowed item, he happily kept their children engaged to allow the parent to work undisturbed.

Most of the molesters interviewed considered themselves to be exceptionally "nice" people who went out of their way to help others, and they saw this characteristic as unrelated to their sexual predatory behavior, and something they did not wish to change. A convicted teacher was always available to the children with whom he worked:

> I played father to many of them. I took them to their outings, brought cameras to take pictures for the parents. . . . I'm really good with kids. I'm a really nice guy. All the other times with children [except for the two events for which he was convicted] were not grooming. I really am safe with children. Kids really like me. I'm good with them. I respect them. I allow them to be themselves and value and appreciate who they are.

He was extremely successful with the children and they adored him: "The two boys I molested, their mother kept requesting me for their foster placements. I had them many times."

A mechanic convicted of molesting children believed, "I'm a really nice guy. I'm really focused on kids. I like kids." He described how helpful he was to their parents: "I do things for the adults. I help them out. I tell them about how wonderful their kids are." He was always welcome at social events because of this helpful focus on children. In addition to being very approachable to children, he was also always ready to help do anything for anybody. He never asked anyone to reciprocate: "I don't want any help. I don't accept it." He later reiterated, "I'm always doing something for others. People know I will do anything for them. I never say no."

A retired neighbor described that his victim's

> mother would call me and want me to come down and get her daughter and take her to volleyball practice, to get her picture

taken, run errands. After we'd done what she had to do, we'd go get soft drinks, ice cream, sit and talk little girl stuff. I was grooming her. I'd take her home. I was always doing something for her mother.

A journeyman carpenter pointed out how he never actually volunteered to baby-sit, but felt that somehow his victims' mothers "knew me well enough and trusted me to baby-sit. I guess they thought I was a good guy. I guess the parents felt their kids were safe with me. I'm kind of, like, a nice, sweet person. The parents felt comfortable with me. They'd say, 'He's nice. He's good with kids.'"

A telephone repairman also explained that he was an extremely helpful, nice person: "I'm very helpful. I never say no to anybody. This is to the detriment of my girlfriend. I'll drop whatever I'm doing if someone needs help and go help them." He added, "I'm always helpful. I might have been more willing to do things so I could be with kids. I'd offer to take the kids somewhere."

A number of child molesters described how they would specifically assure the parents by introducing the topic of child molesters. "I'd say things like, 'You can never be too careful these days. Make sure you don't let this sweet child of yours go with someone who is not trustworthy. You know there's a lot of rapists around.' That gets them agreeing with me, and means they think I'm trustworthy."

A computer technician described his behavior toward the families whose daughters he molested: "I was just a friend doing things a friend would do. Helping them move." He also specifically chose friends who had difficulty parenting their children. He met the parents in bars and then, after becoming friends with the family, would make himself available. He elaborated how relieved the parents would be to get a break from their kids: "With the adults, as long as the kid is having a good time and is not in their hair, then that would be fine."

A truck driver said:

> I liked doing things. If someone asked me to do something for them or help them work on something, I'd be over there. If friends needed to move or were going to have a garage sale, my wife and I would go over there. I'd never go myself to help

somebody, especially if it was a woman. I'd always bring my wife with me. The guys would be no problem. Whenever anyone needed help, we wouldn't say no. We wanted to be helpful.

Another molester insisted that his helpfulness was independent of his molesting behavior. "I was always trying to be helpful. If someone wanted some work done, well, there was a spirit of coop- eration among everybody." He further elaborated that all the neigh- borhood children played in his yard, and he would frequently end up baby-sitting the children: "Oh yeah. They trusted us. We were baby-sitting. We were responsible for them."

A counselor always made himself available to parents and of- fered to baby-sit their children. "I would tell them about how great their kid was. Reward them, build them up by saying their kid's a good kid. What I appeared to be was really caring and thoughtful and good for the kids."

A postal carrier considered himself to be a very helpful guy: "I was always nice to the neighbor." He helped with the yard work and solicited the neighbor's input on any remodeling decisions that might impact his view. This was the same neighbor whose daughter he molested.

While many of the interviewed molesters viewed themselves as generous and helpful, they never asked for help in return: "Usually I never asked. Usually I was the one to the rescue. I never de- manded something." More than one molester considered this gener- osity a possible marker for adults to notice: "Someone that's overly friendly, that goes out of his way and doesn't ask for the same thing back, that's a clue."

Peerlike Play

Children need adult involvement, guidance, and direction.

All of the molesters interviewed described their behavior toward children as "being on the child's wavelength." Those who abused small children reported playing games with them and anticipating their needs. Those focused on older children talked about siding with them in arguments, talking with them as a friend about sexual matters, and generally behaving like another teenager. Many molesters agreed that this should be alarming to adults.

Molesters see this as a strength. Li (1991) extols the virtues of this when he summarizes that to "many pedophiles, the childhood world represents the best of life, while the adult world the worst. Pedophilia is not primarily a matter of sex, but of love, of being wanted, of childhood enjoyment, of things that the adult world cannot provide" (p. 135). One molester reported, "I am very much a Peter Pan, the boy who never grew up. That is why boys are attracted to me. I don't look down upon them as kids. I regard them, and they me, as 'all boys together.' My deep love for boys for so many years is so much a part of me psychologically that growing up would be impossible" (Li, 1991, p. 136). Behaving like a child is an opportunistic way to gain access: "Most pedophiles try to establish a mutual relationship with them, to act like children when they are with them" because "the pedophile wants to introduce himself to the boy's world as an equal, a participant, to be as a boy is, to feel as boys feel" (Brongersma, 1991, p. 155).

Similar themes were repeated by each of the molesters studied. One said, "I'm really focused on kids. I like kids. I think like them. I'm on their wavelength. When a kid is in the room, my focus is on the kid. I'm more interested in the kids than in the adults. I am a kid." Another described that he was always able to be nice with his children: "My wife will lecture the kids. When they tell me something, I will tell them about something I did as a kid. I'll talk to them at their level. I'll tell them what I know they want to hear." Yet another considered, "I'm just a big kid myself. . . . I'm a kid. I'm fourteen years old," when in fact he was forty-nine years old. Another molester pointed out, "I wouldn't be with the adults." He considered his behavior toward other adults to be rude. He was usually extremely self-centered. Yet his behavior around teenage girls was different. With the kids, "I was the one to volunteer. I'll give you a ride." Whenever he was with teenage girls he "acted too hip." He'd engage them in peerlike conversation and make such comments as, "What's your boyfriend up to? We'll have to get you on the pill."

A young woman referred to this:

> My dad's really weird. For instance, I was, like, twelve and I
> had a boyfriend over. So we're all sitting at the family table.
> My seventeen-year-old brother's got a friend over. I've got a
> friend over. My mom's there. We're talking about just what-
> ever. All of a sudden my father looks across the table and he
> says to my friend, "Wow, my daughter's breasts are really
> starting to grow, don't you think?" He says this like regular,
> just like he might say to my mom "Good gravy, dear." That
> was really common. Everybody would just say that was my
> dad.

Molesters frequently noted that their conversations with children
were often sexual in nature.

An older man elaborated, "I'm a very nice guy, I'm very considerate, and I certainly played well with the kids. I always wanted to
play with the kids. I always included her [victim] and fixed her
whatever she wanted. The little girl thought I was a nice guy." As he
further described how he would have seemed with kids, he stated:

Even though another interviewed molester claimed not to care
for children, he felt that children were attracted to him and stated, "I
play good with them. I get along with children all right." Another
man stated, "My wife enjoyed me getting along with her daughters
because they were hard to get along with." Whereas he was usually
self-centered and rude to most people, he was always thoughtful
and considerate to her daughters: "I befriended the girls. I was
always taking their side, giving them things," which he felt was out
of character for him.

> I guess the only thing I can think of is that I was too nicey-nice
> with the kids. In a way I was like a grandparent. I really
> spoiled them. I let them do whatever they wanted to do. Watch
> whatever TV show they wanted to watch. I could relate to
> them. I didn't mind having them around, even noisy kids.
> They [the parents] felt comfortable with me because I wasn't
> annoyed with little kids. The parents felt safe. They'd say such
> things as, "He's nice. He's good with kids. They like him.

They're not afraid of him." I treated the kids well. I was nice. I always wanted to play with the kids.

A middle-aged molester said, "I'm just a kid myself. I play with the kids on the kids' level. I talk to the kids." Then he added, "I'd spend more time with the kids than with the grown-ups. I'd end up with all the kids at the parties. I'm on their wavelength. As they got to be older [sixteen or seventeen], I wasn't on their wavelength."

Another molester described how good he was with kids:

> I'm like a kid myself. I relate with whatever they're doing. If they want to go swimming, hey, I'll take them swimming. If they want to play baseball, no problem. Let's play catch. Want to play with puzzles? No problem. Want to watch TV? No problem. It was easy to do whatever they wanted to do. That was the center of my life. That was what I was doing. . . . If I was in a room full of adults, and there were kids playing, I'd just break off from the adults to see how the kids were doing or to interact with the kids. And if the kids wanted something, I'd never shoo them away. I'd just drop what I was doing and I'd go with the kid.

One molester did not think he was particularly good with kids: "I never put myself in a position of authority over kids. I was more of the good guy. I always tried to be the good guy. I planned the fun things. I was really nice." Another molester in his fifties demonstrated this peerlike response in describing his thirteen-year-old victim: "I started manipulating her because I believed she was so naive and so young. We thought we were falling in love without any regards to the age difference between us. I would want to talk to her on her level and we could communicate."

In each of these cases, the molester described playing with the children "on their level." Children already have peers with whom they interact. Their contact with adults should enrich their lives, provide opportunities for learning, and help give them direction. Adults who behave like children to curry favor with children are exploiting the implied position of authority their advanced age automatically confers upon them.

The molesters' wives viewed this same behavior as an alliance between the molester and child against them. With hindsight, they felt this should have alerted them to the abuse: "He played with the kids like a kid" and, in that play, deliberately sided with "my child against me. I was always made to feel like the bad guy, the enforcer. I was the one who would have to say no, break off the play to enforce bedtime, turn off the television to prevent them from watching an adult movie."

An adult daughter who had been sexually abused by her father described, "One thing my dad always did was when my mom would say 'No,' he would say 'Yes.' When my mom would say 'Yes,' he would say 'No.' For years I was convinced that my mother wanted nothing but the worst for me." A mother whose husband molested their daughter noticed that her husband always contradicted her decisions:

> When I told my daughter, "No, you can't go," he would turn around and let her go. Then there was the time when he let her have the car. I came home and asked, "Where is the car at?" and he answered that "She got in the car and took off." He just let her have the car.

Another daughter whose father sexually abused her said that her father just

> threw the car keys at me when I was thirteen years old. I had asked him if he would drive me somewhere and he threw the keys at me and said, "It's just around the block. Drive yourself." He never asked for the keys back so I drove since. I wouldn't drive with my mother around, but my dad didn't care.

Margaret Carruthers also developed a peer relationship with her victims, which included siding with her students against adult rules or restrictions. Silva (1990) was an adult inviting young children over for "sleepovers," outings more typically seen among young friends. Adult molesters often view the children they target as "best friends," resulting in behavioral interactions that resemble what one might expect between youngsters who lack adult guidance.

A woman whose niece was abused by her husband reported:

> What really tipped me off was, I'd come home from work and he had his friends over and my niece was there. They were all drinking wine coolers, and she wanted one. She was fourteen years old. I said, "No, you can't have one," and I left the room. When I came back there she was drinking a wine cooler. I was just infuriated. I was pissed off. That's what tipped me off. Why would he allow my niece to have alcohol? I got mad, and he said, "Oh, stop it. She can have a drink." That really bothered me. I didn't want to be a part of it. So I'm the bitch. I'm the one bringing down the party.

Prefer the Company of Children

> *Look out for adults who primarily interact with children and do not socialize with their peers.*

Most of the molesters under study preferred the company of children. Many adults enjoy working with children and help guide children in their roles as teachers, scout leaders, coaches, etc., but molesters prefer the company of children to that of other adults, much as a heroin addict seeks out contact with anyone who has heroin. Often their involvement with children ceases abruptly as those children outgrow the age of interest. Many molesters marry women with young children, then divorce those women when the children get too old, only to find another ready-made family with children in the right age range. Mr. Martin was easily able to do this and went through three marriages, each time to women with young children. All the children subsequently provided him with innumerable opportunities to be a doting grandfather.

Mr. Smith spent most of his time every day interacting with children. He attended their birthday parties, he played with them on the school grounds, he baby-sat them at night. Although he was married, his family saw very little of him because of his intense involvement with children. He did not form long-lasting relationships with these children. He played with them, then moved on to the next batch as these children grew older and went off to middle school. All those whose birthday parties he religiously attended for three to five years never saw him again, except when he attended their younger siblings' parties, as he was perpetually involved with children at the elementary school level. One middle school student whose birthday parties Mr. Smith had attended for three years said, "When I saw Mr. Smith the other day at a school play, he looked right through me. He didn't even know who I was. He didn't even say hello. He started playing with the kid behind me."

Once again, these are not enduring and meaningful relationships with children or their families; rather, they are opportunistic relationships with children whose age sexually excites the molester. Adolescent boys surrounded Fred. As the boys hit puberty, he lost interest in them, leaving them to wonder what they said or did to end the friendship, while he targeted the next group of budding victims. After they hit adolescence, Mr. Smith no longer acknowledged the very children whose birthday parties he had once attended. Carruthers terminated all contact with her victim after she graduated from high school.

Molesters deliberately spend their time in places that provide them with access to their targets. According to Donna Bouchard's father, Margaret Carruthers "didn't seem to have any adult friends. She was always hanging around with the kids." Donna Bouchard added that Margaret Carruthers "admitted to me once that she would intentionally go places where she knew I would be." This busy involvement precludes having time to develop any adult relationships:

> Marg never really associated with anyone her own age. She always spent time with kids. And if she did have adult friends, then they were the parents of the child she was preying upon. . . . Even though she lived in Debden for almost twenty years, she really never involved herself in any adult activities—she had uncontrolled access to children and teenagers, but she never was an active member of the community as such.

Convicted molester Noyes, who was married and has children, tells other child molesters, "You may believe that only children really understand you. . . . You may actually care about the children on some level. . . . For years I worked with children and had children as my social and emotional friends." Despite his professional status in the community, his marriage and family responsibilities, Noyes looked to the children he abused for emotional strength and comfort and considered those children to be his peers.

Roughhousing and Tickling

> *"It is not molesting because it is 'only' wrestling around, tickling, massaging, touching games, etc." (Robert Noyes). DO NOT TOLERATE WRESTLING, TICKLING, MASSAGE, AND TOUCHING GAMES.*

All the molesters under study described their contact with children as involving frequent roughhousing and tickling games: One elaborated, "I was always handling the kids." The molester who was always sought out by his relatives' children because he engaged in roughhousing and tickling with his nieces and nephews described this same motif: "At family gatherings like Christmas and Thanksgiving, I'd pay a lot of attention to the kids. I'd tickle them." The girls all would cuddle with him and sit on his lap. Other relatives would notice this involvement and say to the twelve- and fourteen-year-old girls, "Get off Uncle's lap; you're bothering him." He added, "They just thought the kids were pestering me. They would say, 'Don't pester him.' They never knew there was anything between us." They certainly never considered the reverse, that the uncle was pestering the children.

Each of the molesters described variations on this theme: "I'd be around the kids, rolling, tumbling. I'd be like another kid." One molester said, "I don't know if I was specially gifted, but I think by now, with all these interviews you've done, you know a lot of molesters put on a good-guy act. I love children. In the family there was a lot of physical contact. You hold them, they sit on your lap, you roughhouse." He described tickling games and roughhousing as something that he routinely did with the children.

Those who molested older children blurred the boundaries of physical contact in other ways as well. Donna Bouchard describes how Margaret Carruthers "had begun to break through my boundaries . . . as early as grade seven, though nothing overtly sexual happened until grade nine. She was a tactile and affectionate person, she said, so she gave me hugs, touched my back, played with my hair, massaged my shoulders and legs . . . most of this she could explain away as 'part of the trainer's or coach's role.' " Much of this touching, aimed at blurring the boundaries, was clearly visible to adults and has been reported again and again by molesters, their victims, and the adults who blindly observed this behavior.

The molesters all agreed that more than any one single visible behavior, the touching, roughhousing, and tickling games served the purpose of desensitizing the child to touch. They also helped establish parental approval for such activities, which were initially at least partially done in full view of the adults. The apparent adult approval would help to confuse the child as the touch later became more sexualized. The roughhousing and tickling games would also create a context for the parents to assume a misunderstanding should the child ever report any sexualized touching. This should not discourage respectful appropriate touching between adults and children. There is no question of the importance of contact comfort to successful child development. Rather, it should discourage tolerance for tickling and roughhousing, which among the treated molesters was generally accepted as simply being too risky to allow.

Insider Status

Worry when someone is instantly accorded insider status.

Molesters violate the usual rules and niceties with such panache and ease that others assume their behavior must be acceptable. It is not necessary to knock on doors, nor must they wait for permission. They utilize the opportunity and leave others wondering what happened, but too embarrassed, shy, or uncomfortable to say anything. One new guest helped himself to an expensive electric razor because his host was growing a beard and mustache. He took it "since you won't be needing this anymore," leaving his host too stunned to say anything. The wife of a man who turned out to be a sexual molester of children recalled, "When I first met him, immediately, I don't think it even popped out of my mouth, but, like, he's weird. But then I said, 'Oh well. He's not really weird. That's just me,' " and she tolerated his numerous violations of the usual codes of courtship.

The charm, friendliness, and ease with which they violate the usually accepted protocols provides molesters with quick opportunities to be seen as trusted members of the families or as old friends. Fred was technically a virtual stranger to the dozens of families he helped by moving in to take care of their children while they left town for week-long holidays. Many of these families had only briefly met him through their children. Similar to Mr. Smith, he instantly reassured them with his winning ways, his familiarity with other families, and the fact that he had already successfully taken care of so many other children. Those families, of course, had been similarly reassured. In each case, he miraculously bypassed the usual careful screening that parents would use before allowing someone to move into the home to care for their children for a week. "Every type of con relies upon distracting us from the obvious. That's how a conversation evolves into a crime without the victim knowing until it's too late" (de Becker, 1999, p. 69). The con artist begins as an absolute stranger who uses catchy details to come to be perceived as someone familiar who can be trusted. "No matter how engaging a stranger might be, you must never lose sight of context. He is what he is; a stranger who approached you" (de Becker, 1999, p. 69).

Although Margaret Carruthers was not a stranger, she managed to use these techniques to ingratiate herself with the family. Donna Bouchard's mother recalled:

> Marg never actually became a "close" friend, but somehow just seemed to slowly wedge her way into our family. We did not have much money and lived some thirteen miles from town, and yet both my husband and I wanted our three children to participate in school and community activities, including sports. We felt it necessary to limit our children to one sport per season.

This became another opportunity for Carruthers to be more closely involved with the family:

> Donna asked to add another nonschool sport to her agenda. Her dad strongly objected, but somehow I was feeling that Donna was needing something more. While we clearly could not afford the expenses of another sport, Marg had offered to

take care of "equipment," and pay for "out-of-town trips." Once I had allowed her to get involved in this manner, I guess I now felt "obligated" to her.

This feeling of obligation is exactly what the molester leverages to advantage.

Accepting boundary violations results in adults inadvertently becoming coconspirators; they have to either acknowledge the error of allowing someone such immediate insider status or assume that an established alliance really exists. Accepting the latter solution inadvertently automatically places the adult in cahoots with the molester. De Becker (1997) refers to this as "forced teaming," with "the use of the word we" to establish a "we're in the same boat attitude. This forced teaming, one of the most sophisticated manipulations, is the projection of a shared purpose or experience where none exists" (p. 53). In the case of the Bouchard family, Margaret Carruthers used such forced teaming to ensure protection against disclosure. After a suicide attempt, when Donna appeared ready to "spill the beans," her mother described how "Marg quickly became 'my best friend,' accompanying me to the hospital [to see Donna], leaving me money when I spent the night in the hospital." Marg quickly became involved in counseling sessions. Donna's mother said, "I still don't understand why or how that really came to be, but she always seemed to be offering to drive the one hundred kilometers to the appointment. Taking time off school never seemed to be a problem. She seemed as concerned about me now, wanting to be my friend, helping me plant a garden that spring. She always seemed to be 'around.'"

When someone miraculously obtains immediate insider status, the relationship should always be more closely scrutinized:

> The first step toward making a good choice is so obvious as to be nearly invisible: be sure it's your choice, not the choice of the new person, and certainly not the choice of the child. People who select your family and inject themselves into your lives are candidates for more careful scrutiny. People who rush the process of friendship are often in some other process en-

tirely. If they seem overly interested in your child, raise your antenna a bit higher. (de Becker, 1999, p. 163)

The families who welcomed Fred into their homes, and left him to baby-sit their children actually hardly knew him before becoming his staunchest allies and most loyal supporters. Having accepted him into their homes, however, and provided him with access to their children, they attributed qualities to him and meaning to their relationship that had no resemblance to his agenda. He had chosen them because of his sexual attraction to their children. He subsequently molested their children because of the opportunities their enthusiasm, support, and invitations into their homes accorded him. His insider status subsequently became his best defense when allegations occurred, with each of the families vociferously coming to his defense and berating those mean-spirited families who credited their children's "stories."

Fails to Honor Clear Boundaries

"No" really does mean "No." RUN WHEN "NO" IS IGNORED.

Through the media, many people mistakenly believe that "No" means "Yes" and is only an invitation for the hero to be more forceful to overcome the shyness that prevented the heroine from acknowledging her heart's desire. Such messages incorrectly undermine the more pressing need for people to be able to manage boundaries and to have those boundaries honored. Inappropriate invasions of personal space, violations of individual rights, and failure to respect other people should not be tolerated, much less encouraged. Helping people to establish and maintain clear boundaries is the basis of psychotherapy (Minuchin, 1974; Beavers and Hampson, 1990; Lerner, 1985; Corey, 1996), where the division between intimacy and enmeshment is frequently confused, leading to innumerable problems in relationships. Such complex terrain is obviously not going to be fully addressed and resolved in this book. What can begin, however, is for the reader to recognize these concerns and understand the importance of establishing and maintaining clear boundaries to protect children.

Setting clear boundaries and expecting them to be honored is the very foundation for creating a safe environment for children. What makes this especially complicated is that the boundaries need to keep changing as children grow and develop, requiring increasingly more independence and autonomy, while continuing to need structure, nurture, and guidance. Rather than supporting this complex process, molesters help blur the boundaries, creating confusion for both the adults and the intended victims. Most of Mr. Smith's ardent supporters experienced initial discomfort with his involvement with their children but discounted those initial feelings: "Once I got to know him I decided he was really okay." The resultant enthusiastic support then became an invitation for subsequently further blurring and confusing roles and rules.

Remember, for most people, it is extremely difficult to set and maintain appropriate limits of contact and interactions with others under the best of circumstances. Molesters skirt around the usual rules with their helpfulness, their charm, their boldness, and by simply getting directly involved with the children without prior initial approval. After their relationships with the family, school, and adult community, as well as their contact with the child, are a fait accompli, it becomes almost impossible to enforce the boundaries. This is how molesters confuse the adults and, subsequently, is exactly how they also confuse the child victim into assuming responsibility for the abuse.

If a feeling of obligation and debt has been established, or a violation of boundaries has been previously tolerated, this is all the more reason to go back to first principles and enforce the normally adhered to boundaries. It means drawing a line in the sand and graciously reiterating the rules to that person. If the person cannot, or will not, adhere to those rules, then that person's involvement with children should be considered worrisome:

> Declining to hear "no" is a signal that someone is either seeking control or refusing to relinquish it. . . . The worst response when someone fails to accept "no" is to give ever weakening refusals and then give in. Never relent on "no". . . even [with] someone who seems to have the best intentions. And never let him think you're open to negotiation. (de Becker, 1997, p. 54)

Numerous boundary violations may be perfectly harmless or simply represent cultural or lifestyle differences. That the violations appear harmless enough is no reason to ignore them or fail to reiterate the rules. The other person's response becomes crucial. For instance, one mother described a neighbor who always dropped in without knocking. She said, "I don't want anyone coming into my home until I've opened the door to let them in." Although the neighbor's behavior might have been harmless enough, it presented an ideal opportunity to practice presenting the ground rules. This mother said, "I just couldn't tell her. It seemed so harsh. There she would be with a plate of cookies, and I was supposed to tell her not to come in?" This mother chose to keep the door locked, thereby requiring the neighbor to knock instead. However, she could just as easily have said, "I love having you drop by. I need you to knock first and wait for me to invite you in." Most friendships flourish when people can be trusted to make their needs clearly known, rather than expecting others to second-guess what they are thinking or feeling.

In the cases under study, molesters deliberately violated boundaries precisely to see what would happen. Just as they tested the waters with children to identify which ones could be more easily victimized, they similarly tested adults. Those adults who caved in to small boundary violations proved to be more easily manipulated. This subsequently revealed their children also to be safer targets to molest. Mr. Smith never returned to the homes where the parents clearly and directly told him to leave. Mr. Martin never baby-sat those children whose parents did not tolerate the bathing activities. Fred quit calling and inviting on outings those adolescent boys whose parents clearly said, "Stop calling my son." Mr. Clay never had children staying after school whose parents called and clearly followed through on insisting their children come straight home after school; he knew better than to consider their children good targets. The adult community needs to learn to say "No" and mean it when small visible boundary violations occur.

The molesters who reported wrestling, roughhousing, and tickling the children never once heard an adult ask them to stop. Yet numerous mothers described not liking some of the play and saying stop. However, the way they said "No" was not forceful. One wife said:

> My husband molested my daughter when she was nine, and he came and told me. Of course, the way they tell things is not very direct. He said he was educating her. He had read a book that when a father educates a daughter sexually then they're more comfortable in their marriage and they're more accepting of sex. Of course, he said he wouldn't do any more than just touch her. That's all he was going to do, and it kind of goes along with his personality because he was always trying out new things. My answer to him was "That's stupid. Don't do that." I never thought he would do it again. It's such a stupid idea, why would he do that again? I believed that was the end of it.

As it turned out, he had already been molesting this daughter and his two sons for years, and he knew that his wife's brief response of "Don't do that" was meaningless.

Another wife reported that she was "always very suspicious. But my husband just kept convincing me, telling me 'No, you're just imagining things. Quit thinking like that." When she observed specific behaviors she did not approve of, he would laugh at her, or "he ignored me and just continued doing what he was doing." A daughter described her father as only manipulating those he perceived as weaker:

> He never manipulated a man, although I've seen him yell at some little men. I've seen him manipulate women. But I've never seen him stand up against a strong woman. He was kind of crafty. He was pretty smart for what he did. But at the same time, what I noticed was, the stronger the woman, the more he backed off.

Her mother worried about the family's safety upon his release from prison. The daughter counseled her mother to stand firm:

> He never once threatened my aunt or ever yelled [at] any strong women he knew. The reason I say stand firm is that I know the type of woman my mom has become. She has what it takes to be

strong. And I know the type of man my daddy was. He was a person who manipulated only weak women.

Another woman quit tolerating her husband's verbally abusive treatment of their infant daughter only when she thought, "Nobody off the street could talk to my daughter that way, so how come he's so privileged?" That insight opened her eyes. As a result, she quit allowing behavior from her husband that she would never accept from a perfect stranger. What she then saw eventually led to his incarceration.

What additionally makes establishing and maintaining boundaries so difficult are the constantly changing requirements of children as they grow and develop more autonomy. There are no boundaries at all between caretakers and their newborn infants. Then, as children develop, the task becomes one of separating enough to provide them with ever-increasing amounts of responsibility and independence, without doing so too rapidly and abandoning them prematurely. This continual dance between enmeshment and disengagement (Beavers and Hampson, 1990) is also significantly impacted by the expected developmental milestones: beginning school, hitting adolescence, becoming an adult, and starting a family of one's own (Minuchin and Fishman, 1981). Supervising this journey requires adults to develop a healthy balance of structure and nurture, while providing opportunities for increased independence, with appropriate levels of support, supervision, and involvement (Clarke and Dawson, 1998). Even under the most ideal circumstances, this is a difficult balance to achieve successfully. Sexual molestations invariably significantly interfere with this process.

Goes on the Offensive

The best defense is a good offense. Expect this, stand firm, and do not be intimidated.

If one thinks of these molesters as narcissists, and/or closet narcissists, then their tendency to attack when confronted is predictable. Therapists long ago learned not to confront narcissists (Masterson, 1988) because they will go on the attack while being unable to hear the concern: "The narcissistic disordered self will exploit opportunities for freedom and independence to gain narcissistic, not real, self-gratification and will fiercely battle any authority that would infringe on the individual's sense of entitlement" (Masterson, 1988, p. 105).

This is consistent with the experiences people have when trying to confront even minor or seemingly harmless transgressions in this population. The complainant can be made to feel in the wrong and guilty. This is because of how narcissists respond to any perceived criticism, no matter how slight:

> There is extreme vulnerability to criticism or being ignored, together with a strong wish for love, support, and admiring deference from others. . . . If the support is withdrawn, or if there is any evidence of lack of perfection, the self-concept degrades to severe self-criticism. Totally lacking in empathy, these persons treat others with contempt, and hold the self above and beyond the fray. (Benjamin, quoted in Millon, 1996, p. 401)

Even the slightest challenge to any behavior can elicit disproportionate rage. One wife described a lifetime of placating her husband, who was a deacon of the church, a highly placed professional, and, as was later revealed, an extremely active sexual molester of children:

> If I would oppose him about anything, even disagree about a choice of carpet color, he'd become very silent and just go on being silent for days and days. Finally, because I couldn't stand it any longer, and I couldn't stand all this tension in the house, I would go and apologize. I'd tell him, "I'm sorry I didn't whatever," or "I'm sorry it happened, and will you forgive me?" and "Blah, blah, blah."

Another wife agreed, adding that "they have to go to such great levels to convince you that they're right. A healthy person doesn't have to do that." After her husband was charged, he continued to explain it away. "He went on and on about how he had read this in a book. How you educate your daughter by touching her in a sexual way, and it's a healthy, normal thing to do. It was this article that led him astray. This is the document that would save him. It was all the fault of the article." When his wife finally found this article, however, "it proved that he was a sex offender," but she was too cowed to bring it to his treatment provider. This wife, who was an upstanding member of a Christian community, married to the choir director of the church, who worked in a prestigious nationally recognized job, described how "he tried to look so good, which is why he rolled a lot of shit off his lips."

Even minor transgressions seem to bring others to defend the aggressor and blame the victim. For instance, a mother called the school after her ten-year-old daughter had been physically attacked on the playground by an eleven-year-old boy. She called to get a phone number so she could let his parents know. "If that had been my son, I would have wanted to know. It would be an opportunity to teach my son how to behave." The principal did not consider that necessary because "he's a very nice boy. He comes from a very good family." Although that might have been true, the mother pointed out that "what he did was not nice." The principal defended the boy, minimized the event, reiterated that he came from a very nice home, and insisted the boy was only flirting. The girl must have provoked the attack and "liked the attention." This interaction recapitulates what typically occurs with allegations of wrongdoing. The accused is "nice," comes from a "good home," the events are minimized, and the victim is blamed. Addressing this counterattack requires nerves of steel and a broken-record approach, politely repeating the request numerous times. In this case, the principal finally followed through only because the girl's parents continued to insist that the information needed to be relayed to the boy's parents.

Another playground incident involved a small boy who was seriously injured by a boy twice his size. The school preferred not to call it an assault, instead giving it the spin that the boys were equals settling a dispute. If anything, they might need assistance mediating their disagreement. When the parents called the police to consider filing assault charges, the policeman who worked in that school told them the victim would be charged for assault if the predator was. This counterattack by the police finally disappeared when the parents were unwilling to be cowed by both the school district and the police officer. Only then was the case properly investigated. To ignore these transgressions would incorrectly miss opportunities to educate and prevent further violence.

In the case of Mr. Clay's students, the parents found themselves under attack from the very beginning. When they first complained to the principal, they were told "little boys will tell stories." The principal told the teacher whose child had also been molested by Mr. Clay that she was not to discuss the situation with anybody. The school superintendent advised the parents to stop maligning this man's character. Finally, when they went to the teacher's union representative for advice, he told them if they did not stop "hounding" this man they would be sued for libel. In the case of Mr. Smith, the school district told those parents who complained about his activities to stop making false accusations, although no accusations were ever made.

Wives who were themselves sexually abused have their own abuse thrown in their face when they question blatantly inappropriate behavior. One husband was seen leaving his daughter's bedroom at night while furtively zipping up his pants. When his wife inquired what he was doing, he told her, "Just because you were sexually abused you see sexual abuse everywhere. You're really sick, and you should get help." Another wife wondered why her husband was bathing their ten-year-old daughter and was told to "quit imposing your dirty thoughts and sexual abuse on us."

In the case of Noyes, the initial allegations led to his resigning from the school, with "the understanding that he would be effectively blackballed out of teaching" (Margoshes, 1986, p. B3). His personal physician, who was well aware of his sexual proclivities, called one of the mothers who had witnessed Noyes's behavior, "asking her not to call [the] police." The mothers had gone to the principal, who also "talked them out of going to the police and assured them that Noyes would never teach again" (p. B3). Seven months later, Noyes's personal physician signed a statement that "Noyes was 'in good health and does not suffer from any condition which would prevent carrying out the duties of a full-time teacher.'" The school feared a defamation suit should they drum him out of the profession, even though the school superintendent had attended therapy sessions during which Noyes's pedophilia was discussed, which documented that the superintendent clearly knew the extent of Noyes's sexual proclivities. Instead, the district facilitated his move to another school district. When the new principal checked out his references, he was told "if you hire this guy, he'll do a good job for you." Nothing was said about the sexual abuse. Another principal who subsequently hired Noyes to teach in yet another district recalled asking the reference, " 'Is there anything I should know about this person before I hire him?' [and was told] 'everything is fine' " (p. B3). Paralleling the Clay case, powerful forces came to Noyes's defense to protect him from a police investigation and to keep the school district fearing a defamation suit. One school assistant superintendent pointed out that "there were no charges laid, and we had absolutely nothing to go on. Anything else was insinuation " (p. B3).

Each case requires steadfast conviction. Graciously and politely reiterate the required principles. Use the broken-record approach. Do not be confused by intimidation and justification. Remember the mother who was not distracted when the principal minimized, tolerated, and exonerated unacceptable behavior and then blamed the aggression on her daughter, "who must have been asking for the assault by flirting."

Protecting children from potential child sexual abuse requires clarity about child sexual abuse and confidence in refusing to let the boundaries get blurred. This is essential to avoid letting others set the agenda, control the situation, and ignore reasonable standards of conduct. Remember that tolerating small transgressions not only creates opportunities for molesters to gain safe access to children but also fails to model to children the very behaviors they also need to learn and practice. Learning to say "no" with grace and certainty to those whose behavior seems problematical does not interfere with friendships, but does send potential molesters away. Those who are interested in opportunities to molest children will not invest their time with adults who do not tolerate their charm.

Chapter 10

Summary

The same dilemmas that individuals encounter when being charmed by these seemingly respectable child molesters are replicated at a societal level as greater numbers of molesters and their advocates become more organized and prolific in espousing tolerance of child sexual abuse. Their methods are subtle and increasingly successful; they publish in support of their agenda, politick against their opposition, and infiltrate the public domain. The methods they use approximate how, individually, they charm and lull the adult community. They write articles that appear to be scholarly works, which gain authority because they are subsequently reviewed in respectable journals (Talbot, 1999). Upon close examination, however, the material under review refers to research (Kincaid, 1998) that is, in many cases, revealed to be written by individuals openly advocating pedophilia (Brongersma, 1991; Li, 1991; Jones, 1991; Thorstad, 1991; Schmidt, 1991) under the guise of science. The stated goal of molesters and their advocates is to normalize and decriminalize child sexual abuse. They recommend that it be referred to as "intergenerational intimacy" (Schmidt, 1991, p. 2) or "cross-generational love" (Thorstad, 1991, p. 256), rather than the "harsher" language that they believe unnecessarily prejudices people against sex with children. This theme is increasingly echoed in ever more scholarly looking works (Rind, Tromovitch, and Bauserman, 1998), which many argue to be "advocacy masquerading as science" (Editorial, 1999, p. 2). With this increased exposure, and successful inroads by child sexual abuse advocates into more mainstream publications, others are thrown into the morass of faulty reasoning, as they try to counter this pseudoscience directly. Yet the very act of directly addressing these articles confers undeserved credibility on the authors and their arguments (Finkelhor, 1991).

These writers espouse the "benefits" of child sexual abuse and criticize opponents as failing to be in touch with their own sexual arousal to children (Kincaid, 1998). They ascertain that everyone experiences sexual arousal to children, creating the circular argument that those who disagree are in denial (Brongersma, 1991). They disorient the general public in myriad other ways: Failing to accept child sexual abuse is tantamount to not tolerating cultural diversity and denigrating traditional ethnic practices. With the same aggressive support they use to put individuals and their supporters on the defensive, they collectively confuse communities by arguing that restricting their behavior violates the individual freedoms so cherished by everyone in a democratic society.

They also criticize publications addressing the harm caused by child sexual abuse as irrelevant because such studies ignore more pressing concerns that endanger children, such as physical abuse and neglect (Kincaid, 1998; Jenkins, 1998). This approach would be similar to arguing that books about cancer should be trivialized because heart disease is of greater importance. Addressing concerns about child sexual abuse does not diminish that other areas of child safety also need attention, nor does research about cancer negate the need for heart disease education. Yet child safety proponents find themselves arguing moot points that distract from the issues at hand, which only serves to validate arguments and publications undeserving of such acknowledgment. They also argue that sexual arousal to children is a normal human response and that those who deplore it are denying their own desires. The best defense is a good offense, and molesters successfully use these and other arguments to place advocates for child safety on the defensive, much as they do to individuals trying to protect children.

Were child sexual abuse a physical disease such as cancer, then the prevalence data alone would classify it as an epidemic. Child sexual abuse may not be a contagious disease, but it spreads and flourishes when coupled with secrecy, isolation, and confusion. Thus, denial, silence, and lack of clarity become tantamount to giving support and approval to those who would molest. Silence and a failure to act decisively also send the message that adults are incapable of providing children the opportunity to safely develop and mature.

The current political climate is especially worrisome, as increasingly more people begin to accept a shift in focus away from these concerns by minimizing the damage, blaming the victims, glorifying the behavior, or insisting that reports of abuse are fabricated. As such trends gain continued acceptance, children will increasingly be left to fend for themselves, while the adults are overtly or covertly confused or intimidated into silence. As the adults are cowed, so are the children. Sexual abuse disclosures were almost nonexistent in other eras and are decreasing again. Yet the sexualization of children and tolerance for sexual deviancy under the guise of acceptance of individual differences and diverse lifestyles appear to be on the rise.

People should not confuse the love, intimacy, affection, and caring so necessary for successful child development with the sexual intimacy appropriate between equals. Harlow's studies (cited in McConnell, 1980) described how love is a primary reinforcer and noted that children deprived of love fail to thrive. In his studies, Harlow was referring to contact comfort, not sex. The seductive blurring of boundaries, with slippery talk suggesting that sexual caresses exemplify the wholesome contact comfort that children do need, confuses and harms. Children need hugs, warmth, and wholesome touch (Clarke and Dawson, 1998), not sexual caresses.

Tolerance for individual freedoms and liberties is being confused with allowing those in a position of power to abuse those in their care. This perspective would mistakenly allow people to accept self-serving arguments of lust, not only as necessary rights that should be granted to all members in a free society, but as essential to child development.

Those who have a hidden agenda help to generate the confusion. Their desire allows them to ignore the ethical constraints that most people accept. Their ease at deceiving lulls the people who love them into giving them credence and acceptance precisely because most people cannot fathom the depth of their willingness to lie. As one wife of a child molester said: "I used to think that he told the truth but lied a little bit. Now I realize he lies a lot and tells the truth a little bit." Accepting their lies as truth further empowers the sex offender. Another mother continues to live with her husband, whose lies of devotion and loyalty help her to believe "that I love him very much," thus abandoning all three of her children—even though her upstanding, seemingly well-respected, and financially stable husband not only molested all three of her children as well as the neighbor children, but also molested the family dog. Where is the line drawn between healthy sexuality and sexuality run amok?

In this particular case, the father's sexual abuse of the dog provided clarity for the daughter. "I just feel like my dad's pathetic. Why would he do that to me, or my dog? What that taught me is he's a sick man. That cleared it up for me right then. It was because of things like the dog that I can say 'that's psycho' and not blame myself." It failed to provide clarity for the mother, however, who remained in the relationship long after the children were removed from the home, even though she had learned that "he did other odd things along the way . . . that were weird and awful. It brought it to my attention how dangerous he was to be around children." Yet she continues to live with him because "I really love my husband," while abandoning her daughter, who felt that "if something had been found out by fifth grade, I would have wanted to stay with my mom. But now it's too late for that."

The clarity society needs was provided by an adult victim who asked the following of this mother:

> How could this be love? I think this is sick. I think anyone who stays is sick. You can't watch him twenty-four hours a day, seven days a week, to make sure he's not molesting other children. You can't see everything he's doing. Why would you want to be his baby-sitter? He gets to continue with his life, have a home, have a wife. Your daughter has to leave. I think deep down she's upset that you chose to stay with him and not support her. You could be repairing your relationship with your children.

The sexual abuse of children should not be tolerated. Supporting, justifying, minimizing, and ignoring behavior that harms the innocent hurts everyone. It is the task of all sane and responsible adults to assist in protecting children from harm. To do so takes open eyes, courage, and knowledge. One of the mothers concluded that after her children disclosed, and after years of therapy, she realized that the markers identifying her husband as a child molester had all been there, but that she had been blind to the information: "Being with him was like being in a foreign country. You could see all the signs, but you didn't know how to speak the language. I saw the signs, but I didn't know what they meant." Her eyes were open and she had the courage. She just did not have the knowledge.

Hopefully, this book will contribute to keeping children safer by providing a little more of that knowledge. May all adults have the courage and wisdom, individually and together, to take on the difficult challenge of protecting children from being sexually molested.

Appendix

Legal Definitions

Sexual abuse definitions vary only slightly from state to state. Washington laws are summarized here to provide a general framework for the reader. According to the Washington State Criminal Code, Title 9A RCW (1994), child sexual molestations include rape, molestation, and sexual misconduct. Rape charges involve sexual intercourse, whereas child molestation charges involve sexual contact. Charges vary from first to third degree, depending on the age differential of the victim and the perpetrator, and the age of the victim. Sexual misconduct involves sexualized activity with a child between the ages of sixteen and eighteen, with the distinction between first and second degree being that of sexual intercourse versus sexual contact.

Both sexual intercourse and sexual contact are also clearly defined. Sexual intercourse is defined as penetration of the anus or genitalia by any object, while sexual contact involves any sexualized touching.

Rape of a child in the first degree. (1) A person is guilty of rape of a child in the first degree when the person has sexual intercourse with another who is less than twelve years old and not married to the perpetrator and the perpetrator is at least twenty-four months older than the victim.

Rape of a child in the second degree. (1) A person is guilty of rape of a child in the second degree when the person has sexual intercourse with another who is at least twelve years old but less than fourteen years old and not married to the perpetrator and the perpetrator is at least thirty-six months older than the victim.

Rape of a child in the third degree. (1) A person is guilty of rape of a child in the third degree when the person has sexual intercourse with another who is at least fourteen years old and not married to the perpetrator and the perpetrator is at least forty-eight months older than the victim.

Child molestation in the first degree. (1) A person is guilty of child molestation in the first degree when the person has, or knowingly causes another person under the age of eighteen to have, sexual contact with another who is less than twelve years old and not married to the perpetrator and the perpetrator is at least thirty-six months older than the victim.

Child molestation in the second degree. (1) A person is guilty of child molestation in the second degree when the person has, or knowingly causes another person under the age of eighteen to have, sexual contact with another who is at least twelve years old but less than fourteen years old and not married to the perpetrator and the perpetrator is at least thirty-six months older than the victim.

Child molestation in the third degree. (1) A person is guilty of child molestation in the third degree when the person has, or knowingly causes another person under the age of eighteen to have, sexual contact with another who is at least fourteen years old but less than sixteen years old and not married to the perpetrator and the perpetrator is at least forty-eight months older than the victim.

Sexual misconduct with a minor in the first degree. (1) A person is guilty of sexual misconduct with a minor in the first degree when the person has, or knowingly causes another person under the age of eighteen to have, sexual intercourse with another person who is at least sixteen years old but less than eighteen yeas old and not married to the perpetrator, if the perpetrator is at least sixty months older than the victim, is in a significant relationship to the victim, and abuses a supervisory position within that relationship in order to engage in or cause another person under the age of eighteen to engage in sexual intercourse with the victim.

Sexual misconduct with a minor in the second degree. (1) A person is guilty of sexual misconduct with a minor in the second degree when the person has, or knowingly causes another person under the age of eighteen to have, sexual contact with another person who is at least sixteen years old but less than eighteen years old and not married to the perpetrator, if the perpetrator is at least sixty months older than the victim, is in a significant relationship to the victim, and abuses a supervisory position within that relationship in order to engage in or cause another to engage in sexual contact with the victim. (Title 9A RCW, pp. 20-21)

(1) *Sexual intercourse* (a) has its ordinary meaning and occurs upon any penetration, however slight, and (b) also means any penetration of the vagina or anus however slight, by an object, when committed on one person by another, whether such persons are of the same or opposite sex, except when such penetration is accomplished for medically recognized treatment or diagnostic purposes, and (c) also means any act of sexual contact between persons involving the sex organs of one person and the mouth or anus of another, whether such persons are of the same or opposite sex.

(2) *Sexual contact* means any touching of the sexual or other intimate parts of a person done for the purpose of gratifying sexual desire of either party or a third party. (Title 9A RCW, p. 18)

References

Abel, G., Becker, J., Mittleman, M., Rouleau, J., and Murphy, W. (1987). Self-reported sex crimes of nonincarcerated paraphiliacs. *Journal of Interpersonal Violence, 2*(1), March, pp. 3-25.

Abel, G., Becker, J., Murphy, W., and Flanagan, B. (1981). Identifying dangerous child molesters. In R.B. Stuart (Ed.), *Violent behavior: Social learning approaches to prediction, management, and treatment* (pp. 116-137). New York: Brunner/Mazel.

Abel, G., Mittelman, M., and Becker, J. (1985). Sexual offenders: Results of assessment and recommendations for treatment. In M. Ben-Aron, S. Huckle, and C. Webster (Eds.), *Clinical criminology: The assessment and treatment of criminal behavior* (pp. 191-205). Toronto: University of Toronto and M & M Graphic, Ltd.

Abel, G. and Osborn, C. (1992). The paraphilias: The extent and nature of sexually deviant and criminal behavior. *Clinical Forensic Psychiatry, 15*(3), September, pp. 675-687.

Abel, G., Rouleau, J., and Cunningham-Rathner, J. (1986). Sexually aggressive behavior. In W. Curran, A.L. McGarry, and S.A. Shah (Eds.), *Forensic Psychiatry and psychology: Perspectives and standards for interdisciplinary practice* (pp. 289-313). Philadelphia, PA: F.A. Davis Company.

Ageton, S. (1983). *Sexual assault among adolescents.* Lexington, MA: Lexington Books.

Alsop, P. (1988). *Opening doors.* Music video. Moose School Productions.

American Psychiatric Association (APA) (1987). *Diagnostic and statistical manual of mental disorders,* Third edition, Revised. Washington, DC: Author.

American Psychiatric Association (APA) (1994). *Diagnostic and statistic manual of mental disorders,* Fourth edition. Washington, DC: Author.

Anderson, P.B. and Struckman-Johnson, C. (Eds.) (1998). *Sexually aggressive women: Current perspectives and controversies.* New York: The Guilford Press.

Arndt, B., Jr. (1991). *Gender disorders and paraphilias.* Madison, WI: International Universities Press, Inc.

Asch, S.E. (1956). Studies of independence and conformity: A minority of one against a unanimous majority. *Psychological Monographs, 70,* p. 416.

Asch, S.E. and Zukier, H. (1984). Thinking about persons. *Journal of Personality and Social Psychology, 46,* pp. 1230-1240.

Ashley, A.M. and Houston, D.A. (1990). Legal, social, and biological definitions of pedophilia. *Archives of Sexual Behavior, 19*(1), August, pp. 333-342.

Associated Press (1995). Nine-year-old blamed for sex assault. *The Olympian,* January 5, p. A9.

Associated Press (1998). FBI busts alleged child-porn rings. *The Olympian,* September 14, p. A8.

Awad, G. and Saunders, E. (1991). Male adolescent sexual assaulters: Clinical observations. *Journal of Interpersonal Violence, 6*(4), December, pp. 446-460.

Badgley, R. (1984). *Sexual offenses against children: Report of the committee on sexual offenses against children and youths.* Ottawa, Ontario: Government of Canada.

Bagley, C., and Ramsey, R. (1986). Sexual abuse in childhood: Psychosocial outcomes and implications for social work practice. *Journal of Social Work and Human Sexuality, 4,* pp. 33-47.

Bandura, A. (1986). *Social foundations of thought and action: A social cognitive theory.* Englewood Cliffs, NJ: Prentice Hall.

Bates, C. (1994). *Beyond dieting: Relief from persistent hunger.* Courtenay, British Columbia: Tsolum River Press.

Bavelas, J., Chovil, N., and Coates, L. (1993). Language in sexual assault judgements. *Summary of a Project Funded by the B.C. Ministry of Women's Equality,* January-June. Report from a university. University of Victoria. APA manual, p. 209.

Beavers, W.R. and Hampson, R.B. (1990). *Successful families: Assessment and intervention.* New York: W.W. Norton and Company.

Beck, J. and van der Kolk, B. (1987). Reports of childhood incest and current behavior of chronically hospitalized psychotic women. *American Journal of Psychiatry, 144*(11), November, pp. 1474-1476.

Becker, J. and Kaplan, M. (1991). Rape victims: Issues, theories, and treatment. *Annual Review of Sex Research, 2,* pp. 267-292.

Becker, J. and Quinsey, V. (1993). Assessing suspected child molesters. *Child Abuse and Neglect, 17*(1), pp. 169-174.

Becker, J. and Skinner, L. (1994). Behavioral treatment of sexual dysfunctions in sexual assault survivors. In I.R. Stuart and J.G. Greer (Eds.), *Victims of sexual aggression: Treatment of children, women and men* (pp. 211-233). New York: Van Nostrand Reinhold Company.

Becker, J. and Stein, R. (1991). Is sexual erotica associated with sexual deviance in adolescent males? *International Journal of Law and Psychiatry, 14*(1/2), pp. 85-95.

Berliner, L. and Conte, J. (1990). The process of victimization: The victims' perspective. *Child Abuse and Neglect, 14*(1), pp. 29-40.

Black, C. and DeBlassie, R. (1993). Sexual abuse in male children and adolescents: Indicators, effects, and treatments. *Adolescence, 28*(109), Spring, pp. 123-133.

Boyle, C. (1985). Sexual assault and the feminist judge. *Canadian Journal of Women in the Law, I,* pp. 93-107.

Braun, B.G. (1990). Dissociative disorders as sequelae to incest. In R.P. Kluft (Ed.), *Incest related syndromes of adult psychopathology* (pp. 227-246). Washington, DC: American Psychiatric Press.

Brehm, S. and Kassin, S. (1993). *Social psychology.* Boston, MA: Houghton Mifflin Company.

Briere, J. (1984). *The effects of childhood sexual abuse on later psychological functioning: Defining a post-sexual-abuse syndrome.* Paper presented at the Third National Conference on Sexual Victimization of Children. Washington, DC: Children's Hospital National Medical Center, April.

Briere, J. (1992). *Child abuse trauma: Theory and treatment of the lasting effects.* Newbury Park, CA: Sage Press.

Briere, J. and Elliott, D. (1994). Immediate and long-term impacts of child sexual abuse. *The Future of Children, 4*(2), Summer/Fall, pp. 54-69.

Briere, J. and Runtz, M. (1989). University males' sexual interest in children: Predicting potential indices of "pedophilia" in a nonforensic sample. *Child Abuse and Neglect, 13*(1), pp. 65-75.

Brongersma, E. (1991). Boy-lovers and their influence on boys: Distorted research and anecdotal observations. *Journal of Homosexuality, 20*(1/2), pp. 145-173. Binghamton, NY: The Haworth Press.

Brown, M. and Gilligan, C. (1992). *Meeting at the crossroads: Women's psychology and girls' development.* New York: Ballantine Books.

Browne, A. (1987). *When battered women kill.* New York: The Free Press.

Browne, A. and Finkelhor, D. (1986). Impact of child sexual abuse: A review of the research. *Psychological Bulletin, 9*(9), pp. 66-77.

Brownmiller, S. (1975). *Against our will: Men, women, and rape.* New York: Bantam Books.

Burnam, M., Stein, J., Golding, J., Siegel, J., Sorenson, S., Forsythe, A., and Telles, A. (1988). Sexual assault and mental disorders in a community population. *Journal of Consulting and Clinical Psychology, 56*(6), pp. 843-850.

Butler, S. (1978). *Conspiracy of silence: The trauma of incest.* San Francisco, CA: New Glide Publications.

Caplan, P. (1993). Don't blame mother: Scapegoating and myths often keep natural allies apart. *Ms. Magazine, 2*(12), September, p. 96.

CARE (Child Abuse Research in Education) Productions (1985). Classroom Safety Training Materials. Surrey, British Columbia: CARE.

Carmen, E., Rieker, P., and Mills, T. (1987). *Victims of violence and psychiatric illness.* Washington, DC: American Psychiatric Press.

Carnes, P. (1983). *The sexual addiction.* New York: CompCare Publications.

Chesney-Lind, M. (1997). *The female offender: Girls, women, and crime.* Thousand Oaks, CA: Sage Publications.

Clarke, J.I. and Dawson, C. (1998). *Growing up again: Parenting ourselves, parenting our children,* Second edition. Center City, MN: Hazelden.

Cloud, J. (1998). A matter of hearts. *Time Magazine, 151*(17), May 4, pp. 60-64.

Coates, L., Bavelas, J., and Gibson, J. (1994). *Discourse and society.* London: Sage Publications.

Cohen, W. and Boucher, R. (1972). Misunderstandings about sex criminals. *Sexual Behavior, 2*(2), p. 57.

Committee for Children (1996). *What do I say now? How to help your child from sexual abuse.* Video. Committee for Children. Seattle, WA.

Conte, R., Wolf, S., and Smith, T. (1989). What sexual offenders tell us about prevention strategies. *Child Abuse and Neglect, 13*(2), pp. 293-301.

Cook, G. (1989). Grooming male children: A brief overview. Unpublished document.

Coontz, S. (1992). *The way we never were.* New York: Basic Books.

Cooper, W.H. (1981). Ubiquitous halo. *Psychological Bulletin, 90*(2), pp. 218-244.

Copeland, L. (1976). *Sexual abuse of children.* San Francisco, CA: Queen's Bench Foundation.

Corey, G. (1996). *Theory and practice of counseling and psychotherapy,* Fifth edition. Pacific Grove, CA: Brooks/Cole Publishing Company.

Craig, M.E. (1990). Coercive sexuality in dating relationships: A situational model. *Clinical Psychology Review, 10*(4), pp. 395-423.

Crepault, C. and Coulture, M. (1980). Men's erotic fantasies. *Archives of Sexual Behavior, 9*(6), pp. 565-581.

Crews, F. (1994a). The myth of repressed memory. *The New York Review of Books, XLI*(19), pp. 54-59.

Crews, F. (1994b). Victims of repressed memory. *The New York Review of Books, XLI*(20), pp. 49-59.

Dana, R.H. (1993). *Multicultural assessment perspectives for professional psychology.* Boston, MA: Allyn and Bacon.

Daro, D. (1998). Prevention of child sexual abuse. *Future of Children, 4*(2), Summer/Fall, pp. 198-223.

de Becker, G. (1997). *The gift of fear: Survival signals that protect us from violence.* New York: Little Brown and Company.

de Becker, G. (1999). *Protecting the gift: Keeping children and teenagers safe (and parents sane).* New York: The Dial Press.

De Francis, V. (1969). *Protecting children of sex crimes.* Denver, CO: American Humane Association.

de Young, M. (1988). The indignant page: Techniques of neutralization in the publications of pedophilia organizations. *Child Abuse and Neglect, 12,* pp. 583-591.

DeAngelis, T. (1995). A nation of hermits: The loss of community. *The APA Monitor, 26*(9), pp. 1-46.

Delin, B. (1978). *The sex offender.* Boston, MA: Beacon Press.

Doe, Jane (aka, Pamela Freyd) (1992). How could this happen? Coping with a false accusation of incest and rape. *Issues in Child Abuse Accusations, 3*(3), pp. 154-165.

Donnelly, J. (1989). *Universal human rights in theory and practice.* Ithaca, NY: Cornell University Press.

Drieblatt, I. (1982). *Issues in the evaluation of the sex offender.* A presentation at the Washington State Psychological Association Meeting. Seattle, Washington, May.

Editorial (1999). Science, politics, and pedophilia. *Psychological Science Agenda, 12*(5), September/October, pp. 1-2.

Eibel-Eibesfeldt, I. (1990). Dominance, submission, and love: Sexual pathologies from the perspective of ethology. In Feierman, J.R. (Ed.), *Pedophilia: Biosocial dimensions* (pp. 150-175). New York: Springer-Verlag.

Elliott, M. (1993). *Female sexual abuse of children.* New York: The Guilford Press.

Elliott, M., Browne, K., and Kilcoyne, J. (1995). Child sexual abuse prevention: What offenders tell us. *Child Abuse and Neglect, 19*(5), pp. 579-594.

Elmer-Dewitt, P. (1995). Cyberporn. *Time Magazine, 146*(1), pp. 38-45.

Fehrenbach, P., Smith, W., Monasterasky, C., and Deisher, R. (1986). Adolescent sexual offenders: Offender and offense characteristics. *American Journal of Orthopsychiatry, 56*(2), April, pp. 225-233.

Feierman, J.R. (Ed.) (1990). *Pedophilia: Biosocial dimensions.* New York: Springer-Verlag.

Ferracuti, F. (1972). Incest between father and daughter. In H.L.P. Resnick and M.E. Wolfgang (Eds.), *Sexual behaviors.* Boston, MA: Little Brown and Company.

Festinger, L. (1957). *A theory of cognitive dissonance.* Stanford, CA: Stanford University Press.

Finkel, K. (1984). Sexual abuse of children in Canada. *Canadian Medical Association Journal, 130*(2), pp. 345-348.

Finkel, K. (1987). Sexual abuse of children: An update. *Canadian Medical Association Journal, 136*(4), February 1, pp. 245-252.

Finkelhor, D. (1978). *Sexual victimization of children in a normal population.* Paper presented to the Second International Congress on Child Abuse and Neglect, September, pp. 11-15.

Finkelhor, D. (1979a). *Sexually victimized children.* New York: The Free Press.

Finkelhor, D. (1979b). What's wrong with sex between adults and children? Ethics and the problem of sexual abuse. *American Journal of Orthopsychiatry, 49*(4), October, pp. 692-697.

Finkelhor, D. (1981). The sexual abuse of boys. *Victimology: An International Journal, 6,* pp. 71-84.

Finkelhor, D. (1982). Sexual abuse: A sociological perspective. *Child Abuse and Neglect, 6,* pp. 95-102.

Finkelhor, D. (1984). *Long term effects of sexual abuse in child sexual abuse: New theory and research.* New York: The Free Press.

Finkelhor, D. (1991). Response to Bauserman. *Journal of Homosexuality, 20*(1/2), pp. 313-315.

Freeman-Longo, R.E. and Wall, R.V. (1986). Changing a lifetime of sexual crime. *Psychology Today, 20*(3), March, pp. 58-64.

Freund, K., and Kuban, M. (1994). The basis of the abused abuser theory of pedophilia: A further elaboration on an earlier study. *Archives of Sexual Behavior, 23*(5), October, pp. 553-563.

Freyd, J.J. (1994). Personal perspectives on the delayed memory debate. *Treating Abuse Today, 3*(5), pp. 13-20.

Freyd, W. (1995). *Letter to WGBH.* Reported by Kenneth Pope at the Washington Psychological Association Annual Meeting, October 21. Tacoma, WA: Washington Psychological Association.

Frude, N. (1982). The sexual nature of sexual abuse: A review of the literature. *Child Abuse and Neglect, 6*(2), pp. 211-223.

Gagnon, J. (1965). Female child victims of sex offenses. *Social Problems, 13*(2), pp. 176-192.

Gale Research (1995). *Gale's quotations: Who said what?* (CD-ROM). Gale Research Incorporated.

Gannett News Service (1995). Molesters fool many with 'nice guy' syndrome. *Olympian,* December 10, p. A12.

Gardner, R.A. (1993). True and false child sexual abuse allegations. *Workshop for Mental Health Professionals,* October 28, Orlando, Florida.

Glickauf-Hughes, C. and Wells, M. (1995). Narcissistic characters with obsessive features: Diagnostic and treatment considerations. *American Journal of Psychoanalysis, 55*(2), pp. 129-144.

Goleman, D. (1985). *Vital lies, simple truths: The psychology of self-deception.* New York: Simon and Schuster.

Goodwin, J. (1985). Credibility problems in multiple personality disordered patients and abused children. In R.P. Kluft (Ed.), *Childhood antecedents of multiple personality* (pp. 1-20). Washington, DC: American Psychiatric Press.

Green, R. (1987). Exposure to explicit sexual materials and sexual assualt: A review of behavioral and social science research. In M.R. Walsh (Ed.), *The psychology of women: Ongoing debates.* New Haven, CT: Yale University Press.

Greenberg, N. (1979). The epidemiology of childhood sexual abuse. *Pediatric Annals, 8*(5), May.

Groth, N. (1979). *Men who rape: The psychology of the sex offender.* New York: Plenum.

Groth, N., Burgess, A., Birnbaum, H., and Gary, T. (1978). A study of the child molester: Myths and realities. *LAE Journal of the American Criminal Justice Association, 41*(1), Winter/Spring, pp. 17-22.

Halliday, L. (1985). *Sexual abuse: Counseling issues and concerns.* Campbell River, BC: Ptarmigan Press.

Halliday, L. (1995). *Sexual abuse in Canada: An update.* Presented at the International Women's Day Conference at Comox, BC, by the British Columbia Teacher's Federation, May.

Halliday-Sumner, L. (1997a). *Sexual abuse: Disclosures.* Courtenay, British Columbia: LAlyn Publications.

Halliday-Sumner, L. (1997b). *Sexual abuse: Working with first nations people.* Courtenay, British Columbia: LAlyn Publications.

Halliday-Sumner, L. (1997c). *Sexual offenders in Canada: A directory.* Courtenay, British Columbia: LAlyn Publications.

Hamilton, G.V. (1929). *A research in marriage.* New York: Albert and Charles Boni.

Hare, R.D. (1991). The Hare psychopathy checklist, Revised. Toronto, Ontario: Multihealth Systems.

Hare, R.D. (1993). *Without conscience: The disturbing world of the psychopaths among us.* New York: Pocket Books.

Harms, R., James, D., Beland, K., Anderson, M. (1986). *Talking about touching.* Seattle, WA: Committee for Children.

Harms, R. and van Dam, C. (1992). *Child abuse prevention: What the educator needs to know.* Olympia, WA: Office of the Superintendent of Public Instruction.

Heakes, G. (1999). Shock, anger over kiddie porn ruling. *Province,* January 17, p. A2.

Hergenhahn, B.R. (1992). *An introduction to the history of psychology.* Belmont, CA: Wadsworth Publishing Company.

Herman, J. (1981). *Father daughter incest.* Cambridge, MA: Harvard University Press.

Herman, J. (1986). Histories of violence in an outpatient population. *American Journal of Orthospsychiatry, 56,* pp. 137-141.

Herman, J., Perry, C., and van der Kolk, B. (1989). Childhood trauma in borderline personality disorder. *American Journal of Psychiatry, 146(4),* April, pp. 490-495.

Ingrassia, M., Nayyar, C., Miller, S., and Mabry, M. (1995). Calvin's world. *Newsweek,* September 11, pp. 60-66.

Jacobson, N.S. and Gurman, A.S. (Eds.) (1995). *Clinical handbook of couple therapy.* New York: The Guilford Press.

James, B. and Nasjleti, M. (1983). *Treating sexually abused children and their families.* Palo Alto, CA: Consulting Psychologists.

Jenkins, P. (1998). *Moral panic: Changing concepts of the child molester in modern America.* New Haven, CT: Yale University Press.

Jones, G.P. (1991). Study of intergenerational intimacy in North America: Beyond politics and pedophilia. *Journal of Homosexuality, 20(1/2),* pp. 275-296.

Joseph, C. (1995). Scarlet wounding. *The Journal of Psychohistory, 23(1),* pp. 2-17.

Kaplan, M., Abel, G., Cunningham-Rathner, J., and Mittleman, M. (1990). The impact of parolees' perception of confidentiality of their self-reported sex crimes. *Annals of Sex Research, 3(3),* pp. 293-393.

Keith-Spiegel, P. and Koocher, G. (1985). *Ethics in psychology: Professional standards and cases.* New York: Random House.

Kempe, R. and Kempe, H. (1984). *The common secret: Sexual abuse of children and adolescents.* New York: W.H. Freeman and Company.

Kerr, M. and Bowen, M. (1988). *Family evaluation: An approach based on Bowen theory.* New York: W.W. Norton and Company.

Kessler, R.C., McGonagle, K.A., Zhao, S., Nelson, C., Hughes, M., Eshlemann, S., Wittchon, H., Kender, K. (1994). Lifetime and 12-month prevalence of *DSM-III-R* psychiatric disorders in the United States. *Archives of General Psychiatry, 51(1),* January pp. 8-19.

Kilpatrick, D., Best, C., Veronen, L., Amick, A., Villephonteaux, L., and Ruff, G. (1985). Mental health correlates of criminal victimization: A random community survey. *Journal of Consulting and Clinical Psychology, 53(6),* pp. 866-873.

Kincaid, J.R. (1998). *Erotic innocence: The culture of child molesting.* Durham, NC: Duke University Press.

Kinsey, A.C., Pomeroy, W.B., Martin, C.E., and Gebhard, P.H. (1948). *Sexual behavior in the human male.* Philadelphia, PA: Saunders.

Kluft, R. (Ed.) (1985). *Childhood antecedents of multiple personality disorder.* Washington, DC: American Psychiatric Press.

Kluft, R.P. (Ed.) (1990). *Incest related syndromes of adult psychopathology.* Washington, DC: American Psychiatric Press.

Kolb, B. and Whishaw, I.Q. (1996). *Fundamentals of human neuropsychology.* New York: W.H. Freeman and Company.

Landis, J. (1956). Experience of 500 children with adult sexual deviance. *Psychiatric Quarterly Supplement, 30*(1), pp. 91-109.

Langer, E. (1989). *Mindfulness.* Reading, MA: Addison-Wesley.

Langevin, R., Wrighty, P., and Handy, L. (1989). Characteristics of sex offenders who were sexually victimized as children. *Annals of Sex Research, 2*(3), pp. 227-253.

Lanktree, C., Briere, J., and Zaidi, L. (1991). Incidence and impact of sexual abuse in a child outpatient sample: The role of direct inquiry. *Child Abuse & Neglect, 15*(4), pp. 447-453.

Lee, K. (1985). Six sex laws violate rights, says judge: Teacher acquitted. *Times Colonist,* (Victoria, British Columbia), June 15, p. A2.

Leo, J. (1993). Pedophiles in the schools. *U.S. News and World Report,* October 11, p. 37.

Lerner, H.G. (1985). *The dance of anger: A woman's guide to changing the patterns of intimate relationships.* New York: Harper & Row Publishers.

Lerner, H.G. (1993). *The dance of deception: Pretending and truth-telling in women's lives.* New York: HarperCollins Publishers.

Levine, M. and Perkins, D. (1987). *Principles of community psychology.* New York: Oxford University Press.

Li, C.K. (1991). The main thing is being wanted: Some case studies on adult sexual experiences with children. *Journal of Homosexuality, 20*(1/2) pp. 129-143.

Linson, A. (Producer) and Caton-Jones, M. (Director). (1993). *This boy's life.* (Film). Available from Warner Home Video, Burbank, CA.

Lloyd, C. (1987). Sex offender programs: Is there a role for occupational therapy? *Occupational Therapy in Mental Health, 7*(3), Fall, pp. 55-67.

Loewenstein, R. (1990). Somatoform disorders in victims of incest and child abuse. In R.P. Kluft (Ed.), *Incest: Related syndromes of adult psychopathology* (pp. 75-112). Washington, DC: American Psychiatric Press.

Loftus, E. (1991). *Witness for the defense.* New York: St. Martin's Press.

Loftus, E. (1993). The reality of repressed memories. *American Psychologist, 48*(5), pp. 518-537.

Lukianowicz, N. (1972). Incest I: Paternal incest. *British Journal of Psychiatry, 120,* pp. 301-313.

Malamuth, N. (1981). Rape proclivity among males. *Journal of Social Issues, 17*(4), pp. 138-157.

Margoshes, D. (1986). Noyes: How the system failed. *The Vancouver Sun,* Wednesday, June 11, p. B3.

Marriott, M. (1995). Stealth baby-sitting. *Newsweek,* August 14.

Masson, J. (1984). *The assault on truth: Freud's suppression of the seduction theory.* New York: Farrar, Strauss and Giroux.

Masters, W.H., Johnson, V.E., and Kolodny, R.C. (1988). *Human Sexuality.* Glenview, IL: Scott-Foresman/Little Brown College Division.

Masterson, J.F. (1988). *The search for the real self: Unmasking the personality disorders of our age.* New York: The Free Press.

Mayer, A. (1992). *Women sex offenders: Treatment and dynamics.* Holmes Beach, FL: LP Learning Publications, Inc.

McConnell, J. (1980). *Understanding human behavior,* Third edition. New York: Holt, Rinehart and Winston.

Meloy, R. (1988). *The psychopathic mind: Origins, dynamics, and treatment.* Northvale, NJ: Jason Aronson, Inc.

Miller, A. (1990). *Banished knowledge: Facing childhood injuries.* New York: Doubleday.

Millon, T. (1996). *Disorders of personality.* New York: John Wiley and Sons, Inc.

Minuchin, S. (1974). *Familes and family therapy.* Cambridge, MA: Harvard University Press.

Minuchin, S. and Fishman, H. (1981). *Family therapy techniques.* Cambridge, MA: Harvard University Press.

Mohr, J.W., Turner, R.E., and Jerry, M.B. (1964). *Pedophilia and exhibitionism.* Toronto, Ontario: University of Toronto Press.

Money, J. (1986). Statement on pornography. *SIECCAN Journal* (The Sex Information and Education Council of Canada), *1*(2), Winter, pp. 23-27.

Money, J. (1990). Pedophilia: A specific instance of new phylism theory applied to paraphilic lovemaps. In J.R. Feierman (Ed.), *Pedophilia: Biosocial dimensions.* New York: Springer-Verlag.

Murphy, W., Haynes, M., Stalgaitis, S., and Flanagan, B. (1986). Differential sexual responding among four groups of sexual offenders against children. *Journal of Psychopathology and Behavioral Assessment, 8*(4), pp. 339-353.

Nolan, R. (1998). Standoff ends in surrender. *The Olympian,* November 6, pp. A1-A2.

Nolan, R. (1999). Sex assault awareness is protection. *The Olympian,* April 12, p. A8.

Owen, D. (1999). Golf: It turns out to be a very risky business. *The New Yorker,* April 12, *75*(7), pp. 52-57.

Patten, S., Gatz, Y., Jones, B., and Thomas, D. (1989). Posttraumatic stress disorder and the treatment of sexual abuse. *Social Work,* July, *34*(4), p. 381.

Peters, S. (1984). The relationships between childhood sexual victimization and adult depression among Afro-American and White women. Unpublished doctoral dissertation, University of California, Los Angeles.

Pipher, M. (1994). *Reviving Ophelia.* New York: Ballantine Books.

Pipher, M. (1996). *The shelter of each other: Rebuilding our families.* New York: Ballantine Books.

Pope, K. (1995). FMSF scientific and advisory board as described by the FMSF. Washington Psychological Association Annual Meeting, October 21. Tacoma, Washington.

Plummer, T. (1991). The Ophelia syndrome. *BYU Today*, January, pp. 25-38.

Putnam, F. (1985). Dissociation as a response to extreme trauma. In R.P. Kluft (Ed.), *Childhood antecedents of multiple personality* (pp. 65-98). Washington, DC: American Psychiatric Press.

Quinsey, V., Harris, G., Rice, M., and Cormier, C. (1998). *Violent offenders: Appraising and managing risk*. Washington, DC: American Psychological Association.

Ratican, K. (1992). Sexual abuse survivors: Identifying symptoms and special treatment considerations. *Journal of Counseling and Development, 71,* September/October, pp. 33-38.

Reuters News Service (1999). Many pedophile tourists turning to Latin American destinations. *The Vancouver Sun*, November 27, p. A22.

Revised Code of Washington/RCW (1994). *Washington Criminal Code.* Title 9A RCW.

Revitch, E., and Weiss, R.G. (1962). The pedophiliac offender. *Diseases of the Nervous System, 23,* pp. 73-78.

Rind, B., Tromovitch, P., and Bauserman, R. (1998). A meta-analytic examination of assumed properties of child sexual abuse using college samples. *Psychological Bulletin, 124*(1), pp. 22-53.

Rispens, J., Aleman, A., and Goudena, P. (1997). Prevention of child sexual abuse victimization: A meta-analysis of school programs. *Child Abuse and Neglect, 21*(10), October, pp. 975-987.

Rosenthal, R. and Jacobson, L. (1968). *Pygmalion in the classroom: Teacher expectation and pupils' intellectual development.* New York: Holt, Rhinehart and Winston.

Roys, D.T. (1995). Psychoeducation for incarcerated sex offenders in Georgia correctional institutions. *The Network, 13*(1), pp. 53-57.

Ruedrich, S. and Wilkinson, L. (1992). Deviant sexual responsiveness on penile plethysmography using visual stimuli: Alleged child molesters vs. normal control subjects. *Journal of Nervous and Mental Disease, 180*(3), pp. 207-208.

Rush, F. (1980). *The best kept secret: Sexual abuse of children.* New York: McGraw-Hill Book Company.

Russell, D.E.H. (1983). The incidence and prevalence of intrafamilial and extrafamilial sexual abuse of female children. *Child Abuse and Neglect, 7,* pp. 133-146.

Russell, D.E.H. (1984). *Sexual exploitation: Rape, child sexual abuse, and workplace harrassment.* Beverly Hills, CA: Sage Publications.

Salter, A.C. (1988). *Treating child sex offenders and victims.* Newbury Park, CA: Sage Publications.

Salter, A.C. (1995). *Transforming trauma: A guide to understanding and treating adult survivors of child sexual abuse.* Newbury Park, CA: Sage Publications.

Sanford, L. (1980). *The silent children: A parent's guide to the prevention of child sexual abuse.* New York: McGraw-Hill Book Company.

Saylor, M. (1979). *A guided self-help approach to treatment of the habitual sex offender.* Paper presented to the Twelfth Cropwood Conference, Cambridge, England, December 7-9.

Schetky, D.H. (1990). A review of the literature on the long-term effects of childhood sexual abuse. In R.P. Kluft (Ed.), *Incest related syndromes of adult psychopathology* (pp. 35-54). Washington, DC: American Psyhiatric Press.

Schlank, A. and Cohen, F. (1999). *The sexual predator: Law, policy, evaluation, and treatment.* Kingston, NJ: Civic Research Institute.

Schlessinger, L. (1996), *How could you do that?* New York: HarperCollins.

Schmidt, G. (1991). Foreword: The debate on pedophilia. *The Journal of Homosexuality, 20*(1/2), pp. 1-4.

Schmitt, D. (1994). *Readings in social psychology: Perspectives on individual behavior.* New York: Simon and Schuster.

Schoemer, K. and Chang, Y. (1995). The cult of cute. *Newsweek,* August 28, pp. 54-58.

Schwarz, R. and Gilligan, S. (1995). The devil is in the details: Fact and fiction in the recovered memory debate. *The Family Therapy Networker, 19*(2), March/April, pp. 21-23.

Scully, D. (1980). *Men who control women's health.* Boston, MA: Houghton Mifflin Company.

Sedney, M.A. and Brooks, B. (1984). Factors associated with a history of childhood sexual experiences in a nonclinical female poulation. *Journal of the American Academy of Child Psychiatry, 23*(2), pp. 215-218.

Sgroi, S. (1985). *Handbook of clinicial intervention in child sexual abuse.* Lexington, MA: Lexington Books.

Silbert, M. (1994). Treatment of prostitute victims of sexual assault. In I.R. Stuart and J.G. Greer (Eds.), *Victims of sexual aggression: Treatment of children, women and men* (pp. 251-270). New York: Van Nostrand Reinhold Company.

Silva, D.C. (1990). Pedophilia: An autobiography. In J.R. Feierman (Ed.), *Pedophilia: Biosocial dimensions* (pp. 464-493). New York: Springer-Verlag.

Singer, K. (1989). Group work with men who experienced incest in childhood. *American Journal of Orthopsychiatry, 59*(3), pp. 468-472.

Singer, P. (1991). Ethics. *The New Encyclopedia Britannica,* Volume 18, Edition 15, p. 492-521.

Slovenko, R. (1971). Statutory rape. *Medical Aspects of Human Sexuality, 5,* pp. 155-167.

Snyder, M. and Swann, W.B. (1978). Behavioral confirmation in social interaction: From social perception to social reality. *Journal of Personality and Social Psychology, 36,* pp. 1202-1212.

Solomon, R.L. (1980). The opponent-process theory of acquired motivation. *American Psychologist, 35,* pp. 691-712.

Steinem, G. (1983). *Outrageous acts and everyday rebellions.* New York: Holt, Rhinehart and Winston.

Summit, R. (1982). Beyond belief: The reluctant discovery of incest. In M. Kirk-patrick (Ed.), *Women's sexual experience: Explorations of the dark continent* (pp. 33-65). New York: Plenum Press.

Summit, R. (1989). The centrality of victimization: Regaining the focal point of recovery for survivors of child sexual abuse. *Psychiatric Clinics of North America, 12*(2), June, pp. 413-430.

Talbot, M. (1999). The truth about child abuse and the truth about children: Against innocence. *The New Republic,* March 15, *220*(11), pp. 27-39.

Taylor, R. (1984). Marital therapy in the treatment of incest: Social casework. *The Journal of Contemporary Social Work, 65*(4), pp. 195-202.

Templeman, T. and Stinnett, R. (1991). Patterns of sexual arousal and history in a "normal" sample of young men. *Archives of Sexual Behavior, 20*(2), pp. 137-150.

Terman, L.M. (1938). *Psychological factors in marital happiness.* New York: McGraw-Hill.

Thorstad, D. (1991). Man/boy love and the american gay movement. *Journal of Homosexuality, 20*(1/2), pp. 251-274.

Trickett, P.K. and Schellenbach, C.J. (Eds.) (1998). *Violence against children in the family and the community.* Washington, DC: American Psychiatric Association.

Vance, H.B. (Ed.) (1998). *Psychological assessment of children: Best practices for school and clinical settings.* New York: John Wiley and Sons, Inc.

van Dam, C. (1987). *A safety and first aid manual for the prevention and treatment of child sexual abuse.* Port Coquitlam, British Columbia: M.D. Angus and Associates Ltd.

van Dam, C. (1996). How child sexual molesters groom adults to gain access to children. Doctoral dissertation. Cincinnati, OH: The Union Institute.

van Dam, C. and Bates, C. (1986). Book Review of Masson's *The assault on truth: Freud's suppression of the seduction theory. The British Columbia Psychologist,* Fall, pp. 51-53.

van Dam, C., Halliday, L., and Bates, C. (1985). The occurrence of sexual abuse in a small community. *Canadian Journal of Community Mental Health, 4*(1), pp. 105-111.

van der Kolk, B. (1988). The trauma spectrum: The interaction of biological and social events in the genesis of the trauma response. *Journal of Traumatic Stress, 1*(3), pp. 273-290.

van der Kolk, B. (1994). The body keeps score: Memory and the evolving psycho-biology of posttraumatic stress. *Harvard Review Psychiatry* (pp. 253-265). Massachusetts General Hospital, Trauma Clinic. Boston, MA: Harvard Medi-cal School.

van der Kolk, B., Perry, J., and Herman, J. (1991). Childhood origins of self-destruc-tive behavior. *American Journal of Psychiatry, 148*(12), December, pp. 1665-1671.

van der Kolk, B. and van der Hart, O. (1989). Pierre Janet and the breakdown of adaptation in psychological trauma. *American Journal of Psychiatry, 146*(12), December, pp. 1530-1540.

Virkkunen, M. (1975). Victim precipitated pedophilia offenses. *British Journal of Criminology, 15*(2), pp. 175-180.

Wade, C. and Tavris, C. (1990). *Psychology,* Second edition. New York: Harper-Collins.

Walsh, M.R. (1987). *The psychology of women: Ongoing debates.* New Haven, CT: Yale University Press.

Ward, T., Hudson, S.M., and Marshall, W.L. (1995). Cognitive distortions and affective deficits in sex offenders: A cognitive deconstructionist interpretation. *Sexual Abuse: A Journal of Research and Treatment, 7(1),* pp. 67-84.

Wegner, D. and Schaeffer, D. (1978). The concentration of responsibility: An objective self-awareness analysis of group size effects in helping situations. *Journal of Pesonality and Social Psychology, 36,* pp. 147-155.

Weinberg, S.K. (1955). *Incest behavior.* Secaucus, NJ: Citadel Press.

Weiss, J., Rogers, E., Darwin, M.R., and Dutton, C.E. (1955). A study of girl sex victims. *Psychiatry Quarterly, 29,* pp. 1-27.

Westerlund, E. (1992). *Women's sexuality after childhood incest.* New York: W.W. Norton and Company.

West Vancouver Policemen's Association (WVPA) (1986). *Child sexual assault.* West Vancouver, British Columbia: Author.

Whorf, B. (1941). The relation of habitual thought and behavior to language. In L. Spier (Ed.), *Language, culture, and personality* (pp. 75-93). Menasha, WI: Sapir Memorial Publications Fund.

Whitmire, R. and Hale, E. (1995). Child molesters get away with it. *The Olympian,* Sunday, December 10, pp. A1-A2.

Wiebe, A. (1999a). Woman tells of assaults by teacher. *Prince Albert Herald,* January 26, p. A1.

Wiebe, A. (1999b). Carruthers claims she was used in relationship. *Prince Albert Herald,* January 29, p. A2.

Wolfe, F.A. (1985). *Twelve female sexual offenders.* Paper presented at Next Steps in Research on the Assessment and Treatment of Sexually Aggressive Persons (Paraphiliacs), pp. 52-58. St. Louis, MO: March 3-5.

Wright, L. (1994). *Remembering Satan: A case of recovered memory and the shattering of an American family.* New York: Alfred A. Knopf.

Wyatt, G. and Powell, G. (1988). *Lasting effects of child sexual abuse.* Newbury Park, CA: Sage Publications.

Wylie, M. (1993). Shadow of a doubt. *The Family Therapy Networker, 17*(5) September/October, pp. 18-30.

Additional Resources

Adolescent Sexual Abuse Prevention Project
240 North James St., Suite 103
Newport, DE 19804

American Humane Association, Children's Division
63 Inverness Dr. East
Englewood, CO 80112-5117
<http://www.americanhumane.org>

Center for Child Protection
Children's Hospital and Health Center
3020 Children's Way Box 5017
San Diego, CA 92123
<http://www.chasd.org/ccphome.htm>

Linda Halliday-Sumner has a very helpful Web site:
<http://www.breakingthesilence.com>

The National Clearinghouse on Child Abuse
and Neglect Information
330 C St. SW
Washington, DC 20447
<http://www.calib.com/nccanch>

Prevent Child Abuse America
200 South Michigan Ave., 17th Floor
Chicago, IL 60604
<http://www.childabuse.org>

The Safer Society Foundation
P.O. Box 340
Brandon, VT 05733
<http://www.safersociety.org>

Index

Page numbers followed by the letter "b" indicate a box; those followed by the letter "n" indicate a note.

"Above reproach," 3, 5, 38, 102, 103
Access
    to child victims, 8, 11-12
    Mr. Smith, 13
"Accidental slips," 43, 46, 47-48
Accidents, molester denial, 127
Addiction, child molesters, 91-92, 129
Adolescents, deviant sexual behavior in, 78, 85-86
Adult community, grooming process, 37, 38, 39, 87-88, 89b, 96-103, 143-144
Affect disorders, 65, 66
After-school child care, 46, 86
Age, child sexual abuse, 76
Age discrimination, 135
Alcohol abuse, 60b, 66, 94-95
Amnesty for Child Sexuality, 135
Amygdala, 65
Anal fissures, 69
Anger, 61
Anorexia, 65
Anxiety disorders, 60b, 63, 66

Baby-sitters, as molesters, 83, 84, 86, 99, 107, 116-117, 153
Balmoral Junior Secondary School, Robert Noyes, 28
Bed wetting, 43
Being There, 163

Biosocial learning theory, child molesters, 91
Blame the victim, 94, 122, 124-125, 127-128, 129-131, 191
"Bogeyman," 81
Borderline personality disorder, 64-65
Bouchard, Donna, 30-36, 141, 152-153, 158-159, 180, 181-182
Boundaries, development of, 189
Boundary setting, 185-189
Boundary violations, 68, 171, 182, 183, 184, 186-187
    Mr. Martin, 157-158
    Mr. Smith, 13-14, 15, 51-52, 59, 124, 155, 158, 186
    warning sign, 144, 145b, 157-158
Bribery, Mr. Smith, 13, 14, 51, 102
Bulimia, 65

Camp counselor, Robert Noyes, 28
Canada
    child pornography, 58
    childhood sexual abuse impact, 66
    incarceration of sexual offenders, 78
Candy, Mr. Smith, 13, 14, 15, 48, 51-52, 59, 102
Care Kit, The, 138-139
Career choices, child molesters, 11-12

Carruthers, Margaret (case study
    five), 6n, 30-36
  disclosure, 141
  insider status, 183-184
  offensive action, 158-160
  peer-like relation, 152-153, 178
  physical contact, 33, 34, 181-182
  preference for teenagers, 180
  privacy violations, 50-51
Case studies
  One (Mr. Smith), 12-16, 47, 48,
    51-52, 59, 100-103, 109, 111,
    124, 141-142, 145, 147, 151,
    155, 156-157, 179-180, 183,
    186, 187, 192
  Two (Jeffrey Clay), 16-25, 41-42,
    47, 48, 58-59, 105, 110, 124,
    145, 151, 155, 164-167, 187,
    192
  Three (Mr. Martin), 25-27, 48, 99,
    152, 157-158, 159
  Four (Robert Noyes), 6n, 27-30,
    44, 47, 124, 145, 149,
    180-181, 192-193
  Five (Margaret Carruthers), 30-36,
    50-51, 141, 152-153, 178,
    180, 181-182, 183-184
Characterological disorders, 64
Charm
  child molesters, 1, 3-4, 11, 39,
    162-169, 183
  interventions against, 169
  warning sign, 143-149, 145b
Child molestation, legal definitions
    of, 201, 202
Child molesters
  advocacy for, 195-196
  characteristics of, 8, 82, 109, 151,
    169, 171, 172
  child target characteristics,
    104-108
  community support for, 11, 16
  defense of, 131-132, 158-160,
    191-193
  denial mechanism, 127-135

Child molesters *(continued)*
  explanations of behavior, 90-92
  identifying potential, 8, 137-138
  justifications of, 8, 90, 95-96, 130
  misconceptions about, 81, 85,
    126-127
  preference for children, 144, 145b,
    153-154, 179-181
  reputation of, 3, 5, 12, 144-145
Child pornography, 57-58, 79, 94
Child Protective Services, 43
Child sexual abuse
  absence of clarity about, 42-44
  dynamics of, 7
  invisibility of, 5
  legal definitions, 49, 201-203
  minimization of, 58-59, 67, 89,
    197-198
  mores, social/cultural, 8, 58,
    67-68, 71-73
  predatory behavior, 1-3, 5, 6
  prevalence of, 7, 37, 75, 76-77,
    123-124, 196
  problem of, 57-60
  psychological definitions, 49-52
  psychological harm, 60-69
  research definitions, 44-45
  research on, 44-45
  social denial of, 122-127
  social impact of, 7
Child sexual abuse guidelines,
    medical exam, 43
Child victims, characteristics of,
    104-108
Childhood Sensuality Circle, 94, 134
Children
  fashion trends, 120
  grooming process, 8, 37, 38, 52,
    87-88, 89b, 103-113
  molesters preference for, 144,
    145b, 153-154, 179-181
  objectification of, 121
  self-defensive strategies, 4
  sexual attraction to, 89b, 90-92
  social attitudes toward, 115-117

Citizen of the Year, 11, 27
Clay, Jeffrey (case study two), 16-25
  boundary setting, 187
  community defense, 145, 164-165, 167, 192
  nescience, 41-42, 58-59, 124, 158, 164-165
  peer-like play, 151
  physical play, 47, 48, 155
  teaching competence, 165-166
  touch desensitization, 110
  victim targeting, 105
  wife of, 23-24
Closet narcissist, 168, 169, 189
Coaching
  Carruthers, Margaret, 30, 31, 32, 33-34, 35, 26
  voyeurism, 50-51
Coercion, child sexual abuse, 50, 61
Cognitive dissonance; adult grooming process, 100, 101
Committee for Children, 38
Community policies, child sexual abuse, 8
Community support
  child molesters, 146, 148-149
  Smith, Mr., 14-15, 101-103, 147
Complaints
  Clay, Jeffrey 17-20, 22
  Noyes, Robert, 29
  Smith, Mr., 14-15, 102, 103
Confidante, Margaret Carruthers, 32, 33-34
Confirmation bias, 102
Conformity studies, adult grooming process, 101-102
Consent, child sexual abuse, 69-71, 128-129
Contributing to the delinquency of a minor, prevalence of, 85
Conviction
  Carruthers, Margaret, 30
  Noyes, Robert, 29-30
Cook, Mr., 96-97, 107-108, 110-111, 167-168

Coquitlam Junior Secondary, Robert Noyes, 29
Counseling, of children, 22-23
"Cross-generational love," 195
Cultural issues, child sexual abuse, 8, 58, 67-68, 71-73
Cultural relativism, 71-73
Curriculum, child sexual abuse prevention, 22
"Cute," 91, 95, 119

Denial
  of child molester, 127-135
  of child sexual abuse, 122-127
  neutralization process, 92b, 93-94
  psychological term, 124
Depression, 60b, 66, 68
Desensitization, child victim, 103-104, 110-112, 182
Diagnostic and Statistical Manual of Mental Disorders, Fourth Edition (DSM-IV), criteria for:
  characterological disorders, 64
  narcissist, 168
  pedophilia, 55, 56
Diagnostic and Statistical Manual of Mental Disorders, Third Edition, Revised (DSM-III-R), criteria for
  multiple personality disorder, 65
  pedophilia, 55
  somatoform disorders, 64
Differentiation, 68, 106-107
Disclosure, 140-141
Discounting, 124
Dissension condemnation, neutralization process, 92b, 94
Dissociation, 34
Dissociative disorders, 65
Dissociative identity disorder, DSM-IV, 65
Distancing, 61

Dodd, Westley Allan, 46
Drug abuse, 60b, 66, 94-95

Electra complex, 122
Emic perspective, 72, 73
Emotional memory, 65
Emotional reactivity, 61
Enlightened viewpoint,
        neutralization process, 92b,
        94
Entertainment industry, role of, 120,
        125-126
Environmental clues, child
        molesters, 91
Ephebophilia, 53
Ethical issues, child sexual abuse,
        69-71
Ethical realism, 72
Ethical relativism, 72-73
Etic perspective, 72
Exclusive pedophilia, 55
Exhibitionism, 79
    as sexual abuse, 44
Exposure, prevalence of, 85
"Eye contact," grooming technique,
        107, 146

False memories, 75-76
False Memory Syndrome Foundation
        (FMSF), 147-148
Family
    characteristics of targeted, 99
    friends/members, molestation
        perpetrators, 83, 84, 85
Fantasy, child sexual abuse, 54-55,
        79
Fashion trends, role of, 119-120
Fathers, molestation perpetrators, 83,
        84
Females
    abuse unreported, 85
    blaming the victim, 125

Females *(continued)*
    child sexual abuse of, 75
    offenders, 56, 86-87
Films, sexualization of children,
        95-96, 120
Fixated offenders, 53
Fliess, Wilhelm, 122
Fondling, as sexual abuse, 44-45
"Foot-in-the door technique," 100,
        171
Foster children, Mr. Clay, 25
Framing, child molester, 101
Fred, child molester, 2-3, 155-156,
        180, 183, 185, 187
Freedom, 8
Freud, Sigmund, 64, 89, 122
Frottage, 58, 79

Girls, male preference training,
        118-119
"Good touch, bad touch," 138
Grant, Hugh, 100
Grooming process
    adult community, 37, 38, 39,
        87-88, 89b, 96-103, 143-144
    Carruthers, Margaret, 30, 31, 35
    child victims, 8, 37, 38, 52, 87-88,
        89b, 103-113
    dynamics of, 89b, 90-113
    Letourneau, Mary Kay, 87
"Grooming themselves," 127
Group home, Robert Noyes, 28

Handicapped children, Mr. Clay, 25
Health services, increased utilization
        of, 60b, 63, 64, 66
Helpfulness
    child molesters, 170-174
    interventions against, 170
    warning sign, 143-144, 145b,
        150-151
Henry, Joe, 104
Hobbies, child molesters, 11
Hostility, 61

Hypervigilance, child molesters, 169, 171
Hysteria, 64

Identification, child victim, 103-108
Image management, child molesters, 96, 99, 103, 146-147
Incest
    definition of, 53
    justification of, 130
    prevalence of, 85, 125
    runaways, 67
Incest offenders, definitions of, 52-55
Indecent exposure, prevalence of, 85
Indecent liberties, prevalence of, 85
Individual liberties, 8
Individuation, 68
Informed consent, child sexual abuse, 70-71
Injury denial, neutralization process, 92b, 93
Insider status
    child molesters, 182-185
    warning sign, 144, 145b, 156-157
"Intergenerational intimacy," 195
International policies, child sexual abuse, 8
Internet, child pornography, 57, 79
Intervention guidelines, 162b
Interventions, 8, 193
Intimacy, 61, 185
Isolation
    Carruthers, Margaret, 32-33, 35
    child victim, 103-104, 112
    family targets, 99

Jackson, Michael, 100
Justification
    child sexual abuse, 8, 90, 95-96, 126-135
    grooming process, 89b

"Kiddie porn," 79, 120
"Kissfeeding," 119
Klein, Calvin, 79

Lacunas, 124
Lap sitting, as sexual abuse, 51
"Lazy" offenders, 52
Learned helplessness, 62
Learning disabilities, 65
"Lesbian, The," 35
Letourneau, Mary Kay, 6n, 59, 87, 167, 168
Lewd behavior, prevalence of, 85
Lolita, 70
Love, child development, 197

Male fantasies, sexual abuse, 79
Males
    child sexual abuse of, 75
    offenders, 56, 78-79, 86, 87
    sexual arousal of, 90-91, 95
    sexual needs of, 90, 117-118, 121-122, 126, 127
    and unreported abuse, 85
"Markers," 31-32
Marriage, child molesters, 11
Martin, Mr. (case study three), 25-27
    bathing children, 48, 171
    boundary setting, 187
    boundary violations, 157-158
    peer-like play, 152
    single mothers, 99, 179
Massage, 42-43
"Master teacher," 31
Mental health services, increased utilization of, 63
Minimization
    child molester defense, 132, 134
    child sexual abuse, 58-59, 67, 89, 198
Modeling, entertainment industry, 120

Molestation
  extent of, 77
  legal definitions, 201
  perpetrators of, 83
  types of, 85, 86
  unreported, 85
Money, Mr. Smith, 13, 14, 51, 102
Moral issues, child sexual abuse,
  69-71
Mothers, blaming of, 130
Motivation, child sexual abuse, 53
Multiple personality disorder (MPD),
  65
Music teachers, 12

Name recognition, 99-100
Narcissists, personality traits,
  168-169, 189-191
National policies, child sexual abuse,
  8
Nechako Valley High School, Robert
  Noyes, 28-29
"Nervous breakdowns," 66
Neutralization, process of, 92b,
  92-96
Nonexclusive pedophilia, 55
North American Man-Boy Love
  Association (NAMBLA), 57,
  93, 94, 95-96, 134-135
Norwegian Pedophile Group, 135
Noyes, Robert (case study four), 6n,
  27-30
  community defense of, 192-193
  nescience, 44, 47, 124, 145, 149
  preference for children, 180-181

Objectification
  of female children, 121
  of women, 117, 121, 125
Obscene phone calls, 79
Obsessive-compulsive disorder, 60b,
  63
Oedipal complex, 122

Offensive action
  narcissists, 189-190
  warning sign, 144, 145b, 158-160
Ophelia Syndrome, 118
Opponent-process learning theory,
  child molesters, 91
Opportunistic behavior, molesters, 1
Oral sexual contact, 44

Pair bonding, 91
Panic attacks, 60b, 63
Parenting dysfunction, 60b, 68,
  106-107
Pedophile Information Exchange
  (PIE), 135
Pedophiles
  definitions of, 52-56
  justifications of, 90, 95-96, 130
Pedophilia, 47, 53
  advocacy of, 195-196
  DSM definitions, 55, 56
"Peeping Toms," 86
Peer-like behavior
  Carruthers, Margaret, 152-153,
    178
  child molesters, 108-109, 174-179
  child victim, 103-104, 108-110
  Clay, Jeffrey, 151
  Martin, Mr., 152
  Smith, Mr., 109, 151
  warning sign, 144, 145b, 151-153
Peers, sexual relations with, 45
Peers relationships, as sexual abuse,
  50
Personality disorders, 60b
"Pervert," 81
Physical abuse, child molesters,
  91-92
Physical contact, child molesters, 45,
  51, 154-156, 158, 181
Physical education teachers, 12
Physical play
  child molesters, 110, 112, 181-182
  Clay, Mr., 16, 21-22, 47, 110

Physical play *(continued)*
 Smith, Mr., 13, 14, 15, 47
 warning sign, 144, 154-156
Physical trauma, 69
Piaget, Jean, 70
Plethysmography, arousal
  measurement, 54
Police investigation
 Clay, Mr., 19
 Noyes, Robert, 30
Pornography
 availability of, 94
 dehumanizing role, 120-121
Post-traumatic stress disorder, 60b,
  65-66
Power
 child sexual abuse, 70
 sexual abuse, 34-35, 46, 50
 therapeutic relationship, 69
Pregnancy, 69
Prevalence, of child sexual abuse, 7,
  37, 75, 76-77, 123-124, 196
Prevention, 8, 38-39
 child-centered, 4, 38, 137-142
Prisoners
 child sexual abuse, 67
 sexually related offenses, 77-78
Privacy, invasion of, 33, 50-51
Prostitution, and child sexual abuse,
  67
Psychiatric disorders, child sexual
  abuse, 60b, 62, 64-66, 68
Psychological damage, child sexual
  abuse, 60-69
Psychopaths, 87-88, 103, 146

Rap music, 125
Rape
 legal definitions, 201
 prevalence of, 85
"Red flags," 31-32
Regressed offenders, 53
Regressive narcissist, 168
Rene Guyon Society, 57, 93, 94, 134

Reputation
 of child molesters, 3, 5, 12,
  144-145
 Clay, Mr.,18, 145
 Noyes, Robert, 145
 Smith, Mr., 12-13, 14, 145
Responsibility, child victim,
  103-104, 113
Role disturbance, Margaret
  Carruthers, 33
Roughhousing
 child molesters, 110, 112, 181-182
 Smith, Mr., 13, 14, 15
Runaway children, incest
  victimization, 67

Same-sex abuse, 34
School authorities,
 support for Mr. Clay, 17, 18, 20,
  21, 22, 41, 42
 support for Mr. Smith, 13
Screening checklist, sex offenders,
  145b
Secondary prevention, 137-138
Secrecy, sexual abuse, 49, 61
Self-injury, 63-64, 65
Self-perception theory, adult
  grooming process, 100
Sex education, 132
Sex offenders, 52
 characteristics of, 82, 151
 gender of, 56
 research, in defense of, 131-132
Sexual abuse, working definition,
  50b
Sexual Abuse Victims Anonymous
  (SAVA), 83
Sexual activity
 child molesters, 109
 sexual abuse, 49
Sexual aggression, toleration of, 126
Sexual arousal
 in males, 90-91, 95
 and violence, 120

Sexual attraction, grooming process, 89b, 90-92
Sexual contact, legal definition of, 201, 203
Sexual delusions, 66
Sexual development, 45
    disruption of, 60-61
Sexual dysfunction, 60b, 66
Sexual experience, molester's initial, 92
Sexual expression, pedophile need for, 90, 117-118, 126, 127
Sexual intercourse
    legal definition of, 201, 203
    as sexual abuse, 44-45, 49-50
Sexual minority, pedophiles, 57, 71-72, 73
Sexual misconduct
    legal definitions, 201, 202
    young males, 79
Sexual molesters, definitions of, 52-56
Sexual preoccupation, 66
Sexual talk, as sexual abuse, 49, 109, 176
Sexually transmitted diseases, 69
"Shared negative hallucination," 48
Sheldon, hostage taker, 145
Single parents, as targets, 99, 107, 116
Smith, Mr. (case study one), 12-16
    adult grooming, 100-103
    boundary violations, 13-14, 15, 51-52, 59, 124, 155, 186, 187
    community defense of, 145, 147, 192
    insider status, 156-157, 183
    nescience, 47-48
    peer-like behavior, 109, 151
    preference for children, 179-180
    safety program, 141-142
    touch desensitization, 111
Social attitudes, 8
Social services, increased utilization of, 60b, 63

Social work, child molestation as, 127-128
Social workers, Mr. Clay, 18-19
Social/cultural mores, child sexual abuse, 8, 58, 67
Somatoform disorders, DSM-III-R, 64, 65
Stadler, Matthew, 95-96
Stare, of psychopaths, 88
Statutory rape, prevalence of, 85
Stepfamilies, molestation risk, 83
Stepfathers, molestation perpetrators, 83, 84
"Stranger danger," 4, 81
Strangers, as molesters, 83-84, 85, 86
Stress, 115, 116, 126
Studiegroep Pedofilie, 135
Substance abuse, 66
Suicidal ideation, 60b, 63, 65
Supervision, absence of, 115, 116

"Teacher of the Year," 148
Teachers, 12
    Carruthers, Margaret, 30, 31, 32, 33-34, 35, 36
Teacher's union, defense of Jeffrey Clay, 23-24, 42, 192
Therapists, defense of child molesters, 131-132
Therapy
    for abusers, 46
    Clay, Jeffrey, 24
    Noyes, Robert, 28, 29
    victim treatment, 43-44
This Boy's Life, 162
Tickling
    child molesters, 181-182
    Clay, Mr., 16, 47
    Smith, Mr., 13, 14, 15
Time, for children, 115
Timing, child molester, 101
Touch, desensitization of, 110-112, 182

Touching
   Carruthers, Margaret, 33, 34,
      181-182
   Clay, Mr., 17-18, 19, 20, 23, 41
   Martin, Mr., 26, 48
   as sexual abuse, 43-44
Trust relationship
   grooming process, 97
   violating, 49-50, 68, 69

Uncles, molestation perpetrators, 83

Victimization denial, neutralization
      process, 92b, 93-94
Voyeurism, sexual abuse, 49-51, 79
Vulnerability, child victims, 104-108

Warning flags, 37, 144
Wergrupp Pedophilie, 135
Wives, blaming the victim, 129-131
Women
   infantalization of, 119
   mutilation of, 73
   social attitudes toward, 117-122
"Wonderland," child pornography,
      57-58

THE HAWORTH MALTREATMENT AND TRAUMA PRESS ®
Robert A. Geffner, PhD
Senior Editor

IDENTIFYING CHILD MOLESTERS: PREVENTING CHILD SEXUAL ABUSE BY RECOGNIZING THE PATTERNS OF THE OFFENDERS by Carla van Dam. (2000). "The definitive work on the subject . . . . Provides parents and others with the tools to recognize when and how to intervene." *Roger W. Wolfe, MA, Co-Director, N. W. Treatment Associates, Seattle, Washington*

POLITICAL VIOLENCE AND THE PALESTINIAN FAMILY: IMPLICATIONS FOR MENTAL HEALTH AND WELL-BEING by Vivian Khamis. (2000). "A valuable book . . . a pioneering work that fills a glaring gap in the study of Palestinian society." *Elia Zureik, Professor of Sociology, Queens University, Kingston, Ontario, Canada*

STOPPING THE VIOLENCE: A GROUP MODEL TO CHANGE MEN'S ABUSIVE ATTITUDES AND BEHAVIORS by David J. Decker. (1999). "A concise and thorough manual to assist clinicians in learning the causes and dynamics of domestic violence." *Joanne Kittel, MSW, LICSW, Yachats, Oregon*

STOPPING THE VIOLENCE: A GROUP MODEL TO CHANGE MEN'S ABUSIVE ATTITUDES AND BEHAVIORS, THE CLIENT WORKBOOK by David J. Decker. (1999).

BREAKING THE SILENCE: GROUP THERAPY FOR CHILDHOOD SEXUAL ABUSE, A PRACTITIONER'S MANUAL by Judith A. Margolin. (1999). "This book is an extremely valuable and well-written resource for all therapists working with adult survivors of child sexual abuse." *Esther Deblinger, PhD, Associate Professor of Clinical Psychiatry, University of Medicine and Dentistry of New Jersey School of Osteopathic Medicine*

"I NEVER TOLD ANYONE THIS BEFORE": MANAGING THE INITIAL DISCLOSURE OF SEXUAL ABUSE RE-COLLECTIONS by Janice A. Gasker. (1999). "Discusses the elements needed to create a safe, therapeutic environment and offers the practitioner a number of useful strategies for responding appropriately to client disclosure." *Roberta G. Sands, PhD, Associate Professor, University of Pennsylvania School of Social Work*

FROM SURVIVING TO THRIVING: A THERAPIST'S GUIDE TO STAGE II RECOVERY FOR SURVIVORS OF CHILDHOOD ABUSE by Mary Bratton. (1999). "A must read for all, including survivors. Bratton takes a life-long debilitating disorder and unravels its intricacies in concise, succinct, and understandable language." *Phillip A. Whitner, PhD, Sr. Staff Counselor, University Counseling Center, The University of Toledo, Ohio*

SIBLING ABUSE TRAUMA: ASSESSMENT AND INTERVENTION STRATEGIES FOR CHILDREN, FAMILIES, AND ADULTS by John V. Caffaro and Allison Conn-Caffaro. (1998). "One area that has almost consistently been ignored in the research and writing on child maltreatment is the area of sibling abuse. This book is a welcome and required addition to the developing literature on abuse." *Judith L. Alpert, PhD, Professor of Applied Psychology, New York University*

BEARING WITNESS: VIOLENCE AND COLLECTIVE RESPONSIBILITY by Sandra L. Bloom and Michael Reichert. (1998). "A totally convincing argument. . . . Demands careful study by all elected representatives, the clergy, the mental health and medical professions, representatives of the media, and all those unwittingly involved in this repressive perpetuation and catastrophic global problem." *Harold I. Eist, MD, Past President, American Psychiatric Association*

TREATING CHILDREN WITH SEXUALLY ABUSIVE BEHAVIOR PROBLEMS: GUIDELINES FOR CHILD AND PARENT INTERVENTION by Jan Ellen Burton, Lucinda A. Rasmussen, Julie Bradshaw, Barbara J. Christopherson, and Steven C. Huke. (1998). "An extremely readable book that is well-documented and a mine of valuable 'hands on' information. . . . This is a book that all those who work with sexually abusive children or want to work with them must read." *Sharon K. Araji, PhD, Professor of Sociology, University of Alaska, Anchorage*

THE LEARNING ABOUT MYSELF (LAMS) PROGRAM FOR AT-RISK PARENTS: LEARNING FROM THE PAST—CHANGING THE FUTURE by Verna Rickard. (1998). "This program should be a part of the resource materials of every mental health professional trusted with the responsibility of working with 'at-risk' parents." *Terry King, PhD, Clinical Psychologist, Federal Bureau of Prisons, Catlettsburg, Kentucky*

THE LEARNING ABOUT MYSELF (LAMS) PROGRAM FOR AT-RISK PARENTS: HANDBOOK FOR GROUP PARTICIPANTS by Verna Rickard. (1998). "Not only is the LAMS program designed to be educational and build skills for future use, it is also fun!" *Martha Morrison Dore, PhD, Associate Professor of Social Work, Columbia University, New York, New York*

BRIDGING WORLDS: UNDERSTANDING AND FACILITATING ADOLESCENT RECOVERY FROM THE TRAUMA OF ABUSE by Joycee Kennedy and Carol McCarthy. (1998). "An extraordinary survey of the history of child neglect and abuse in America. . . . A wonderful teaching tool at the university level, but should be required reading in high schools as well." *Florabel Kinsler, PhD, BCD, LCSW, Licensed Clinical Social Worker, Los Angeles, California*

CEDAR HOUSE: A MODEL CHILD ABUSE TREATMENT PROGRAM by Bobbi Kendig with Clara Lowry. (1998). "Kendig and Lowry truly . . . realize the saying that we are our brothers' keepers. Their spirit permeates this volume, and that spirit of caring is what always makes the difference for people in painful situations." *Hershel K. Swinger, PhD, Clinical Director, Children's Institute International, Los Angeles, California*

SEXUAL, PHYSICAL, AND EMOTIONAL ABUSE IN OUT-OF-HOME CARE: PREVENTION SKILLS FOR AT-RISK CHILDREN by Toni Cavanagh Johnson and Associates. (1997). "Professionals who make dispositional decisions or who are related to out-of-home care for children could benefit from reading and following the curriculum of this book with children in placements." *Issues in Child Abuse Accusations*